THE IMAGE OF THE ARMY OFFICER IN AMERICA

Contributions in Military History

C. Robert Kemble

THE IMAGE OF THE ARMY OFFICER IN AMERICA

Background for Current Views

Contributions in Military History
Number 5

Greenwood Press
Westport, Connecticut • London, England

Library of Congress Cataloging in Publication Data

Kemble, Charles Robert, 1925—
    The image of the Army officer in America.

    (Contributions in military history, no. 5)
    Bibliography: p.
    1. United States. Army—Officers. I. Title.
II. Series.
UB413.K45   301.15'43'355332   72-814
ISBN 0-8371-6383-8

Library of Congress Catalog Card Number: 72-814
ISBN: 0-8371-6383-8
First published in 1973

Greenwood Press, a division of Williamhouse-Regency Inc.
51 Riverside Avenue, Westport, Connecticut 06880

Manufactured in the United States of America

In Memory of Roy H. Kemble

Contents

Preface

If it is important that we reach a deep understanding of our civil-military relations, then we must thoroughly examine our habits of thought in this area. We most often consider civil-military matters in the terms used by the political scientist: constitutional, political, and administrative factors, and how they shape military policy and functions. These are at the core of most of our studies. And they should be, for they undoubtedly are the most immediately consequential aspects. Yet these relationships, the sociologists remind us, operate within, and take much of their tone from, a larger civil-military climate, a climate that conditions every relation, every trust, every interaction. In this sense, it is as important for us to be cognizant of what the nation "feels" the military leader to be as to understand what he in fact is. As the politician, the university president, or the businessman are all very well aware today, "image" can often be as consequential as reality.

The mythology and demonology which surround the military figure in America are extensive. Part-truth, part-imagination, they have accumulated over the years, augmented and reshaped by every generation. This is hardly surprising when we consider that the nation's picture of its career soldiers has been largely acquired secondhand. Except in wartime, day-by-day professional contacts have been limited for the most part to military-related industries and agencies of the government. Even in wartime, it is mostly just our young men, and often only a fraction of them, who are added to the civil-military equation.* With such limited direct associations, America's vision of the profession of arms has necessarily been filtered through a variety of minds and media. What have been the results? The several answers are much of the burden of this study.

What follows is the first of a planned two-part cultural-historical study of America's conceptions of, and attitudes toward, the military professional. I have long hoped that someone else would examine this and a number of associated questions, for, in spite of my efforts to the contrary, there must be some bias when a military careerist examines America's views of its soldiers. All the same, I hope no more discoloration occurs here than when those trained in other fields step back to look at their own particular professions and how they have fared in the nation's esteem. And if one accepts the not uncommon contemporary picture of the unimaginative, highly organized, coldly rational "military mind," then what follows should have at least those "virtues." My hope, however, is that this study has been informed by the mixture of tendencies which inspirits one whose adult life has been stretched between being a teacher of humanities and an enlisted and professional soldier.

---

*We talk as if limited warfare were unusual for the United States, but only twice in our history (during the Civil War and World War II, a total of about nine years) have we engaged in "unlimited" warfare. And never with the total involvement that some other nations have experienced.

Acknowledgments

This study was accomplished with the support of the Department of English at the United States Military Academy. The research, a continuing effort for four years, was assisted by the George Washington University Library, the Library of Congress, the Department of the Army Library, the Office of the Chief of Military History, the United States Military Academy Library, and too many considerate people to name here.

The work was considerably facilitated by the National War College where, as a research fellow, I had the advantages of time and location for the completion of the first phase of this study.

I wish especially to thank Clarence Mondale for his thoughtful guidance; Colonel Thomas E. Griess, Howard Merriman, and David Cooke for their advice; Jack Capps, Robert Moore, and Keith Kemble who read the text; and Robert H. Walker, with whose assistance the study was initiated. Doris Marsh and Frances Mandarano have, at different phases, been indefatigable not only in preparing the text but in assisting in the continuing research. Geneva Gardner provided a major assist in the final editing. Mostly, I thank my wife, not only for bearing with me, but for typing and proofing what seemed endless notes and drafts.

THE IMAGE OF THE ARMY
OFFICER IN AMERICA

We must unload traditional stereotypes of "the military mind,"
along with other conceptual baggage carried along from a
time when war-peace was a useful dichotomy. . . .
—Daniel Lerner

Chapter One

Introduction

The officers of the army are less identified with the country
. . . than any other class of citizens.
—North American Review, 1826[1]

This is not a history of the United States Army or a study of its leaders, and it is not a discussion of past military policies or events. It is, instead, an investigation of how, over the years, our nation has developed certain ways of viewing the military profession and professional; and it attempts to identify at least some of the basic, though often contrary, impulses behind those conceptions. This volume, as the first of an intended two-part study, deals mainly with nineteenth- and early twentieth-century developments and their lasting influences on the image of the military leader in the United States.

That we have need of a more comprehensive understanding of the subject than now exists is underlined by the persistence of certain distorted notions, such as the idea that America's attitudes toward its military institutions have been generally clear-cut, essentially static, and (except in wartime) traditionally uncongenial. According to another common thesis, there has been nothing much more complicated in the history of our civil-military relationships than a running battle between two neatly defined forces: militarism and anti-militarism. But even a cursory examination of the multi-figured image of the army officer projected by recognized leaders of American thought denies such simplistic formulas.

Consider just a sampling. To John Marshall, as to most of our early biographer-historians of the Federalist strain, the military leader was a noble figure whose character was strengthened by the rigors of war. By contrast, contemporary authors of the then popular "sentimental novel" were regularly picturing army officers as the lascivious offspring of an amoral squirearchy whose favorite pastime was despoiling hapless young virgins. And according to the early republican press, the officer corps was a collection of Benedict Arnolds or, at best, members of the distrusted Society of Cincinnati plotting to seize national power.

By the 1830s, a new "historical school" of novelists, including James Fenimore Cooper and his imitators, was featuring gallant and decorous young military heroes who were the exemplification of "proven" values and virtues. At about the same time, Davy Crockett and many of his congressional colleagues were complaining about unduly favored and ineffectual "West Point aristocrats." The United States Commissioner of Education, on the other hand, saw West Pointers as the ideal combination of an enlightened education and inner discipline. To pacifist-minded William Ellery Channing, *all* military careerists were hired killers, but to our leading antebellum historians, whether democrats like George Bancroft or the more patrician-inclined like Jared Sparks, America's gallery of great heroes continued to be filled in large measure by military figures.

The postbellum army was to Horace Greeley a collection of shiftless nobodies, but to Congressman James A. Garfield and cartoonist Thomas Nast, professional soldiers were abused yet selfless national servants. To *The Nation's* crusading editor, E. L. Godkin, the estimate depended upon the occasion. To social scientist William Graham Sumner, military leaders were the personification of various inherited class traits—admirable and otherwise. To labor spokesman Henry George, officers were tyrants. To literary leader William Dean Howells, soldiers personified devotion to duty in an age of moneygrubbing. To the late-century expansionists, America's military men were foot-draggers. To Andrew Carnegie and the "business pacifists," they were warmongers.[2] And so on.

Still more revealing is the fact that America's seminal minds have conspicuously contradicted not only each other, but themselves, on this matter at one time or another; for the conflict evoked by the figure of the army officer has actually dwelt as much *within* the American mind as *between* American minds. Over the years, our leading social theorists have dreamed aloud of eliminating warfare and class distinction and regimentation. Yet they have frequently viewed the professional warrior, operating in a hierarchal institution with discipline as its cornerstone, with unhedged respect. James Fenimore Cooper is one notable case of such juxtaposed opinions. Seeing America's antebellum military leaders as part of an essential "aristocracy of worth," yet personally committed to furthering America's democratic ideals, Cooper could at once draw admiring literary portraits of officers-and-gentlemen and passionately denounce Sir Walter Scott's affection for hereditary rank. As a historian-biographer, he enthusiastically authored both *The Lives of Distinguished Naval Officers* and *The Cruise of the Somers: Illustrating the Despotism of the Quarter Deck . . .* , whose contrasting titles speak the range of his critical mind.[3]

Historian George Bancroft worshipped Andrew Jackson as a *citizen*-soldier, but as Secretary of the Navy Bancroft fathered the Naval Academy at Annapolis to train career officers, and in the 1870s he modeled himself so completely after the then renowned Prussian military professionals that he was on occasion mistaken for a retired German officer.[4] Emerson, certainly one of the most influential minds of his century, spoke strongly against regimentation and felt that "a company of soldiers is an offensive spectacle." Still, he was delighted with West Point's contribution to America, declaring in 1863 that it should be encouraged to turn out a "true aristocracy," or a "power of the Best." And, in his later years, he asserted that in most occupations "they only prosper best who have a military mind . . . with energy and sharpness."[5] Such an array of contrary opinions is but one indicator of the complexity of the subject and the requirement for further examination.

★

It has only been in the last fifteen years or so that there has been any collected weight of thoroughgoing studies in the general field of military thought and affairs. With a few notable exceptions, earlier works lacked depth, objectivity, and balance. They were likely to be either the unevenly researched castigations of dedicated opponents of the military profession or the adulations and apologias of military romancers and defenders. Unfortunately, both varieties are still very much with us. Recently, however, there have been some substantial and valuable contributions to the study of military sociology, education, and history, as well as civil-military political theory and practice. The attempt here is to build upon these and complement them with a cultural-historical examination of America's developing conception of the military professional.

In order to gain the overview inherent in this objective, a wide variety of media have been examined, ranging from pacifist lectures to literary reviews, from educational theory to labor thought, from histories to novels. Even so, no attempt has been made at a grass roots public opinion poll. The emphasis has been on the image of the military career-ist as seen and broadcast by leaders and shapers of Ameri-can thought.

To make this initial investigation manageable and to establish a foundation for subsequent study, the main atten-tion here has been focused on the officer of the regular army in the period between the War of 1812 and the Span-ish War. The enlisted soldier has been excluded because he has been, unfortunately, of little interest to America. It is the commissioned officer who has symbolized the profes-sion of arms to the nation. The decision to concentrate on the figure of the army officer at the exclusion of his navy counterpart was, from a standpoint of scholarship, a more difficult judgment. For most of the nineteenth century, cer-tainly, the former provides us a better sounding board. After 1815, and before 1898, our military experiences were more land than sea affairs and the army was more involved in civil affairs, like enforcing frontier laws and policing labor riots.

★

The answers to the question "How *has* America pictured its military professionals?" are not available in any body of neatly assembled exposition. While numerous discussions of war as an institution are on record, there is little explicit analysis of the military service as a career. Moreover, the commentary about the professional soldier which is most easily tracked down, and therefore most often quoted, is generally shortsighted or slanted, coming from such sources as pro-military service journals, anti-military pacifist writings, and vote-seeking harangues from the political arena. These materials are an indispensable part of the overall picture and have been included here, but with due cognizance of their origin.

With such limitations to direct approaches, a typological analysis of the military images to be found in a broad variety of writings becomes, in my opinion, an especially revealing study. America has long had a tendency to reduce its military men to stereotypes. Any easily identified group suffers this, but the army officer has been particularly susceptible. Aways set off by his unusual occupation and his uniform, he has often been physically separated from American society as well. All these factors considered, there is, this study contends, as much to be learned about the nation's attitudes toward the profession of arms from the military personifications in novels, plays, histories, essays, and biographies* as from the opinions asserted in service journals, congressional records, and pacifist broadsides.

The sections and chapters following have been organized chronologically and thematically in order to examine the thrust of America's collective impressions of its military leaders. Within this broader structure, however, the discussion often centers on representative social elements, for in one sense this is very much a study of differing points of view. Identifiable interest groups—progressive educators or

---

*Poetry, too; but because the poet *qua* poet's view of the professional soldier is particularly difficult to search out and often more descriptive than analytical, I eliminated poetry as a major source in this study.

labor leaders, for instance—tell us not only how a segment of America has pictured the military careerist, but why.

On the other hand, the reader will find here only limited discussions of American military history or military policy. There are two reasons. For one thing, these are matters for other works and can be found elsewhere. More important, there is at times startlingly little correlation between events in these areas and attitudes toward the army officer. In the realm of political-military policy, for example, some of our most vocal expansionists (like the War Hawks of 1812 or the more militant politicians of the 1840s) have had noticeably little affection for regular soldiers. We cannot therefore neatly equate expansionism and admiration for the military profession, as some would have us do. Nor does our military history demonstrate any long-term relationship between battlefield performances, good or bad, and attitudes toward the performers. After some notably poor showings by militia forces, Americans maintained their faith in the militia system; and, conversely, while the Mexican War revealed a new proficiency in the professional ranks, it brought only a temporary suppression of a mounting criticism of the regular army. Even the Civil War, as we will see, was not immediately decisive in reshaping the picture of the military careerists; nor were the army's bureaucratic bunglings of the postwar era, its unsung frontier services, or its sometimes comic-opera, sometimes highly professional, efforts in the Spanish-American War. In short, a history of America's military policies, achievements, and shortcomings does not in itself show us how or why this nation has looked at its soldiers in certain ways.

If there is any single thesis that might be declared at the outset, it is this: the periods *between* our wars have been surprisingly more decisive in shaping our conceptions of the military leader than we have to date generally understood. Because the years between 1815 and 1899, for example, were marked by periods of prolonged peace, scholars tracing our civil-military affairs have tended to slight much of the "middle century." Generally, they dutifully examine the beginnings—the constitutional foundations—of the armed forces. Once past the post-Revolution debates and the War of 1812, however, they prefer to skip most of the Jacksonian era, pause briefly at the Mexican War, give due attention to the Civil War, then leap another generation or more to the Spanish War and America's late-century overseas ventures. In short, they skip from war to war, getting as quickly as possible over the ground between our eighteenth-century civil-military foundations and the "modern period" of America's twentieth-century extracontinental involvements.

That procedure may be adequate for reviewing specific aspects of national policy or particular political-military problems during times of crisis. But it ignores a much broader perspective, assuming, erroneously, that the relationships between our armed forces and civil society are significantly affected only in times of military stress. It forgets that, even if constitutionally grounded, those relationships are not legal-political constants functioning in a social vacuum, but human associations strongly conditioned by the ever-changing cultural climate.

In actuality, as the following chapters should make clear, this nation's conceptions of its armed forces and leaders have evolved through historic stages. Thus, our present attitudes and outlooks toward the military are, to a considerable extent, dependent on what has gone before. To slight the militarily less exciting portions of our past then, is to misunderstand the continuously developing nature of our civil-military relationships and to ignore the important extramilitary, nonpolitical factors involved. Even at those times when the navy was rusting in drydock and the tiny regular army was lost from sight on the frontier, America was nurturing attitudinal patterns toward the armed forces that remain basic to our outlooks today.

Finally, there is a need to mention that America's

philosophy of war has itself been extremely contradictory. This should prove no surprise. It is certainly not peculiar to the history of the United States. But unlike some other peoples, we have perpetuated a number of myths, such as the half-truth that commonplace Americans are always great fighters but have a unique reluctance to go to war. The whole truth seems to be something else.

In fact, four overlapping national outlooks on warfare come quickly to mind. One persistent approach (founded on our Enlightenment-inherited faith in progress and human perfectibility) has been to see armed conflict as an outdated barbarism lingering on the horizon of civilization. Past wars, like the American Revolution, may have contributed to man's advancement, but that day should be gone.

Another view (stemming more from Puritan thought) has seen war in an Old Testament sense. Military power in the hands of Evil is evil, but righteous wars are divinely supported. Military adventurism is thus wrong, but the vigorous prosecution of war in defense of high ideals is not only acceptable, but a duty. Stated negatively, America has supported warfare enthusiastically only when it could be rationalized as a crusade of some sort. This was the most basic of our nineteenth-century philosophies on war and it apparently still is.

Third, pure pacifists—and Edward Burns and Merle Curti tell us there have been few—have seen all wars as wrong.[6] But most who have professed pacifism have been willing to suspend that faith, and even urge the nation to battle, for causes *they* saw as righteous, as the Civil War proved in the case of Thoreau, Charles Sumner, Emerson, Garrison, and others.

Fourth, few Americans—military or civilian—have advocated warfare for its own sake or for the sake of exploitation; but throughout our history there has been a persistent idea that wars are periodic requirements in the grand scheme of things, ordained tests of great nations. War as a necessary catharsis is an idea that has not been foreign to America's religious leaders, among others.

In fine, this nation has had no consistent outlook toward war. As a consequence, the very base of reference, the plane to which public opinions of the military officer have been related, has been uneven. Beginning from philosophically lumpy foundations, America has established and justified some remarkably different visions of its military leaders. The American environment, especially since 1815, has promoted a man-of-action's indifference to philosophical consistency; and rather than develop long-term and well-defined policies, we have "grown" a variety of attitudes toward war and military affairs. With them, we have also nurtured some diverse and revealing conceptions of officership—images of lasting influence. It is those basic figures and the attitudes they reflect that we will examine here.

SECTION ONE

THE POINT OF DEPARTURE, 1775-1800

In charting the changing makeup of the military figure in America's thought and imagination, one begins with a fairly apparent but seldom noted truth: from before the Revolution through much of the nineteenth century, army officers were considered "military gentlemen." Wide variations of this picture developed, but the officer-and-gentleman remained the basic image for generations.

This military-leader-as-a-patrician idea invited a variety of responses ranging from respect and admiration to distrust and contempt. However viewed, the officer was seldom pictured realistically. He was romanticized or caricatured. To his more ardent admirers, he was a figure from the past of whom there were too few still extant. He was an Americanized *preux chevalier*: refined, intelligent, supple, gentle, brave, honorable, skillful in horsemanship, and well-trained in the use of weapons. Yet, ideally, he was also somehow Puritan in his morality and republican in his political outlook; and he associated easily wit'⸱ the soldier of basic American stock, a man of fewer social attributes and less formal learning, but of greater physical and equal moral strength. Together these two were an unbeatable team leading America to its destined achievements.

To his more severe detractors, the military gentleman was no such admirable combination of the best of Old and New World traits. He was not part American; he was un-American: an amoral, effeminate, deceitful, overly refined, worthless man of leisure, a burden on the economy and a threat to freedom and equality. And to most of our leading writers up to and beyond the Civil War, he was at different times a variation of either of these, and often some combination of both.

Even though the military gentleman notion persisted for three-quarters of the century or more, there were important developments during that time. The image was fragmented, assigned different social and military roles, dressed in different uniforms, condemned, praised, and ignored. In the process, certain habits of thought were established and certain stereotypes congealed. To understand these developments, we need to establish a point of departure, and to do so we look first at the new nation's conception of officership at the close of the eighteenth century.

Chapter Two

Officers-and-Gentlemen Americanized: Patrician But Puritan Military Artists[1]

War must be carried on systematically, and to do it, you must have good officers, . . . Gentlemen, and Men of Character . . . activated by Principles of honour, and a spirit of enterprise.

—General George Washington[2]

[The evil Lt. Belcour] possessed a gentle fortune, and had a liberal education; dissipated, thoughtless and capricious . . . self, daring self, was the idol he worshipped, and to that he would have sacrificed the interest and happiness of all mankind.

—from **Charlotte Temple** by Susanna Rowson[3]

The new nation's impressions of officership were clearly founded on the customs of Europe which for centuries had related class codes with theories of military art and leadership. Those long-established views were at first not discarded, but only modified, by the Americans. Although a formative feature of the New World's military experience was, and would continue to be, its geographical remove from Europe, in some ways the Old World influences proved all the greater because of this isolation. Lacking firsthand experience in "conventional" affairs, the American people, even after their revolution, continued to look back to Europe for their military as well as social standards—including their models of officership.

The prototype of the Western military leader in vogue at the time of the Revolution had taken form during what today's military historians call "the age of limited engagement." For over two hundred years, military activity in Europe had been restricted by a variety of sociological, political, and economic factors. War was considered an extension of state policy and, as such, an instrument for the ruler's use—though not one to be employed casually. European populations were unarmed and monarchs were hesitant about putting weapons in their hands; besides, war was becoming increasingly expensive and if used too frequently could severely drain a nation's financial power. For these and other reasons, armies were, as Walter Millis deftly put it, "by an admirable economy . . . drawn, generally speaking, from the least productive elements at the two ends of the social scale." Even so, they were costly and, in Daniel Boorstin's words, the idea of recruiting and "throwing away a whole generation of young men—as happened at Verdun and on the Somme in 1916—would have appalled an eighteenth century king or general." In an entire and decisive year of the War of the Spanish Succession, for example, the combined British army and navy lost fewer men killed in action than did the Union army in one day at Fredericksburg in the Civil War.[4]

For two centuries, the guiding spirit in military affairs was one of restraint. It was characterized by the writings of Grotius and Vattel, who (in 1625 and 1758, respectively) formalized the laws of peace and war in an effort to regularize and reduce war's savageries. Battles were generally considered tactical contests fought not by entire armed nations, but by small regular armies on "playing fields" at the call of the monarchs. The concern for economy and other factors produced a geometric sort of warfare of position and block-type maneuvers that avoided costly pitched battles. The very nature of the existing weapons system, with limited effective range, demanded massed formations in order to gain striking power. So too did the fact that the basic soldiers were often impressed into service and did not possess sufficient motivation or reliability to permit other than mass control.

In any event, the rigid discipline and the intricate parade-ground evolutions of the day were not merely militaristic ritual, but the means by which army officers, like naval commanders, brought to bear the massed broadsides of their units. The junior leader's role was to maneuver his unit into battle and, if necessary, as the British saying still goes, "show them how to die." The senior commander put himself in position to view as much of the battlefield as possible, and to move his "chesspieces" to gain sufficient advantage to cause the enemy to sue for peace. Mass destruction of the opposing forces was considered uncivilized and total victory was not usually the goal.[5]

Under these conditions, military leaders were not the rigorously schooled full-time professionals of later years, but members of the "better" classes temporarily serving their monarch. While soldiers were often the sweepings of society, the officers were sons of nobility or members of the rising commercial classes seeking social advancement. They were, at best, experienced mercenaries or cultured adventurers who, by virtue of their social position, had acquired a knack of command.

Hand in hand with this system went the presumption that "military command was an art, like music or sculpture, which required inherent talent. Military competence could not be transmitted or learned; it was a product of purely subjective factors." That long-held theory was modified only slightly during the eighteenth-century Age of Reason. The nobility continued to argue that only men born to high station were fit for officership, while the military writers of the Enlightenment held that it was the "natural" aristocracy who made the best commanders. Either way, whether his position was founded on inherited station or inborn talent, the officer was expected to be a gentleman "born to command" and by instinct (genius) a military artist rather than a methodical military scientist.[6]

In short, the officer's social strata, his qualifications for leadership, and his methodology—his artistry—were all of the same package.

★

There is substantial evidence that America absorbed much of that tradition, if not all of its European social niceties and refinements. Our founders generally recognized a need for a leading class, and eventually two solutions emerged: Adams' idea of a carefully controlled gentry and Jefferson's *aristoi*.[7] Military leadership was no exception; as in Europe, higher ranking officers, whether chosen from the gentry or the "natural aristocracy," were expected to be officers-and-gentlemen.

As is often pointed out, there was in that time strong fear, envy, and suspicion directed toward all men of power, and there was the New World's particularly deep distrust of standing armies. Washington himself was fearful of military dictatorship, and he urged his colleagues to keep a watchful eye on the army. Samuel Adams went even further. "If an officer drank to the army before toasting the Congress Sam wanted to cashier him out of the service as a potential

Caesar." Madison felt that "a standing army is one of the greatest mischiefs that can possibly happen," and Governor Randolph reported to the Virginia convention that "with respect to a standing army, I believe there was not a member in the Federal Convention who did not feel indignation at such an institution."[8]

But apprehensions about overly powerful military institutions were reservations to an otherwise common regard for patrician-styled leaders of proven mettle and loyalty. Indeed, the deep-seated American fear of standing armies *demanded* that officers be men of the best possible background and training so that they would not be tempted to prostitute their commission. The early military commissions made this clear, reminding the recipient that his appointment was based on "special trust and confidence." During the war, Washington complained repeatedly about the scarcity of gentlemen in his officer corps and argued that "they ought to have such allowances as will enable them to live like, and support the Characters of Gentlemen; and not be driven by a scanty pittance to . . . low and dirty acts."[9] And to most of the emerging nation, their commander-in-chief was only one of the outstanding gentlemen who led the army that eventually won them liberty. Lafayette, Von Steuben, Pulaski, Kosciusko, and other European aristocrats were eagerly welcomed to help offset deficiencies in America's military discipline and artistry; and they were admired accordingly.

Nor did appreciation of the military patrician end with the war. There is a whole body of American writings—historical, fictional, biographical, dramatic, and topical—which demonstrates the continuing admiration for officers *as a class*. As later pacifists would repeatedly complain, "Men of letters . . . have been the leading agents [glorifying war]. . . . They have written its histories; they have composed its songs and ballads; they have emblazoned the warrior's deeds."[10] Of our early writings which "emblazoned the warrior's deeds," perhaps best known are those of the postwar historians, described by historiographer Harvey Wish as men of "upper middle class status that usually went hand-in-hand with a conservative social outlook despite [their] fervent expressions of liberal nationalism."[11] Writers like William Gordon and David Ramsay drew word portraits of military leaders in the heroic proportions of a Peele or Trumbull painting.[12] The early theatre (such as it was) shows case after case of patrician-type military heroes. Not only were Generals Warren, Greene, Putnam, Prescott, and others—regardless of their diverse backgrounds—portrayed as conventional officers-and-gentlemen, so too were fictional figures with fitting names like Colonel Steel and Captain Strong.[13]

The founding fathers were themselves largely of the patrician class, and many had officer experience or aspirations. They were part of "the better kind of people" who "found themselves set off from the mass by a hundred visible, tangible, and audible distinctions of dress, speech, manners, and education". The idea of a high-ranking officer as anything but a gentleman—albeit an American version—was not acceptable to the cultivated classes. Alexander Hamilton, with characteristic bluntness, wrote to John Jay, "Let officers be men of sense; but the nearer the soldiers approach to machines perhaps the better." In the same vein, Washington had expressed concern that if the "men consider, and treat [officers] as an equal; and . . . [they are] mixed together as one common herd; no order, nor no discipline can prevail. . . ." Some twenty years later, President Jefferson urged William Wirt to "come into Congress, . . . and after obtaining the standing which a little time will ensure you, you may look, at your own will, into the military, and judiciary, the diplomatic . . . [and] be assured of being engaged through life in the most honourable employments." Whether Federalist or Republican in slant, the early formulators of our national thought showed a consistent respect for the profession of arms as an "honourable employment." Because they distrusted standing armies, they figured that leadership in the military, as elsewhere, should come from a class considered more trustworthy and better qualified than most commoners.[14]

All the same, there had been from colonial days a distinctly middle class tone to America's military matters and manners. including its view of officership. Long before the Revolution, the colonial experience had bred a number of habits uniquely American and "unconventional." The nature of the opponents (raiding savages instead of drilled battalions), the weapons (designed for aimed-fire hunting rather than short-range massed volleys*), the military objectives (defense of home and family rather than checkmating an opposing army) all contributed. It even showed in the way the Revolutionists fought. They frequently resorted to methods that violated the accepted rules of the day. They infiltrated guerrilla forces behind British lines and aimed at individuals in battle; and, in a practice which particularly angered the British, they shot at opposing officers, "who as gentlemen were supposed to be inviolate from bullets."[15]

But America's modifications of Europe's military codes went far deeper than a mere disregard of the customary preferential treatment for young aristocrats on and off the battlefield. With the Revolution a success, the country had an almost psychic requirement to assert its identify, and in so doing to reject Europe—at least in token. Daniel Boorstin has analyzed the anti-European current of thought which prevailed in America for a hundred years. "In the United States," he explains, "until about the beginning of the present century, 'American' and 'European' were not used so much as precise geographical terms but as logical antitheses." This polar framework "served our need and our disposition to describe our national character and posi-

---

*The British muskets were so crude that the manual of arms did not include the command "aim."

tion in elusive, vague, and shifting terms. It . . . required little precision, and demanded little agreement to assert that we stand for everything that Europe is not."

Being unmistakably second-rate in cultural achievements, the new nation chose to claim the superiority of its Puritan-based morality. The influence of this "moral nationalism" on the military image was immediate and pervasive. Utopian America characteristically defined war and the profession of arms as European, not native, institutions. From Washington and Jefferson on, the phrasing of our international policy contained the plea for "the prevention of entanglement" in European affairs, i.e., an avoidance of the barbaric and troublesome past. Likewise, while patrician virtues like honor, courage, courtesy, and self-sacrifice were looked on with favor, any Restoration-styled immorality, any military cliques, or any pretentious trappings were summarily rejected, especially if there was a smell of despotism in the air. The well-known reaction to the Society of Cincinnati, founded in 1783 to honor officers of the Revolutionary Army, is a case in point. It was almost immediately assailed as an effort to create a hereditary military aristocracy. Though Washington was a member, the General Court of Massachusetts condemned it, and the Connecticut legislature refused to grant it a charter. Perhaps the wisest concern of all was expressed by Jefferson, who feared that with the Society, "a distinction is kept up between the civil and the military, which it is for the happiness of both to obliterate."[16]

Distrustful of potential despots and idle aristocrats, utopian, Puritan, middle-class America canonized military heroes who were gentlemen by virtue of their social stratum *and* their exemplary moral character. Though pilloried by political opponents in his lifetime, Washington, almost from the moment of his death, became a legend symbolizing (among other things) the "superiority" of American military leaders over foreign officers because of their greater strength of character. A full century later, O. O. Howard was still telling the officer corps, as so many had before him, to model themselves after the Virginia planter, the greatest military name in all history. "There is a hidden meaning in the name of Washington. . . . This preciousness, this sanctity . . . has for foundation, *character*. No mere physical superiority . . . no expansion of intellect . . . has produced a similar lasting impression."[17]

Conversely, this rationale declared that officers who proved unworthy were probably so because of some character deficiency. Usually it was because they had fallen prey to Europe's amorality. Even in jest, Royall 'Wat' Tyler's highly popular comedy, "The Contrast" (1787), showed the negative side of the ideal-American-gentleman formula. The play revolves around the contrast between Dimple, a British rake who connives to gain liaison with various women, and Colonel Manly, a virtuous, homespun Yankee who has little fondness for either European dandies or intrigue. As the despised Dimple departs, the playwright with ironic wit has him plead to the audience "to observe . . . the contrast between a gentleman, who has read Chesterfield and received the polish of Europe, and an unpolished, untravelled American." While the awkward Manly was hardly meant to depict the ideal military patrician, he clearly serves as the foil for those *not* worthy of national admiration: false aristocrats and unpatriotic mercenaries. As a loyal, if rustic, American, Manly's claim to achievement is "to have humbly imitated our illustrious WASHINGTON in having exposed my health and life in the service of my country without reaping reward."[18]

The antitype of America's military ideal was our first and almost only flesh and blood national villain, General Benedict Arnold. Not, it should be noted, because of either his military profession or his rank, but because he fell victim to European ways. The bread-and-butter pieces of the early American stage were—as one would expect—reenactments of Revolutionary events. The most popular of all were didactic treatments of Arnold's treason, deploring his prostitution of military trust and honor for the sake of feudal finery.[19] So from the nation's very inception, its antihero was a military officer flawed by "un-American" indulgences.

Demonstration of the point is also found in our early fiction, especially in the sentimental novel, which was slanted to middle-class consumption and exceptionally popular in America. As in Britisher Samuel Richardson's widely read originals, the standard plot was the attempted seduction of a virtuous maiden by some handsome and cultivated rake. Since the American novel was virtually born with our Revolution, it is no surprise that the culprits in the favorite works on this side of the Atlantic were often British officers, as in the widely read *Charlotte Temple* and *Amelia; or the Faithless Briton*.[20] Terence Martin, who has studied the social attitudes revealed in our early novels, explains that the authors, "knowing evil to be a fact but believing it not to be an American fact, very often took an obvious course and blamed evil on the decadent culture of Europe. If Evil exists in the United States, [they] reasoned, it is because it has been imported."[21]

But foreign villains could not be imported forever. When the shift to a homegrown variety was made, it was, quite naturally, to the closest local approximation of Europe's "decadent nobility"; namely, an American army officer who took undue advantage of his class and uniform. Major Sanford in Hannah Foster's *The Coquette* (1797) has been called "the most accomplished villain in early American literature," and Mrs. Foster makes it painfully clear that Sanford's sins are very much the result of his Chesterfieldian habits. Nor does the major stand alone as the only reprehensible officer in early American fiction. Quite the reverse. Alexander Cowie, in his survey of *The American Novel*, remarks that reading the sentimental novels of the day "left a girl resolved never to trust any man—least of all a man in uniform."[22]

All this is not to imply that respect for the "true" military

gentleman—even when an enemy—was on the wane in
American letters. William Dunlap's drama, "Andre" (1798),
was only the first of a whole series of tragedies about the
sad fate of that highly admired British gentleman-officer
who, unlike the ignoble Arnold, lived up to his commission
and to the internationally recognized codes of honor, even
as a spy.[23] In like celebration of the soldier faithful to his
calling, J. D. Burk's popular drama, "Bunker Hill," has
General Warren scornfully refuse a British offer to remit
his past "offences" provided he abandon the American
camp.

> Is't goodness to seduce the soldier's worth,
> To rob him of that loftiness of soul
> That pride, which makes him spurn dishonor from him;
> ....
> Is this what now in England is called goodness?[24]

The sentimental novel notwithstanding, the view of the profession of arms reflected in American literature would
remain generally favorable for nearly a century, as we shall
see.

★

From the first days of the nation, the image of the military leader was, one finds, anything but sharply defined.
He was clearly expected to be gentleman-soldier of the
European mode, just as experienced leaders in the Continental Army had often been imported European aristocrats
or had served earlier with British colonial units—as had the
commander-in-chief himself. But certain reservations to this
impression of the officer corps were already visible. The
New World impulse to cast off the past had clearly begun
to color America's conception of the military man, even
before the minutemen stood at Lexington. And Puritan,

middle-class morality had long been looking askance at the uniform and all it implied. The fledgling republic's portraitures of officership were, as a consequence, not often affectionate in tone. They reflected, nevertheless, the general respect then afforded a military gentleman armed with the breeding, instinct, and sense of service associated with the "better" classes.

SECTION TWO

VARIATIONS FROM THE
BASIC MOLD, 1815-1850

The long, exciting and splendid panorama of
revolution and war, which for twenty-five years
absorbed the world's attention and dwarfed all
other interests, vanished more quickly in America
than in Europe, and left fewer elements of
disturbance. . . . In a single day, almost in a single
instant, the public turned from interests and pas-
sions that had supplied its thoughts for a generation, and took up a class of ideas that had been
unknown or but vaguely defined before.[1]

So Henry Adams described the shift in national temper at
the close of the War of 1812.

It was hardly all that sudden, but there were indeed
major adjustments, and the influences on this nation's conception of military men were soon to be seen. Basic military
factors had changed. With "the second war of independence" and the Treaty of Ghent, external threats were
removed for over a century. Unchallenged security soon
became part of the American way of life and thought, and
there was very limited need for competent military regulars.
Those required were, during most of the next eighty years,
detailed to coastal defense positions and frontier outposts,
seldom to be heard from and seldom much noted.

As the military equations were changing, so too was the
entire intellectual climate. Merle Curti wrote of this period:
"No simple formula epitomizes the complex pattern of ideas
that characterizes the thought of the better established
classes in the first three decades of the nineteenth century.
Broadly speaking, the desire for a distinctly American culture, which conservative intellectuals often shared with radi-
cals, conflicted with the continuing cosmopolitan and eclec-
tic tones of intellectual life."[2]

In an era marked by social turbulence and an almost
wholly new military situation, the eighteenth-century view
of army leaders soon began to fragment. New patterns

began to show through. Impressions which had been only barely discernible in the last quarter of the previous century now, under new conditions, became discrete images, distinct enough for separate identification. Recognition of these developing stereotypes is of importance, for their influence endured. Having been implanted in American thought, they formed the basis for future notions—even after the conditions which created them had all but passed.

For clarity of discussion, the next several chapters deal separately with these several "types". It will be necessary, therefore, to keep clearly in mind that America's more profound writers did not hold any such neatly defined attitudes toward the military careerist. The fluctuating reactions to the army officer displayed by the nation's spokesmen reveal instead the inner tensions of an age that was at once sectional yet national in outlook, genteel and democratic in mood, morally conservative but politically progressive, and both European and American in its cultural aspirations.

Chapter Three

The Egalitarian View:
Military Gentlemen As
Unwanted Aristocrats[1]

For many years previous to secession, the profession of arms
had, at the North, fallen from disrepute to contempt. . . . To
be an officer of the Regular Army was, popularly, to be an
idle gentleman, well paid for doing nothing, scarcely worthy
of respect, and assuredly not of esteem.

—General Truman Seymour[2]

33

When authoress Hannah Foster, in 1797, dressed the villainous aristocrat of the sentimental novel in an American army uniform, she was anticipating things to come. In the accumulating democratic folklore of the first half of the nineteenth century, the career officer, like Miss Foster's fictional Major Sanford, took on all the uncomplimentary features previously reserved for sons of the European upper classes. As the expanding nation became increasingly committed to egalitarianism, the description of America's officer corps as reprehensible aristocrats—wealthy, effete, lazy, and immoral—became a common caricature. In literature, for example, Miss Foster's *The Coquette* gained its greatest vogue between 1824 and 1828, and Susanna Rowson's *Charlotte Temple* went on to become America's longest lived novel, going through more than 160 editions.[3] But the military aristocrat characterization was most strongly expressed in the political rhetoric of the Jacksonian era.

From the nation's birth, there had been some men of influence, like the Chief Justice of South Carolina, who insisted that American officers "are generally in their hearts aristocrats, and enemies to the . . . republic." And circumstances in the Jeffersonian era reinforced that early reputation. As historian John Miller summarized the situation, "The Army had been augmented in 1789 for the purpose of defending the country. . . . But when the French failed to invade the United States. . . , the most compelling reason for maintaining a large military establishment was to back up . . . the enforcement of unpopular laws." The officer corps thus incurred the wrath both of indignant taxpayers and of the champions of civil rights. Republican newspapers pictured the army as "a ferocious wild beast let loose upon the nation to devour it." As for the officers, "Our citizens . . . are exposed to the insolence and impudence of every wretch who has sufficient interest to procure a commission."[4]

Following the War of 1812, and especially with the depression of 1819, egalitarian opposition turned more particularly against military expenditures. In Congress, complaints against the privileged officer corps wasting the nation's monies were expressed with vehemence. In 1820, Representative Newton Cannon of Tennessee introduced the first of many resolutions to come, "to inquire into the expediency of abolishing the Military Academy at West Point." Cannon objected to the academy as an aristocratic institution, and he argued that the money expended for West Point should be used instead to train militia officers. When Cannon failed in reelection, several others continued the attack against the "unduly favored military caste." After 1825, Representative Davy Crockett became the worthy successor from Tennessee on this score.[5]

But until the heyday of Jacksonianism, in the late 1820s and the 1830s, the egalitarian critique remained a strident but relatively ineffectual voice. Congressman Cannon and other decriers of military aristocracy were vocal but not yet politically powerful. As one bemused military observer reported in a private letter to the superintendent of the Military Academy, "The Tennessee Cannon, which has been for some time charged and primed, went off a few days since in Congress Hall, pointed as usual against the Army, but I suspect with little effect."[6] He was right. This was the period of John C. Calhoun's considerable influence as Secretary of War (1817-1825), and his widely acclaimed reorganization of the failing War Department gave strength to his formidable defense of the regular army. Though eventually frustrated, Calhoun's faith in an expansible regular force, including a disproportionately large staff of officers to perpetuate essential military skills, represented America's official military policy for the time.[7]

★

It was during the second quarter of the century that the officer corps was confronted by a much more consequential surge of egalitarian opposition. With the democratic plurality of 1824 and presidential victory in 1828, the attacks became increasingly political in orientation and anti-intellectual in temper—even when expressed by some of the intellectual leaders of that day. Where post-Revolution critics had harbored fears that America's military patricians would become the tools of an aspiring monarch, the Jacksonians saw the officer corps not only as a threat to the nation's hard-won liberty, but as dedicated opponents of their newfound democracy as well.

The growing democratic critique of military careerists centered on two basic counts. The first was summed up by the not uncommon question, "Do we need them?" By now the nation was quite clearly secure from external threats, and the three decades of world conflict stretching from the beginning of the Revolution to the end of the War of 1812 were rapidly fading from national memory. Granted, there were governmental spokesmen, notably cabinet members and presidents, who continued to assert the need for the United States to keep apace with developments in the military arts. "The United States may again be involved in war," President Monroe warned; and our land forces must "preserve the science as well as the necessary implements of war." But while Monroe's message was typical of succeeding presidential statements, any suggestion for an army more than barely capable of meeting its immediate frontier requirements was increasingly difficult to justify—especially to frugal and independent-minded agrarians who were, by nature, suspicious of anyone in official position.

Fundamental to this attitude, of course, was America's growing faith in the common man. War, the democrats reasoned, was an occasional and short-lived emergency that could be met by nonprofessionals. Any good white Anglo-Saxon American male could, on short notice, be a successful general—or, for that matter, president of the United States.[8]

"Are career officers fit to command an army representing the New World?" That was the second basic challenge. Since egalitarians saw the officer corps as a closed association for aristocrats, they considered them to be spiritually unsuited to lead soldiers of a democracy. Regular officers, it was presumed, remained tainted with the faults associated with European nobility: moral flabbiness, overrefinement, arrogance, religious pallor, egotism, and pride of caste. No American army built on such leadership could be great. Speaking of military institutions in particular and societies in general, historian George Bancroft wrote, in full caps, in 1835 "ALL THE GREAT AND NOBLE INSTITUTIONS . . . HAVE COME FROM POPULAR EFFORTS."[9]

The two-pronged attack did much to darken the image of the military patrician, a figure broadly admired in the Federalist period. Even so, it must be kept in mind that mainstream Jacksonians did not themselves shy from military involvement or commissions. Most certainly they were not pacifists; their argument was against privilege. They eagerly sought their share of military commands and commissions. Tocqueville concluded (in 1835) that war had a special appeal to the Americans because democracies worship opportunity and carry that spirit to the battlefield. War is an opportunity for easy advancement, a chance for a man to get ahead "by only risking his life."[10] What the opportunistic Jacksonians objected to was the awarding of the coveted commissions in favor of wealth and station. Their declared goal was "to level" the military aristocrats.

In truth, they sought only to replace officer-gentry with self-made, one-generation aristocrats. Jackson, the sometimes regular officer yet democratic hero, was a case in point. Jackson was no primitive of the Davy Crockett mode but a man of property, and "typical, not of the Southwest's coonskin democrats, but of its peculiar blend of pioneer and aristocrat."[11] Likewise, the democrats' military model was just such a blend of self-made soldier and military gentleman.

All the same, their criticism was founded on class contentions, and by the 1830s West Point had become, in egalitarian eyes, the primary symbol of the exclusiveness of the regular officer corps. "The Military Academy had hosts of enemies," one graduate recalled later. "But for the demonstrations of the Mexican War, it would have been abandoned. . . ."[12] The controversies over West Point in the Jacksonian age have been amply reported elsewhere.[13] There is little to be gained here by covering that ground, in detail, once again. It is important, however, to analyze the main ingredients of the mounting hostility, for they reveal some of the complex forces contributing to the increasing alienation of the regular army officer in America.

The central political charges are well summed up in a War Department paper reprinted in the *North American Review* in 1843. The criticisms of West Point over the past several years were being reviewed "because this institution has lately been the object of much censure, and the tenor of the objections . . . show that its character is misunderstood." Demonstrating the strength of the egalitarian opposition, the author recalled that "in June, 1842, the legislature of Connecticut passed a resolve, that the Academy was 'aristocratic and anti-republican,' and ought to be abolished, because a *very large proportion* of the Cadets 'are the sons of wealthy and influential men, who by the interposition of Members of Congress, obtained situations in that institution, to the *almost total exclusion* of poor and less influential men.' " Connecticut's lead, the author noted, was followed by Maine; and these movements "are in imitation of the example set by Tennessee and Ohio, the former having attacked the Academy on the same grounds, in 1833, and the latter in 1834."[14]

The report offered statistical refutations of the charges, but the accuracy of the complaints is not our concern here. What *is* to be noted is that Jacksonian criticism was in certain ways decidedly different from that of the previous period. The Federalists had been seeking, not avoiding, military patricians. Washington had complained of too few, not too many, gentlemen in his army, and he later suggested a school for "instructing a certain number of young Gentlemen in the Theory of the Art of War."[15] And it was, we should recall, Jefferson who eventually founded the suggested Military Academy with an eye toward establishing a military *aristoi*. Unlike Jacksonian equalitarians, our eighteenth-century leaders clearly preferred to place the nation's security (albeit under careful checks) in the hands of those who had had the advantages of cultivation and education.

The Congressional Records of 1815 to 1850 show that the two most common complaints about West Point were: (1) its anti-democratic appointment system and (2) its lack of discipline.[16] The first point is only further demonstration of the difference between Federalist and democratic outlooks. The charge of lack of discipline, on the other hand, reveals yet another aspect of the Jacksonian impression of career officers, one which stands in sharp contrast to a later stereotype, the overdisciplined automaton. To Jacksonian critics, West Pointers were anything but military robots; they were the pampered, unruly, and unmanly sons of the eastern gentry. Allen Partridge, a discredited officer relieved from his faculty position at West Point, found receptive ears in Congress when he charged that Academy training was "*effeminate* and calculated to unfit young men to encounter the fatigues and hardships of war." He described how the cadets, weather permitting, marched "a few times each day over the beautiful lawn in front of their quarters." "*Gentleman* soldiers," he explained, could not be "exposed to the rude assaults of the weather which might injure their *beauty*." Congressman Crockett echoed the charge, saying that West Point men "were too delicate and could not rough it in the army like men differently raised."[17]

Equally significant, the Academy and its graduates were not attacked in this period for intellectual shortcomings, as would be the case later in the century and beyond. West Point was, in fact, almost universally hailed as the nation's outstanding engineering institution. Even the pacifist-minded president of Brown University, Francis Wayland, admitted that West Point graduates did more "to build up the system of internal improvements in the United States than [the graduates of] all other colleges combined."[18] The common complaint of the day was not about the Academy's educational shortcomings, but the reverse. West Point officers were pictured as overeducated "kid glove gentry," and it was suggested that the "tinsels of scholarship" provided there could not substitute for the basic military attributes acquired by more rugged field experiences.[19]

★

Although hardly consistent with the conception of the officer corps as a clique of pampered aristocrats, the country's deeply engrained fear of standing armies, inherited from the Revolutionary days, continued to be a major force in shaping the military image. While western-oriented democrats might see regular officers as soft and unmanly, less primitivistic critics, like Wayland, were concerned that "the very means by which we repel a despotism from abroad, only establishes over us a military despotism at home." Actually there had been no experience since the initiation of the Society of Cincinnati nearly half a century before to give much sustenance to this old concern. The political ammunition was apparently too good to ignore, however. As a senator, former Secretary of War Calhoun felt obliged to chide his congressional colleagues for their convenient fears of the small army scattered in company-size units on the vast frontier.[20]

Despite the facts, the spectre of military despotism stubbornly persisted, and it demonstrates one of the basic historical patterns in American military criticism. Anti-military arguments, especially those of the political liberals, have tended to be additive: old criticisms retain their appeal—and hence are not discarded—even when inconsistent with new lines of attack. Typically, at the very time that Jacksonian democrats were denigrating West Pointers as an un-American elite threatening the government, they were also complaining that too many were resigning from the service. As Britisher Marcus Cunliffe concludes in a penetrating essay on "The American Military Tradition," one finds it "hard to believe that Americans, even in Jackson's era, were genuinely alarmed by the prospect of military overlordship. Rather," Cunliffe perceives, "they [were objecting] to . . . a *European* concept."[21]

Logic aside, the somewhat incongruous pictures of effeminate dandies and threatening military dictators were fused, and foreign observers were baffled by the inconsistency of the whole situation. Godfrey Vigne, reporting on his *Six Months in America*, wrote that "laughable as it might appear, objections have been raised on account of the aristocratical ideas which the young men [cadets at the Military Academy] bring with them into society." And Charles J. Latrobe observed that "the jealousy and suspicion with which even this skeleton of a regular army is regarded by the American people, renders [the officers'] position difficult. . . . West Point Academy . . . is looked upon with mistrust, as nursing a young brood of aristocrats."

To Europeans, accustomed to a well-defined social hierarchy and governments respectful of the profession of arms, America's outlook seemed badly warped. The United States Army officer, they felt, was a victim of his social environment. He had the thankless job of commanding, in their view, "the worst soldier in the world, as regards obedience and discipline, [one who has] been brought up to believe himself equal to the officers who command him." Few of the foreign military observers could, for example, abide with the American army's practice of equal punishments for officers and enlisted offenders. As one wrote, "The whole tenor of [the enlisted men's] lives and conversation . . . are

dissimilar to those of gentlemen. Why, therefore, as long
as such is their deportment, should not their punishment
be widely contradistinguished?"

The foreigners' astonishment also points up the degree
to which America's military institutions had already
departed from Old World ways. More important, it illustrates Cunliffe's point that Jacksonian criticism was in large
measure still directed toward *European* models of
officership—even when, in the eyes of the European
observers, those models did not truly apply.[22]

★

Other factors, also at work, are worth mention. One was
the already established American bias against isolated
minority groups. David Brion Davis' study of "Some
Ideological Functions of Prejudice in Ante-Bellum
America" argues that because the people were supremely
confident of their doctrines and of "the infallible corrective
of public opinion," they considered any self-contained
organizations dangerous. Davis cites the persistent biases
against the Masons and the Catholic Church as cases in
point, but it is difficult to imagine a better illustration than
the isolated brotherhood of regular army officers nurtured
at sequestered West Point in the Hudson highlands and sent
to the lonely frontier. Physically and intellectually out of the
mainstream, they were not, their Jacksonian critics were certain, to be trusted.

Also strong at the time was the nation's proclivity for temporary, volunteer associations and an inherent opposition
to highly traditional and permanent institutions, such,
again, as the Catholic Church.[23] The same critical spirit of
amateurism cast its shadow on the regular soldier. From the
first, the country instinctively preferred the minuteman and
made him an American legend despite the well-documented
fact that volunteer and militia concepts seldom worked with
much efficiency, even in the Revolution.

With the shabby record of the militia units in the War of 1812 close at hand, Jacksonians conveniently chose to remember instead the naval victories and the Battle of New Orleans in which "we licked the men who licked Napoleon." Nathaniel Hawthorne consciously capitalized on this amateuristic bias when he authored Pierce's presidential campaign biography. Contrasting Pierce to his political opponent, General Winfield Scott, Hawthorne wrote, "There is surely a chivalrous beauty in the devotion of the citizen-soldier to his country's cause, which the man who makes arms his profession and is but doing his duty cannot pretend to rival."[24]

To understand the situation fully, there is a negative factor to consider here as well. Most of the traditional military myths and symbols common to older countries were missing in the New World. In the absence of long lines of legendary warriors, uniformed rulers, elaborate military-state ceremonies, and the other trappings of the "grand" military tradition, it was just that much easier for Jacksonian America to see career soldiers as a dangerously un-American elite. Having few counterbalances, the individualistic and amateuristic spirits of the age were almost bound to work against the reputation of a European-founded, closely organized, and traditionally oriented institution like the army.[25]

However inconsistent the characterizations may have been, America's newfound democratic faith and the growing myth of unique destiny could only conceive of the regular army and its leaders as part of the burden of the Old World from which the New was blessedly ordained to be free.

Chapter Four

The Pacifist View: Military Gentlemen As Brutish Mercaries[1]

Slaughter becomes an exalted profession; the marked distinguished employment of what is called a gentleman.

—Douglass Jerrold[2]

The motives which generally lead to the choice of a military life strip it of all claim to peculiar honor. . . . The man who undertakes this work . . . to earn money or an epaulet commits . . . a great wrong.

—William Ellery Channing[3]

Whatever their shortcomings, the poorly paid officers and men of the Continental Army or of the tiny post-Revolutionary establishment had not often faced the charge of being mercenaries. That tag had been commonly reserved for foreign hirelings employed by countries other than their own, such as the widely despised Hessian units used by the British in the American Revolution. It was the nineteenth-century pacifists who were largely instrumental in popularizing the image of the officer corps as a mercenary association of willfully brutal men motivated more by their desire for money, power, and personal advancement than by any sense of national service.

Growing out of utopian hopes for a New World, Enlightenment-inspired cosmopolitanism, and Quaker preachings, the American dream of unbroken peace took on new life with the end of the War of 1812, and new intellectual energy with the concurrent surge of Unitarianism. "No sooner was peace declared in 1815 than two Unitarian ministers, Noah Worcester and William Ellery Channing, took steps to launch a permanent protest against war and an increasing campaign to build peace." Using Worcester's magazine, *Friend of Peace*, and the pulpit as common platforms for its views, the new pacifist cult asserted that, "We have our *slave ships* and our regular army," and warned that, "in a community, in which precedence is given to the military profession, freedom cannot long endure."[4]

Like the egalitarian military opposition, the pacifist outcry gained in voice during the 1830s and 1840s. But if parallel in development, the two were not in harmony. Certainly the often aggressive Jacksonians did not themselves represent the pacifists' ideal of peaceable citizens-of-the-world. James Edmonds was exaggerating, but only slightly, when he asked his readers to reconsider the thirty years from 1830 to 1860. "Never, perhaps in so-called modern times has there been a more swaggering, quarrelsome tribe of folk, speaking one language and marshalled under one flag. They were . . . lusty, prolific, land-hungry, truculent,

. . . and resentful of discipline."⁵ Calhoun, commenting on the America of his own day, estimated that there was no country in the world more inclined to war, for the American people were young in nature and "disposed for adventure of any description."⁶ Indeed, the pacifists, especially the educated New England variety, were as ready to disparage the Jacksonian image as the military gentleman type. "I stand amazed," one wrote, "at the disposition of intellectual men to eulogize war and warriors. . . . The hero of New Orleans or Tippecanoe, with only a modicum of talent or knowledge, leaves the first minds of the land behind them in the race of popularity and power."⁷

The pacifist critique became increasingly uncompromising, lumping together all military men regardless of social, religious, or political affiliations, military record, or nationality. All military affairs were immoral acts and all officers, they declared, sought war. Channing, who remained their most prominent spokesman until his death in 1842, was one of the few to qualify his outlook by stating, "I mean not to deny to military men equal virtue with other classes of society." Just the same, he repeatedly asserted, "How common is it for military men to desire war, as giving rich prizes and as advancing them in their profession. They are willing to slaughter their fellow-creatures for money and distinction."⁸ R. P. Stebbins was more concise, "The *trade* of the warrior is to injure; his sworn duty, to harm; his office, to destroy."⁹

Capitalizing on America's faith in progress, the pacifists often pictured military men as anachronistic representatives of subcivilizations from the past. Charles Sumner characterized both the church and the army as holdovers from feudal institutions and as history's twin promoters of warfare. In his now famous "The True Grandeur of Nations" speech delivered in Boston in 1845, he first lamented the "strange and unblessed conjunction of the clergy with war" and then turned on the soldiers. "From the prejudices engendered by the church, I pass to the prejudices engendered by the army itself. I allude directly to what is called the *point of honor*, early child of chivalry, the living representative in our day of an age of barbarism."[10] Channing expressed much the same idea in different language. "The dress of Europe," he observed, "not many centuries ago was fashioned very much after what may be called the harlequin style. This taste belongs to rude ages and has passed away very much with the progress of civilization. . . . The military man is the only harlequin left us from ancient times. It is time that his dazzling finery were gone."[11]

As "living representatives of an age of barbarism," the nation's officers were presumed to be inhumanly indifferent to suffering, if not wantonly cruel. "On this point," one pacifist wrote, "history is decisive. Warriors have generally been . . . like Attila and Alaric, . . . a species of human tigers, skilled in little else than the art of bloodshed, devastation and misery."[12] Published pacifist collections included detailed and gory accounts of European torture systems, implying that this was the sadistic temper behind all military discipline.

It was on this point that foreign observers again showed astonishment. While the pacifists pictured America's military gentlemen as unfeeling authoritarians, the European military observers often saw just the opposite. To them, the American army was in danger of losing control of its units because it had nearly abandoned discipline, particularly corporal punishment. One wrote, "The mistaken humanity of pride that has forbidden corporal punishment has not apparently substituted any efficient method of maintaining discipline."[13]

Still another theme receiving full play in pacifist expression was the pure waste of military expenditures, particularly the pay and privileges garnered by military "gentlemen of leisure." In his 1845 Boston oration, Sumner pointedly noted that the salary of the captain of the battleship Ohio (then lying in Boston harbor) was $4,500, while "the salary of the President of Harvard is $2,235.00, without leave of absence, and never off duty." The democrat's challenge was, "Who needs a *regular* army?"; but "Who needs an army [at all]?" was Sumner's audacious cry to an audience including high-ranking military men.[14]

*

On balance, the pacifists' influence in the Jacksonian age was not profound. They simply could not make headway in an expansive and nationalistic society. Yet, if most of the country did not embrace their thinking, the influence of their general line of thought when coming from men of the prominence of Sumner, Wayland, and Channing is undeniable. Their pleas, at certain times, were repeated by more broadly influential sources. In 1827, for example, the Washington *National Intelligencer* spoke in typical pacifist generalizations when, during Jackson's campaign for the presidency, it objected to placing *any* military man in authority "because having once tasted of the pleasure of absolute command . . . he may endanger the public peace, at home as well as abroad."[15] And again in the 1840s, a temporary convergence of New England reform thought with the widespread political objections to America's heavy-handed treatment of Mexico gave renewed force to pacifist expression.

It was the pacifists' long-term influence which would prove most important, however. The humanitarian idealists of the antebellum days were, it turns out, establishing the foundation for the much more consequential neopacifist movements of the twentieth century. To appreciate that point (addressed later in this study), it will be necessary to have clearly in mind where the arguments of the antebellum philosophical pacifists differed from the opposition to officership expressed by the more pragmatic mainstream Jacksonians. To contrast:

1. Cosmopolitan-minded pacifists opposed *all* military activities; the more nationalistic Jacksonians did not. They

were supremely proud of America's military victories, and especially those of "democratic" armies like the one at New Orleans.

2. Philosophical pacifists condemned "military tigers"; anti-intellectual democrats condemned effete and cultivated regulars, and they idolized heroes like Crockett and Jackson who were noted for their eagerness to do battle. In the election of 1824, they backed "Andy Jackson who can fight" against "John Quincy Adams who can write."[16]

3. Humanitarian pacifists abhorred the brutality of military discipline; the tougher-minded western leaders were themselves often stern disciplinarians.* Jackson was a prime example, making full use of untempered military justice and command authority to gain obedience from his unruly troops.[17]

4. Idealistic pacifist reformers protested all military expenditures (until needed to fight slavery); opportunistic political liberals constantly sought their "democratic share" of military rank and monies. Representative Cannon, it will be recalled, sought to close the Military Academy and transfer the funds to militia forces.

There were, to be sure, times when their differences were not so sharply pronounced. In depression days, for instance, both the pacifists and the democrats struck hard at governmental demands for taxes to support military institutions in a geographically secured nation. On other points, too, they could at times come remarkably close. Either would have agreed with "Father of the House" Lewis Williams (who served in Congress from 1815 to 1842) when

---

*For decades the New England humanitarians led a fight for total abolishment of corporal punishment and for other service reforms, but Jacksonian Congresses showed little real concern. According to a recent study, it was not until Congress was face to face with the issues of the approaching Civil War that much reform progress was made. Flogging, for instance, was not abolished in the navy until 1850.

he declared that "in our free country persons habituated to military life become, as officers, . . . domineering and intolerant."[18]

United in their attendant zeal for spreading the vision of the career officer as a member of an un-American persuasion, pacifists and democrats made strange bedfellows. All the same, it was largely through their joint efforts that the eighteenth-century officer-and-gentleman myth was fragmented once and for all.

Chapter Five

The Jeffersonian Ideal: Military Gentlemen As Enlightened Men Of Science[1]

You may be assured, my friend, that the diploma of this [United States Military] Academy is received in the world—not only as conclusive evidence that its owner is a gentleman, . . . but also that he is possessed of mental qualifications of no ordinary nature.

—Iver James Austin[2]

Science! Meet daughter of Time thou art
Who alterest all things with thy peering eyes!

—Cadet Edgar Allan Poe[3]

America's vision of officership in the Jacksonian age is not to be discovered by plumbing the views of the pacifists and the political critics alone. If not so vociferous in statement, there is still voluminous commentary which indicates that much of the nation, including most of its intellectuals, continued to see the officer corps in a favorable light. One approach, in line with the precepts of Jefferson in particular and the Enlightenment in general, envisioned a corps of officers drawn from the "natural aristocracy," men who were, at once, scientists, schooled technicians, and military commanders. The Enlightenment optimists presumed that, in the not too distant future, civilization's advance would eliminate war; and, in the meantime, the army's officer corps should be a combination military fire brigade and a reservoir of civil engineers. In peacetime, they would build bridges, canals, roads, and fortifications; in wartime emergencies, they would lead their country in battle.

The idea was not peculiarly American, but the new nation provided a unique opportunity to apply such theories on a grand scale. Jefferson had been quick to perceive this. "After making the Louisiana Purchase, Jefferson . . . [used] the officer corps of the tiny regular army as a source of competent, responsible and thoroughly loyal Federal agents not only to take over but to explore the new domain," men like Meriwether Lewis, William Clark, and Zebulon Pike. It was precisely this vision of an organized body of productive and trustworthy military explorers and engineers that led to the establishment of the Military Academy in 1802. "It is sometimes forgotten," Walter Millis reminds his readers, "that Jefferson, who cut the already small regular army in half, . . . [became] the true father of our whole system of military education."[4]

The concept of the military gentleman as a peacetime scientist-technician took on factual substance as officers from both services made important contributions in civil and military engineering, marine science, and western exploration.[5] West Point, placed appropriately under the control of the chief of Engineers, came to life following the War of 1812. The French Ecole Polytechnique (the Enlightenment-inspired technical school which Napoleon converted into a military academy) became its model. For half a century, military studies were subordinated to military engineering, and military engineering was subordinated to civil engineering. It is a revealing fact that the nation's military college established a Department of Engineering in 1812, but had no Department of Tactics, as such, until 1858. The point can be overplayed, but there is no doubt about the dominance of engineering over military subjects in the early West Point curriculum.[6]

Almost as soon as the officer-technician figure took form in American thought, he began to acquire mythical proportions. And for good reason. He combined the better features of several American hero figures: the intrepid minuteman, the dedicated scientist, the glamorous soldier-adventurer, the respected battlefield commander, and the dauntless pioneer. Appealing to pragmatist and idealist alike, this man could be productive in peacetime and a savior in wartime. Indeed, the idea of devoted soldier-scientists leading a peace-loving nation across the continent would prove the most consistently admired of the various images of officership to emerge in the nineteenth century.

The address of Congressman Thomas Reed to the cadets at West Point in 1827 is one of many striking illustrations of the early fruition of this view. Reed noted with obvious pride that the Military Academy "has become a national object of deep interest to the American people, and to enlightened travellers from abroad." "We have seen," he went on, "a small embryo, planted by the illustrious Jefferson, unfold itself with the progress of the country." Here is a school conceived in the "spirit of science and of liberty." And he added, "Let no one undervalue the sciences which are principally taught at this institution. . . . [They] constitute the basis of all true knowledge." Rejoicingly, he told

the future officers, "Civil engineering will be, for a long
time, the most useful and memorable pursuit. . . . What
a happy destiny awaits you!" Reed's supreme optimism, his
faith in science, his emphasis on military-civil pursuits, his
pride in West Point's Jeffersonian origins—all these were
common to the views expressed by supporters of the
Academy throughout its formative years.[7]

And Reed was right about the interest created among
"enlightened travellers from abroad." After her visit to the
Academy in 1819, young Frances Wright (the Scottish-born,
English-reared, reformer of French materialist philosophy
who was collecting her *Views of Society and Manners in
America* which would bring her international prominence)
nearly bubbled over with enthusiasm for the sheer perfection of a place that trained officers who were to become
"peaceful tillers of the soil," only to bear arms in case of
war. The Academy's purpose "is not," she insisted, "to rear
a band of *regulars*," in her European sense of the word. The
military engineers at West Point, she observed, combined
"the mildness and frankness of manner peculiar to the
American gentleman"—although she ingenuously admitted
her ideas were to a large extent "attributable to General
Swift," a former superintendent and another "enlightened
American officer."[8]

★

Enthusiasm for the technician-soldier concept served as
a balancing force to the growing egalitarian and pacifist-
based criticisms of the profession of arms. In his second
annual message to Congress, President John Quincy Adams
reflected the optimistic social climate then so favorable to
the New World's versatile soldier-engineer. "In a period of
profound peace the conduct of the mere military establishment forms but a very inconsiderable portion of the duties
. . . of the Department of War," the president pointed out.
The army, he noted happily, is "marked with order, reg-

ularity, and discipline"; and is spiritually in tune with the nation. "The officers feel themselves . . . that the glory of a republican army must consist in the spirit of freedom. . . ." Given this situation, the President was sure that his military men would be able not only "to secure our shores" and maintain "orderly relations . . . with the Indian tribes," but also bring about "the internal improvements and surveys for the locations of roads and canals, which . . . may engross so large a share of their benefactions to our country."[9]

The image of the productive soldier-scientist-engineer weathered the democratic attacks of the '30s and '40s quite well. President Jackson, himself at times under attack because of his military background, found it politic to assure the voters that, "considering standing armies as dangerous to free governments in time of peace, I shall not seek to enlarge our present establishment. . . ." But the demands by more outspoken critics for further reductions in the regular officer corps and the closing of the Military Academy went generally unheeded by the president and the Congress at large.* The military technicians, so instrumental in improving and protecting eastern harbors, as well as opening and securing routes to the west, were too useful to be eliminated.[10]

Even at the height of antebellum criticism, the debates concerning the role of a military academy in a free republic were far from one sided. Academy defenders were numer-

---

*Before his election, Jackson publicly admired the Military Academy and referred to it as "the best school in the world", and as president he sometimes urged its support. But Jackson and Sylvannus Thayer, the long-time superintendent, were both strong-willed men and often at odds, particularly over issues of Thayer's authority. On more than one occasion, the president countermanded the Academy's ruling to dismiss cadets (including Jackson's nephew) on disciplinary grounds. Thayer, under attack from Democratic congressmen, eventually resigned in frustration.

ous and influential. Leading educators, like Henry Barnard, were openly proud of an American institution, "world renowned, as West Point justly is. . . ."[11] Horace Mann, though outspoken in his opposition to war, also had high praise for West Point, where he had "rarely, if ever, seen anything that equalled either the excellence of the teaching or the proficiency of the taught."[12]

Men of letters agreed. In *Notions of the Americans*, James Fenimore Cooper declared that "the discipline, order, neatness, respectability and scientific progress of the young men are all admirable. . . . Perhaps no similar institution in the world is superior."[13] Editor and poet William Cullen Bryant was instrumental in the appointment of one of the Academy's professors and later helped his nephew gain admission.[14] Emerson denounced the Jacksonian notion that the Academy was "hotbed of aristocracy" as the "word of some political hack."[15]

The annual reports of the Board of Visitors, composed not only of politicians and military men but a wide variety of respected intellectuals (including Edward Everett, Bancroft, George Ticknor, Mann, and Emerson), were as a rule highly flattering. According to a recent study, the Boards became, during the superintendency of Sylvannus Thayer (1817-1833), "a kind of public relations project . . . [and] the occasional maverick who . . . submitted a strongly critical minority report, carried little weight. . . ."[16] With only occasional flare-ups, the Boards remained essentially sympathetic throughout the period. Not all the reports were as overweening as the view expressed in 1842 by I. J. Austin who stated: "I have been commissioned by the Board of Visitors to express . . . their unanimous opinion when I say, that more high-toned discipline, or better conduct, greater precision and accuracy of thought . . . more triumphant results of that rare and happy union of intellect and industry . . . have never been witnessed by any of our number in any portion of the country." But that tone was far from unusual.[17]

Nor were such praises simply for public display. There is a rather persistent note of surprised admiration on the part of the more skeptical Academy visitors. Ticknor, while serving as a member of the Board of Visitors, wrote privately to his wife: "The institution itself . . . has gratified me beyond my expectations. This feeling, I believe, I share in common with the rest of the visitors, and have no doubt the Academy deserves it. There is a thoroughness, promptness, and efficiency in the knowledge of the cadets which I have never seen before, and which I did not expect to find here."[18]

Ticknor's experience was repeated some thirty years later by Emerson, who came to West Point reluctantly and wrote his wife of his anger when he found that he was expected to stay sixteen days instead of two. But he soon found that "West Point Academy makes a very agreeable impression on me." He noted with pleasure "the military bearing of the cadets, their probity, veracity, self-reliance, loyalty to each other, and superb discipline." He made a sheet of "West Point Notes" and was prepared to tell the cadets "Your ways inspire lively curiosity. I thought two days sufficient. I could willingly spend twenty. . . ."[19]

The Mexican War experience did much to silence the critics of the career officers, particularly of the soldier-technician variety. By general consensus, the engineer-trained West Pointers proved themselves nearly as adaptable to wartime emergency as Jefferson had visualized. Even the critics admitted that the supposedly soft aristocrats gave excellent account of themselves in battle. It is doubtful whether the Academy graduates were yet ready to provide on short notice effective leadership at the highest levels, but old soldier Winfield Scott, for all his pomposity, took care of the strategic requirements, and brilliantly. And it was Scott, still the nation's foremost military figure, who, at the approach of the next war, told the people that "but for our graduated cadets, the [Mexican] War . . . probably would have lasted some four or five years. . . ."[20]

★

When encomia as these (coming from such diverse sources as Scott, Ticknor, and Mann) are posed against the deeply bitter hostility emanating from the egalitarians and pacifists, the remarkable range of feelings toward military careerists that developed in Jacksonian America comes clear. In 1854, Samuel Bayard, a Democratic Congressman (whose son attended the Academy) warned the cadets "you will serve a jealous mistress. . . . Republics *are* ungrateful." In a tone of near apology, he reflected, "There is, too, a deep and deadly repugnance in superficial and unreflecting minds. . . . They fear and hate the soldier. . . . They forget, that according to the history of other republics, the people were always corrupted, before the army became dangerous."[21] At a time when some state legislatures were calling for the end of the "aristocratical institution at West Point," politicians from other states were holding it up as a model for liberal America. "Turn your eyes to this Academy: it is a perfect republic," cried Senator Ashbel Smith of Texas. "Honors are awarded to those who win them. . . . Suppose for a moment, the distinctions of the Academy were awarded not to merit, but conferred as a birthright. . . . The absurdity is hardly greater than that of hereditary monarchs and aristocrats."[22]

What the record clearly demonstrates is this. When viewed as a republican-minded defender of the New World, a soldier-scientist and a productive technician, the regular officer—in spite of the sometimes savage political attacks —was still highly admired. As Bayard put it, "Let the demogogue from the rostrum inveigh against the military chieftain—I would always rather trust the honor of the soldier, than the professions of the mercenary and crafty politician."[23]

Chapter Six

Environmental Modifications: Military Gentlemen As Indian Fighters And Frontier Policemen[1]

[On the American frontier] no one can . . . enjoy the enviable privilege of wearing an epaulet and an embroidered coat. The service is one of real and almost constant privations.

—British Captain Thomas Hamilton[2]

Whatever their training and aspirations, most nineteenth-century officers served an Indian-fighting, frontier-patrolling army. There were those who, in the Jeffersonian spirit, found opportunities to serve science while stationed on the cordon of frontier outposts; but their primary duty was to regulate activities in the new American west. The Louisiana Purchase of 1802 gave the United States an enormous piece of territory. Although British traders and their Indian allies controlled a large portion of it until after the War of 1812, with the war's end western expansion went forward unchecked. With it went most of the regular army.

The military men sent across the Alleghenies were very much out of the nation's sight and mind. When pictured at all, the frontier army was usually seen only in the passing glimpses provided by occasional articles and reports written by western travelers. Surveying early nineteenth-century periodicals, for example, leads one to the conclusion that the educated public was more interested in, and better informed about, Indian customs than the activities of their own army.[3] This is hardly surprising. Cut from 10,000 to 6,000 authorized personnel in 1821, the army was not only small in size, but its units were now far more distant—in more ways than just mileage—from the nation's cultural centers than they had been in the colonial-revolutionary era. There was, moreover, little in the monotonous routines of these distant posts to excite attention back East. As one observer wrote, "Perfectly isolated as these outposts are . . . the soldier [must] . . . kill the hours of a tedious solitude, and beguile away the extreme loneliness of his situation."[4] While Indian "incidents" were not uncommon, large-scale battles, especially in the northwest, were infrequent and seldom prolonged.

In spite of the public's lack of interest, yet another image of the military leader, shaped by his frontier service, was slowly taking form. When pictured as an Indian fighter, the officer-and-gentleman was becoming a less embroidered, more sinewy, figure. Pre-Revolution officers, even when engaged in Indian warfare, had remained rather strictly patrician in type. Like Washington, they had usually served only temporarily on the frontier before returning to their established niche in society. But with the army's displacement westward, the regular officer became much less a product of the British-American culture of the Atlantic coastal strip. The War of 1812 accelerated this mutation by weeding out Revolutionary-generals-gone-to-seed. As historian Richard Hildreth wrote not many years afterward, "By the end of 1813, after a series of defeats and debacles, nearly all of the original generals had been forced out . . . and into their places had stepped younger and abler officers."[5]

With the final battle at New Orleans, Andrew Jackson, half courtier and half Indian fighter, stepped front-stage in America's imagination. It is difficult to gauge accurately the influence of Jackson's immense notoriety on the nation's impression of military careerists. Although he held a commission as a regular officer from 1811 to 1819, Jackson represented for much of the nation almost the opposite. The Battle of New Orleans was quickly mythologized by western "historians" into a victory of nature's nobleman: a victory of the untrained, unpolished, undisciplined, unlettered, but sagacious frontier sharpshooter over "the martinet . . . accustomed to regard neatness and primness as essential virtues of the good soldier." To his enthusiastic biographers, Jackson was greater than "the *mere* officer, who acquired his knowledge of tactics from *books*, and his ideas of subordination from reading the articles of war."[6]

To others, Old Hickory represented quite something else. Under Cooper's pen, Jackson, even on the night of his election defeat of 1824, was every inch a gentleman in grace, style, dress, and deportment. "General Jackson," Cooper has his spokesman in *Notions of the Americans* say, "returned [our] greeting with his usually mild and graceful mien. I watched his manly and marked features narrowly during the courteous dialogue. . . . He left us laughing and conversing cheerfully with some ladies, who induced him to join their party. A minute before, he had been seen congratulating his successful rival with great dignity, and with perfect good nature."[7]

The views are mixed, but the general impression seems clear. As candidate for president, Jackson was, as Arthur Schlesinger reminds us, "known primarily as a military hero"; for many, he remained so throughout his lifetime. And for all his plantation ways and his strings of race horses, he did epitomize, and thus helped popularize, a less urbane species of officer than was represented in America's earlier military lore, founded on the Revolutionary War.[8]

All this is not to suggest that the old standard conception of the officer as a gentleman had lost full currency, even in the case of the isolated frontier patrolman. The most frequent comment of cultivated frontier travelers was their assertion that the officers they met had remained gentlemen despite their "deplorable" separation from civilization. Well-known antiquarian Caleb Atwater gave a glowing description of the officer complement he found at the posts on the upper Mississippi in 1829. The younger leaders, he claimed, were invariably gentlemen, "brave, active, vigorous, energetic, high minded, honorable, strictly honest and correct in . . . deportment. . . . These officers, belonging to the first families in the nation, educated in the very best manner, are induced by their self respect, to conduct themselves in the very best manner on all occasions. . . . As officers, as gentlemen, and as men, I feel proud of them as my countrymen."[9]

Such totally unqualified praise was surely too generous. But, regardless, the picture projected by both foreign reporters and respected American writers, such as Atwater and Governor Cass of the Michigan Territory, was much the same. Still essentially an eighteenth-century patrician, the western commander was nevertheless taking his place in the long line of somewhat unconventional and less refined American military favorites that includes Swamp Fox Marion, Old Hickory Jackson, Tippecanoe Harrison,

Rough and Ready Taylor, Sam Grant, Billy Sherman, "Fustest" Forrest, the postbellum cavalrymen of the western plains, the Rough Riders, Rogers Rangers, and the Green Berets, among others.

★

A less becoming version of the military image was also developing in the West. Not yet widely broadcast in the East, the reputation of regulars as bullying policemen and officious province bureaucrats was fairly common in certain sections by the '30s and '40s. To many settlers, military officers were petty, domineering tyrants, using riffraff troops from the Old World to control the territorial affairs. As in all of these various views, there was a degree of factual basis. The frontier army *was* to a large extent composed of men who had deserted European or American society for one reason or another. In the blunt opinion of one British observer, "the enlisted soldiers were either the scum of the population of the older States, or of the worthless German, English, or Irish immigrants." At times, the number of men of European birth became so great that they gave a foreign complexion to the whole army—a feature which inspired neither great confidence nor affection among the settlers.

The recruitment problem had no easy solution. Obtaining reliable enlistees was almost impossible during some periods. High recruiting standards eliminated too many applicants, and lowering the standards resulted in such poor quality soldiers as to be nearly as much burden as good. Drunkenness was common and desertion rates were appallingly high. In turn, by modern, if not by nineteenth-century standards, the discipline was often brutal. While not usually as callous or pointless as the pacifists suggested, it was dreadfully severe both physically and mentally. Men were required to march for hours or days on end with stone-laden packs for minor offenses and were heartily flogged for more serious ones. Convicted deserters were

generally put to death by firing squad; if not shot, they were
sometimes put through the mental torture of being
required to dig their own graves and were marched to their
place of execution before being told of a lesser sentence.

Local discontent with the military leaders did not, however, generally spring from humanitarian concerns. More
often it grew out of the resentments created among the
unruly settlers by the army's assignment to uphold and regulate federal laws. Enforcement activities put the officer
corps in the unpopular role of frontier referees, and the
resultant antipathies became progressively more acute as
Congress continued to pass acts which required restrictions
on the local sale of liquors and firearms and demanded
punishment for encroachments on Indian territory. As
Francis Prucha summarizes the situation, "To some settlers
the army authority seemed despotic and malicious, the commanding officers petty tyrants; and Americans in general
were willing to believe and spread atrocity stories about
army officers." While the available evidence tends to refute
many of the charges, there was apparently sufficient combined truth and fiction to establish an impression of officership that would continue for decades. Half a century later,
a United States congressman was still maintaining that "we
select men for this [frontier] business of throat-cutting and
brain-bespattering . . . because they are fitted for that particular service."[10]

★

Roughhewn hero of the Indian campaigns or cutthroat
overlord, the frontier officer was gradually becoming a
familiar type. In 1837, Washington Irving published a work
that serves as an excellent indicator both of the influence
of the western service on the shifting images of the military
gentleman and of the intellectual crosscurrents behind
those images. *The Adventures of Captain Bonneville, U.S.A.*[11]
relates the experience of an American officer during three-

and-a-half years of exploration in the Rocky Mountains. Based on Bonneville's carefully kept journals, Irving's account soon became internationally known and the captain himself somewhat of a celebrity. Forty years later, Johns Hopkins' President D. C. Gilman would recall that during his youth "Bonneville . . . was a classic story of adventure among school boys. . . ."[12]

The figure of Bonneville blended several of the different impressions of officership then prevalent in America. He was, in one sense, the military gentleman, an offspring of European culture and gentility. As Irving noted, his father, a Frenchman, "was an excellent scholar; well acquainted with Latin and Greek, and fond of the modern classics"; and the son "inherited something of his father's *bonhommie.* . . ." At the same time, the captain was also representative of the schooled military technician of the Enlightenment mode. His "excitable imagination," Irving tells us, was "disciplined in early years, by mathematical studies . . . at West Point where he acquitted himself very creditably."[13] Later, when stationed in the West, he fulfilled his role of military-engineer by charting unknown territories.

For all that, the basic picture that comes through is neither Old World patrician nor New World soldier-scientist. Captain Bonneville, as Irving perceived, "had strangely ingrafted the trapper and the hunter upon the soldier." This military gentleman of French descent, this West Point trained engineer, became more a representative of the primitive West. His story is really that of the frontier scout leading his little band through Indian territory in the fashion of Daniel Boone. He is the trapper and hunter and small-unit commander relying on his native ingenuity to carry him through.

Irving's authorship itself is indicative of the pervasive influence of the frontier on the image of America's military men. Here was the very model of patricianism writing his third work about the raw American West. As one London literary critic wrote, "What! Washington Irving a buffalo-hunter on the Prairies? . . . It was but yesterday we saw this same Washington Irving in London a quiet, gentlemanly, douce, little, middle-aged man."[14] The urbane Irving had hardly become a buffalo-hunter, but the frontier did have a way of leaving its mark on all comers, writers and military men included.

★

Considering that the army was engaged on the frontier for over a generation even prior to the Mexican War, the most notable point is how slowly the westernized military image took hold. It was not until "Old-Rough-and-Ready" Taylor and others like him drove into Mexico (with a style markedly different from that of their commander, grandiose Winfield Scott) that the constabulary brand of military gentleman became a common figure in America's imagination. For a quarter of a century, from 1815 to 1840, the frontier soldier was generally ignored. As one contemporary foreign observer noted, between wars, "the [American] people care[d] nothing for a set of invisible beings mewed up in some petty forts on the vast frontier."[15]

Chapter Seven

The Persisting Legend: Military Gentlemen As Refined But Virile Patricians[1]

[Captain Arthur Butler had a] decided manly view, . . . his whole bearing, visage and figure, seemed to speak of one familiar with enterprise and fond of danger:—they denoted gentle breeding predominating over a life of toil and privation . . . [and] his profession . . . was seen in his erect and preemptory carriage. . . .

—from **Horseshoe Robinson** by John P. Kennedy[2]

Given the diversity of the cultural forces at work, it was to be expected that America would soon create its own several species of the military leader. What is surprising is that the old eighteenth-century model of officership inherited from Europe remained so firmly entrenched in American lore. With only minor changes, the polished patrician-soldier continued to be one of the most popular figures in American writings. Historical, fictional, biographical, dramatic, and periodical literature of the Jacksonian period abound with examples. The officer-and-gentleman—refined, courtly, elegant, discriminating, and obviously admired —remained a standard image throughout the age of Davy Crockett and triumphant democracy!

Before examining the evidence in detail, certain causes can be suggested. For one thing, following Waterloo, military theory and practice in the entire western world returned in some degree to eighteenth-century precepts. Universal conscript systems developed in the Napoleonic era decayed in exemptions and deferments, and Western armies once again relied upon long-service forces, usually a combination of professionals and long-term volunteers. Britain, for one, almost completely reverted to the volunteer-and-professional system. In the United States, militia enrollments were maintained after the War of 1812, but in practice most of those units degenerated from semi-professional bodies to little more than social gatherings and soon lost their effectiveness as fighting forces.

With the backsliding of "republican" military theories and systems, old attitudes toward officership were revived. In Europe, remnants of the feudal classes made new claims on their ancient prerogatives. The Prussian junkers rejected army reforms and the British gentry reasserted its control over the military by purchasing commissions for its younger sons, as it had in the previous century. Colonial wars of the nineteenth century were once again fought with forces largely officered by sons of the upper class. This counter-wave of military styles was felt in America as well. In Walter

Millis' words, "The code of the 'officer and the gentleman,' not only preserved paying careers for the sons of the Prussian nobility or the British landed gentry; it operated [if less overtly] much farther afield, leading to pistol duels in the American backwoods or enshrining the concepts of chivalric honor, class prejudice and privilege among the young gentlemen . . . [at] West Point."[3]

While this revival of earlier military manners and methods no doubt contributed to the perpetuation of the patrician-soldier ideal in the United States, there were other, more fundamental, forces involved. As a kind of social counterforce to rising Jacksonianism, there was a continuing and very conscious regard for gentlemanship as a style of life. This was an age, Boorstin reminds us, when such an incongruous pair as Davy Crockett and George Washington "both emerged into legendary fame." And W. R. Taylor (tracing the Cavalier and Yankee figures in American literature) has observed that "one of the strangest developments of the egalitarian thirties was the resurgence . . . [of an] essentially anti-democratic and static ideal of a Good Society, with its obvious source in the literature which celebrated the English squirearchy." This affection for upper-class standards was reflected in more than just the belles letters of the period. The noted German traveler and author Francis J. Grund wrote a well-documented account of *Aristocracy in America*, and William Grimshaw, in his popular *History of the United States*, complained that although "aristocratic customs are so generally denounced, . . . there are in the United States more nominal nobility than any country in the world. . . ."[4]

For all the bravado of our more outspoken egalitarians, the United States was still feeling its way into a social-political system that had never been tried before. It was only natural that there would be reservations. Some writers were certain that the path led to national disaster; others at least wished to proceed cautiously. Either way, many of America's spokesmen continued to keep faith in "proven"

ways and values. Spurred by their distaste for egalitarian
enthusiasms, which even democratic booster George Bancroft called "screaming with the mob," social and intellectual
leaders of the age deliberately chose to emulate, with sectional colorations, the upper classes of Europe. "In the
South . . . [it was] a 'democracy' modeled after the society
of pre-Christian Greece, in which a large population of
slaves supported a small population of enlightened
freemen. Moneyed aristocrats in the East . . . adhered to
the stake-in-society theory. . . . Less materialistic patricians
continued to put their trust in family; others, in the learned
professions; and still others (as the Brahmins of Boston),
in both." Young scholars beat a path to the Old World, the
fountainhead of knowledge and accepted customs, and part
and parcel of their admiration was an obvious regard for
the patrician-military codes generally esteemed by that
class.[5]

★

There certainly is no doubting that America's foremost
writers, whatever their reasons, still preferred their officers
as gentlemen. The historians are prime examples. For
them, the patricians of the Revolution remained history's
military paragons. John Marshall, writing *The Life of George
Washington* early in the century, set the tone, for years to
come, in both military biography and Washingtonphilia by
stressing his subject's "strong . . . attachment to a military
life" and his "proud and punctilious feelings of a soldier."
Marshall gave a lengthy account of the young colonial's
military career, emphasing that the national father's
renowned strength of character was shaped by his honorable and rigorous service as an officer of the British army.[6]

The description of the famous Indian ambush of British
forces at the Monongahela River in the French and Indian
War serves as a graphic illustration of Marshall's conception
of officership—as it does with many later writers. Marshall's

account stands in contrast with those of less genteel inclinations who, over the years, chose to magnify General Braddock's aristocratic shortcomings while making young Washington an untainted, almost humble, commander of the Virginia provincial troops. (He was, in fact, Braddock's aide-de-camp.) In the manufactured folklore of Parson Weems, for example, a grossly arrogant Braddock rejects the counsel of the wise, yet modest, young Virginian on how to fight Indians. In one typical Weems vignette, "Smothering his feelings, [Washington] rode toward his men, biting his lips with grief and rage, to think how many brave fellows would draw short breath that day through the pride and obstinacy of one epauletted madman."[7]

Most of our early historians, urbane and federalist by nature, followed Marshall's rather than Weems' lead. They made less of Braddock's shortcomings, while picturing Washington as the epitome of patrician leadership. For Marshall's readers, the young colonel was only the best of several capable officers on the scene—because "he manifested that coolness, that self-possession, that fearlessness. . . . which are so necessary to the character of the consummate soldier." And rather than the "brave fellows" of Weems' account, the British line soldiers were the cowardly villains of the affair. Marshall quotes Washington at length to the point that, "the dastardly behavior of the regular troops (so called), exposed [the officers] who were inclined to do their duty, to almost certain death."[8]

This picture of America's model soldier-hero struggling, along with his fellow officers of the crown, against the uncontrolled fear of the common herd remained standard for four decades. The great chroniclers of the Jacksonian era were of the narrative school, choosing to picture the past rather than analyze it; but whether presented by a Jeffersonian republican like Francis Parkman, a whig like Washington Irving, a southern champion like W. G. Simms, or a democrat like George Bancroft, their portraits of officership were much the same as Marshall's.

Parkman's favorite commanders are clearheaded, natural-born leaders. At Monongahela, Washington is again the model of the enlightened commander, rallying the troops and riding "through the tumult, calm and undaunted."[9] Irving, like Marshall forty years before, explicitly accredits Washington's capacity for greatness to his experience as an army officer. Irving also emphasized the "consummate bravery" of the British regular officers, even though gentlemen of leisure. He wrote, "Washington beheld with admiration those who . . . had appeared to him to have an almost effeminate regard for personal ease and convenience, now exposing themselves to imminent death . . . in the vain hope of enspiriting the men. . . ."[10] Bancroft painted the same scene, giving his greatest credit to the officers who "bravely advanced . . . but were sacrificed by the soldiers, who declined to follow them, and even fired upon them from the rear."[11]

Change the battle and the picture stays much the same. In his *History of South Carolina*, Simms tells how the Americans during the Battle of Eutaw, were on the verge of victory when the men suddenly "dispersed without order among the tents, . . . fastened on intoxicating liquors, and [became] utterly unmanageable." As a result the "officers, nearly abandoned by their soldiers, became conspicuous marks"; and there was "an unhappy loss of valuable lives . . . [including] the gallant Colonel. . . ."[12] To liberal historians half a century later, the class flavor of such accounts would be totally distasteful, as we will see. For the time, however, it was seldom (Richard Hildreth's balanced portraits being the prime exception[13]) that the officer corps of any respected western nation was pictured as less than peerless leaders of scratch troops.

Lavish praises for gentlemen-soldiers filled the pages of the great biographical collections of the day. Officers of such diverse backgrounds as Marion, Washington, LaFayette, von Steuben, and Jackson were cast in the standard mold and lauded equally; and it was made abundantly clear that Benedict Arnold's faults lay in the man, not in his calling. Arnold continued to be an historical personification of "The Rake's Progress," his illustrious army career ruined by yielding "to the temptations of pride and vanity," and by "indulging himself in the pleasures of a sumptuous table and expensive equipage." Collections such as the multi-volume *Library of American Biography* edited by Jared Sparks were filled with moralizing reminders that the converse was equally true: great officers avoided the temptations that accompany high office. Many outstanding soldiers, these works proclaimed, had succeeded; only a few, like Arnold and the now forgotten Charles Lee, had failed the test.[14]

★

Bellitristic literature of the day likewise did much to popularize the gentleman-soldier. On the American stage, the patricians of 1776, rather than Old Hickory or Tippecanoe, remained the military favorites. Putnam, Morgan, Hale, Wayne, Ethan Allen, and others were all popular stage figures—and all were overshadowed by the now legendary Washington. Revolutionary War plays like Burk's "Bunker Hill" were frequently restaged, and more recent works based on the War of 1812 at times took extraordinary care to demonstrate that U.S. victories were won by *conventional* forces and *traditional* gentlemen-officers, not by some rabble of irregulars fighting guerrilla warfare. As one of the characters in N. M. Noah's "She Would be a Soldier" describes the Battle of Chippewa, "The enemy . . . was encountered on the plains. . . . No tangled thicket . . . gave effect or facility to our rifles. . . . Force was opposed to force, skill to skill . . . in regular, disciplined, and admirable order. . . . [And Winfield] Scott rode through the lines, cheering the men and gallantly leading them on. . . ."[15]

Far more influential in this regard than the drama was the new "historical novel"; and ironically, it was James Fenimore Cooper, author of *The American Democrat*, who was the prime literary expositor of military partricianism. Cooper's fictional soldiers are nearly all members of the upper-class dutifully fulfilling their *noblesse oblige*.

The Spy (1821) was this nation's first internationally acclaimed novel, and with it Cooper, like Marshall, set a pattern for a whole school of writers to follow. Subtitled "A Tale of Neutral Ground," the story makes no sharp qualitative distinction between honorable military gentlemen, whether they are fighting for American liberty or are "misguided" Tories. In perhaps the most revealing scene of the book, the impeccably noble protagonist, Major Dunwoodie, is forced to pass judgment on Henry Wharton, his closest friend and brother of his fiancée. Wharton, a loyalist serving as a British officer, has been captured in civilian clothes and turned over to Dunwoodie for further disposition. Reminiscent of Washington and Andre, these two paragons of military gentility face their painful situation with mutual courtesy and without equivocation. The Tory refuses to prevaricate even slightly in order to slip out of the accusation that he is a spy, and Dunwoodie in turn puts his soldier's honor above his deep friendship for the captive and his love for Captain Wharton's sister. Speaking to his fiancée, he declares with typical grandiloquence, "I would this moment die for you—for Henry—but I cannot forget my duty—cannot forfeit my honor; you yourself would be the first to despise me if I did."[16]

If less dramatically portrayed, Cooper's respect for uniformed upholders of the patrician ethic is equally clear in his popular *Leatherstocking Tales*. In the *Last of the Mohicans*, for example, colonial Major Duncan Heyward, British Colonel Munro, and French General Montcalm are all models of eighteenth-century military patricianism. (The antihero, British General Webb, is a haughty coward who refuses to support Munro in crisis, and Cooper makes the comparison to Braddock obvious.) Frontiersman and commoner Natty Bumppo is, of course, Cooper's great creation and the central figure of the Leatherstocking series; nevertheless, it is apparent that the crafty scout is neither meant to represent nor to replace the conventional military type. He does not belong to the world of the gentleman. For Cooper, in military matters as elsewhere, gentility and democracy were both essential to the advancement of American society, but they did not necessarily blend.[17]

★

In understanding the military gentleman in American literature, we need to note that for three decades he had decidedly southern features. And it was not simply because he was often presented by southern authors like Simms and John Pendleton Kennedy. Since the days of Washington and Jefferson, the mid-Atlantic planter class had been the model for the well-to-do throughout the nation and was still highly admired by writers from the North, like Cooper and James Kirk Paulding. As New Yorker Cooper proudly told the world, "In proportion to the population, there are more men who belong to what is termed the class of gentlemen, in the old southern states of America than in any other country of the world."[18]

And while the planter remained a model for patricians, North and South, he was turning more and more to military codes for his ethic and style. John Hope Franklin has provided us book-length description of the growing martial tendencies in *The Militant South*, but perhaps James Edmonds best summed up that section's particular appreciation for professional officership that reached full tide with the Mexican War. "Washington, Jackson, Taylor, Scott—the successful commanders in all the nation's foreign wars—had been Southerners and were the revered idols of most southern youth. A majority of the higher leaders in the Mexican adventure had been southern men. The region had more than its quota of West Point graduates, . . . [and] its share of Regular officers appointed from civil life was twice its right proportion. . . ."[19]

The point is distorted however, unless we also note that the southern-oriented model of gentlemanship and officership so admired in the first four decades of the nineteenth century had not yet become the quick-tempered, pistol-dueling plantation aristocrat that would emerge in the late '40s and '50s. This man was not yet the foredoomed cavalier stoically defending a fading way of life. He was still more late-eighteenth-century Virginian than mid-nineteenth-century Georgian. He looked confidently to the future, not the past. Virile and self-assured, he was a man of action, seldom contemplative and anything but a fox-hunting profligate. His bravery might need bridling, as in Kennedy's *Horseshoe Robinson* when the crafty Sergeant Robinson is required at times to keep his commander in check. "Whist Major, you are a young man and don't study things as I do," he tells patrician-hero Arthur Butler; and with that he leads him around the Tories whom the officer would just as soon fight.[20] But while ready to do battle, the military ideal of the Jacksonian age was no hot-headed sectionalist. He was, instead, a blend of English squirearchy, New World republicanism, and southern gentry. He took his courtly mannerisms from the European texts, but—as can be seen in the stories of Cooper, Kennedy, Simms, R. M. Bird, Paulding, W. A. Caruthers, and D. P. Thompson—he acquired his strength of character from his own nation and its ideals.[21]

Acknowledging that "the southern hero [of antebellum fiction] was a military gentleman," Lucy Hazard, in her study of *The Frontier in American Fiction*, considered William Gilmore Simms's smug hero of *The Yemassee* as typical. "He is well born, well educated, a man of the world, and a gentleman . . . [and Simms] never falls into the democratic fallacy of believing that [the soldiers] are of essentially the same caliber as their commander."[22] Simms' initial description of his hero, Craven, is excellent documentation of Miss Hazard's point and, at the same time, graphically illustrates the blend of Old and New World characteristics seen in the contemporary conception of the ideal military leader. Craven's features were

> moulded finely, so as to combine manliness with as much of beauty as might well comport with it. He was probably six feet in height, straight as an arrow, and remarkably well and closely set. He wore . . . a sort of compound garb, in which the fashion of the English cavalier of the second Charles had been made to coalesce . . . with that which seemed called for by . . . the mode of life prevailing in the region. The resulting costume included a gentleman's blue surcoat *worn over buckskins* with a white Spanish hat "looped broadly up at one of the sides."[23]

Part Old World cavalier; part New World frontiersman!

Kennedy's and Cooper's officer heroes were likewise almost invariably fine-featured, slender, Anglo-Saxon, and refined. They offset a lack of great physical power (too coarse for a gentleman) with intelligence, poise, quickness, and soldierly skills. To balance these attributes, they were often given a yeoman retainer who was crafty, experienced, and of greater strength. For example, Sergeant Horseshoe Robinson, compared to Butler, "was a man of altogether rougher mould. Nature had carved out . . . an athlete whom the sculptors might have studied to improve the Hercules." These men of "rougher mould" (like Cooper's Natty Bumppo and his later creation, Chainbearer) served to complement the thoroughbred gentlemen-officers.[24]

★

Lucy Hazard and the southern influence notwithstanding, the hero of *The Yemassee* was more Stuart in nature and dress than most of his fictional colleagues. Unlike Craven, the model gentlemen-soldiers were not, as a rule, cocky, and were usually reluctant to display their finery. Such "European" features were gradually being stripped away from the more sober American military ideal. Education and cultivation remained important, but the traditional link between the military commission and inherited wealth was increasingly denied. Cooper stated flatly that "a man can neither buy preferment in church, state, army, navy, nor in anything else with his dollars. . . . He can educate his children, and give them manners . . . but there the benefits cease."[25] Accordingly, the patrician-democrat novelists often suppressed their admiration for military gentlemen by keeping them in the background. Cooper did so in *The Last of the Mohicans*, and Kennedy continued the pattern in *Horseshoe Robinson*. Major Heyward and Captain Butler exemplified patrician ideals and carried the romantic leads, but the true heroes were yeomen Natty Bumppo and Sergeant Robinson.

From Puritan days, the relationship between wealth and the gentleman in America has, it seems, been a paradox. As one scholar puts it, there has been "a curious ambivalence toward the things of this world: a suspicion that material prosperity may be an impediment to the inner-life."[26] Clearly, neither the American officer corps nor their literary admirers could have in good faith accepted the British system of purchased commissions and promotions that continued until 1871. The cadets of West Point were repeatedly reminded that, "Here you have been practically taught the moral truth, that money . . . entitles no one to superior rank over his fellows." Alex de Tocqueville observed that the American officer of the '30s stood in sharp contrast to the young European nobleman who "enters the Army in order to find an honorable employment for the idle years of his youth."[27]

Idleness itself was antipathetic to Puritan-founded America, and leading authors sought devices which would allow their protagonists to possess the cultivation considered necessary for leadership, yet avoid the undemocratic and morally damaging influences of undue wealth and leisure. The two heroes in Daniel Pierce Thompson's *Green Mountain Boys* (1839) illustrate the point. One is a commoner who has been trained by European nobility, while the other is a professional officer who has lost his money through the mismanagement of his estate by the father of one of the story's villains. Thus, both have the background and decorum expected of military commanders, yet they are relieved of the stain of actually belonging to the ranks of the well-to-do.[28]

★

Stripping their model American soldiers of aristocratic ostentation and sloth, the leading novelists continued to extol "true" military gentlemen, whatever their nation. In *Horseshoe Robinson*, British Captain St. Jermyn is remarkably like Arthur Butler, "of a graceful and easy carriage, neat figure and a countenance that bespoke of an intelligent and cultivated mind"; and General Cornwallis is accredited with a chivalric grace that causes him to spare Butler's life, at his fiancée's entreaty, "in the spirit of a cavalier who denies no lady's request."[29]

Like the severely aristocratic caricature of the military leader (a product of egalitarian demonology), the incredibly noble patrician officer (a product of upperclass mythology) could be found in nearly all media of national expression. Unlike his opposite number, however, this more flattering view of the military gentleman was, naturally, strongest in the cultural centers along the Atlantic Coast rather than in the Washington political arena or the bumptiously vulgar agrarian West. Whatever their primary locus, these conflicting versions of the military gentleman would remain prominent among the images of the officer corps through much of the nineteenth century.

SECTION THREE

THE BEGINNINGS OF AN END, 1850-1865

The Civil War, according to most historians, marked a major turn in our national thought. But for America's conception of the army officer, it did not. The extended and brutally waged conflict, so significant in the history of modern warfare, marked only the beginning of the end for the patrician-soldier type. The officer-and-gentleman did not, as one is tempted to believe, die with the Old South, for that figure had been as deeply, if somewhat differently, engrained in the Northern culture. He did not give way until late in the century, when he finally succumbed to a combination of contrary forces including military professionalism, social Darwinism, and philosophical naturalism.

What the Civil War era did demonstrate, once again, was the capacity of the military figure to excite painfully contrary reactions. And diverse views of the officer corps were not simply differences representative of sectional attitudes. The real philosophical conflict relating to the profession of arms lay, as it had from the beginnings of this nation, deep in the cross currents of America's political, social and moral persuasions—regardless of sectional emphases.

Chapter Eight

The War Of The Rebellion: Officers As Northern-Styled Gentlemen[1]

The character of the good soldier is one which the world, and we [The Union] least of all, could not afford at present to let die.

—Charles Eliot Norton[2]

One bullet-headed general will succeed another in the Presidential chair. . . . And yet I do not speak of this deprecatingly, since very likely, it may substitute something more real and genuine.

—Nathaniel Hawthorne[3]

At the height of the Civil War, *The Atlantic Monthly* reviewed George Calvert's new book, *The Gentleman*, and stated, "Paradoxical as it may appear, we believe there never was a time when the true and pure standard of gentlemanhood could be more impressively raised and upheld in this republic than now." The question of "What constitutes the Gentleman?" said the reviewer, had obviously been raised "by the preposterous and exclusive claims thereto arrogantly put forth [by the South] . . . in justification of profane and destructive violence to a nation's welfare."[4] Calvert's book and the *Atlantic's* review illustrate two closely related points. During the war, appreciation for patrician leadership in general, and military gentlemen in particular, did not fade in the North; nevertheless, beginning in the 1850s, the southern model was gradually discredited and, with the war, finally cast aside.

The first point is not always understood. There is good reason, after all, to presume that this of all wars (usually described by military historians as the first modern conflict) should have unceremoniously discarded the eighteenth-century gentleman-officer along with his mass formations, close-order maneuvers, and checkerboard tactics. Even more likely, it would seem that, as far as the North was concerned, the war, often billed as "the defense of democracy against southern aristocracy," should have purged any sympathy for patricianism. While such attitudes did, to be sure, contribute to a readjustment of the image of the military leader, there is ample proof that admiration of—in fact, an expressed   need   for—career   officers-and-gentlemen remained strong.

It wasn't the old military-gentleman theory that was considered at fault; it was the southern version that was wrong. As the *Atlantic* reviewer saw it, the war was basically a contest between true and counterfeit gentlemen. That point was dramatized for the Union's benefit in 1863 by Edward Hale's popular *The Man Without a Country*. Hale made clear his admiration for the career officer who, in contrast to the story's anti-hero, Philip Nolan, remained true to the soldier's profession and to the country that "gave him the uniform he wore, and the sword by his side." What Nolan and the Southern leaders had tragically forgotten, the author told his readers, was that officers were a class apart, that the United States had "picked you as one of her own confidential men of honor."[5]

Military gentleman, yes. Plantation nobility, no. That was the new message. Otherwise, although the nature of warfare was undergoing a revolution, civilian impressions of officership were changing much more slowly. The country as a whole, North and South, continued to assume that high-ranking officers *should* possess (if admittedly such was not always the case) an instinctive tactical genius. West Point was persistently criticized during the war for failing to turn out a military virtuoso. "Not that a military education naturally unfits a man for being a great soldier," explained *Harper's Weekly*. "But war being an art, not a science, a man [cannot] be made a first-class painter, or a great poet, by professors and text books; he must be born with the genius of war in his breast."[6] Henry Barnard's *Journal of American Education* (1864) indicates that this antique concept was still strong after four years of "modern" warfare. Even as he was arguing for up-to-date competitive examinations as a democratic means of selecting the West Point cadets, reformer Barnard refused to deny the eighteenth-century "military artist" concept that "no amount of book knowledge can give assurance of the great military genius, 'which must be born and not made.' "[7]

Officers too were reluctant to put aside the old theories and models. It was, surprisingly, the Union generals in the first half of the war who were most especially addicted to past concepts. As T. Harry Williams puts it, "They thought of war as an exercise in bloodless strategy, as a series of maneuvers to checkmate an enemy. . . . Above all—and here George B. McClellan is the supreme example of the type—they envisioned a leisurely, gentlemanly kind of war."

It was not until 1864 that "the North succeeded in bringing into the important command posts . . . men who understood the political nature of the war." Even then, Russell Weigley submits, Grant understood the change only intuitively, while Sherman made a few half-successful attempts to verbalize it.[8]

As old notions of officership stubbornly persisted, so too did the general alignment of opinion toward military training and careerists. Sympathetic voices remained strong. Barnard, from his position as the United States Commissioner of Education, argued for military education in public schools and wrote some nine hundred pages about military schooling in Europe and the United States. Governor J. A. Andrew of Massachusetts, also prominent in educational circles, likewise proclaimed the advantages of a military education; and Francis Parkman told the people of Boston, "We look with hope to see a military element infused into all our schools and colleges."[9] Once again the patricians of the Northeast were speaking out boldly. The Adams family suggested that the North's wartime problems could all be solved by reconstituting civilian and military staffs with "the gently born." Oliver Wendell Holmes expressed open admiration for military gentility, and even clung to a southern-styled belief in the *code duello*: "I don't believe in any aristocracy without pluck as its backbone," he said, and his wartime writings show his pride in the military records of upper-class New Englanders, including his own thrice-wounded son. These men, he felt, had vindicated Boston.[10]

Not atypical of this sort of thought was young Charles Eliot Norton's adulation of the chivalric code. Writing for *Harper's* in 1861, he identified British Major Hodson (William Stephen Raikes Hodson, whose *Twelve Years of a Soldier's Life in India* were recounted from his letters, following his death, by his brother in 1859) as the model for "a noble corps of officers." Norton called him "the *preux chevalier* of our times," and compared him to Lancelot. "Thou were the meekest man and gentlest that ever eate in the hall among ladies; and thou were the sternest knight to thy mortall foe that ever put speare in the rest."[11]

Such poetic encomia considered, there was, all the same, no sweeping return to favor of Old World military types. America's inbred distrust of class codes and manners remained in force. Parkman would growl that "the fallacies of ultra democracy cannot be safely applied to the . . . army"; but he also made clear that America had no use for needless refinements. In letters to the *Boston Advertiser*, he expressed a primitivistic view that the armies of New England, and especially their leaders, were soft and "no longer the best in the world [because] luxury and commerce have emasculated a people naturally war-like."[12] Northern intellectuals like Parkman sought military champions who were conscious of their rank and profession, yet Yankee in their distaste of leisure and republican in their opposition to inherited position.

Perhaps the clearest evidence of the continued democratizing of the military ideal came from the regulars themselves. As the war progressed, those at the top made increasingly clear that they were an *American* species of the military gentleman genus. Grant, when commander of all the Union armies, insisted on wearing a private's coat, and former college president Sherman intentionally spoke in the vernacular to get down to the level of the troops.

★

Despite the continuing vulgarization of the commander's image, egalitarian critics saw the war as an upperclass chess match directed by southern planters and West Pointers, whom they still considered one and the same. Whichever side they were on, they were dangerous military aristocrats. The Brahmins and gentry might have been seeking gentlemen to lead the North, but there were others just as ready to throw them out summarily. Articles in the press repeated the old warnings that war might well "pave the way for a military dictatorship to ride rough shod over the people, and establish a grinding despotism at the expense of justice, constitutional liberty and right."

More damning was the charge that the graduates of the Military Academy were anemic in their patriotism. West Pointers fighting for the South were, one common argument went, living demonstrations of the traitorous tendencies one could expect from all such mercenaries. The Secretary of War himself stated that but for the West Point "defectors," the rebellion would never have become formidable. And the *Cleveland Herald* wrote of Generals Hazen and Seymour, "Both of these Generals were educated at West Point, and inherit from that institution the peculiarity of sentiment that made so many officers lukewarm to their devotion to our cause." (Seymour ardently rebutted, pointing out that 133 southern-raised officers remained with the Union, "while but a squad of northern graduates [19] were traitors.")

Professor Williams has analyzed in some detail "The Attack on West Point During the Civil War." He found that the political critics of the 1860s were largely Republican, not Democratic by party, but that they unabashedly employed most of the old Jacksonian arguments. It was not until after the Union's twin victories at Vicksburg and Gettysburg in July of 1863 that the political antagonists were momentarily stilled and the regular officers basked in a rare moment of general national esteem.[13]

Interestingly, of the several hostile voices, it was the pacifists who were most subdued during the Civil War—if only temporarily. Where before they had made much of the immorality of the invasion of Mexico and those engaged in it, they now found themselves in the vanguard of "the war against slavery." Robert Ingersoll is an interesting case. He professed pacifism even while serving as an officer, and for forty years thereafter he expressed a curious combination of chauvinistic and pacifist ideas. However much can be attributed to his proclaimed pacifist beliefs, he clearly disliked the regulars. During the war, according to biographer Clarence Cramer, he expressed "a militia man's contempt for West Point," and felt that "the North would enjoy no real success until the West Point officers were kicked out of the army." On one occasion he wrote a friend with evident relish a story which was then popular among the men.

Q. What is the meanest kind of dog?
A. Pointer.
Q. What is the meanest kind of pointer?
A. West Pointer.[14]

Ingersoll's distaste for regulars was typical in a way of a major segment of the nation. It was the product of the not unusual, if basically contradictory, American combination of pacifist and Jacksonian tendencies.

These and other antebellum tensions behind the military image remained apparent throughout the war. Nathaniel Hawthorne's conception of officers was a bundle of fascinating contradictions. As an "antiregular" he had earlier written Franklin Pierce's campaign biography stressing the shallowness of the professional officer's valor when compared to the citizen-soldier's, and as a pacifist he had recoiled from the militaristic impulses behind the Mexican War.[15] He did not change these views with the Civil War; nonetheless, at times, he could not suppress open admiration for military life and virtues.

In 1862, the *Atlantic Monthly* carried a two-part article called "Chiefly About War Matters," which speaks the crosscurrents in Hawthorne's mind. Subtitled "By a Peaceable Man," it began by expressing the author's distaste for military influences. "Even supposing the war should end tomorrow . . . what an incalculable preponderance will there be of military titles and pretensions for at least a half a century to come!" Still, Hawthorne saw in war and warriors something noble. He described at length a young officer on General McClellan's staff, "a gallant cavalier, high-booted,

with a revolver in his belt, and mounted on a noble horse.
. . . As I looked at him, it seemed to me that the war had
brought good fortune to the youth of this epoch, if to none
beside. . . . The atmosphere of the camp and the smoke
of the battlefield are morally invigorating; the hardy virtues
flourish in them, the nonsense dies like a wilted weed."

Nor was this appreciation for the "morally invigorating"
aspects of the military life confined to the youthful or the
nonprofessional. Displaying little respect for what he causti-
cally called "the self-commissioned" (politically appointed)
officers whom he found gathered in Washington's Willard
Hotel, Hawthorne felt "it was pleasant, occasionally, to distinguish a grizzly veteran among this crowd of carpet-
knights—that trained soldier of a lifetime, long ago from
West Point, who had spent his prime upon the frontier, and
very likely could show an Indian bullet-mark on his breast.
. . ."16

★

At bottom, neither the nation's basic concept of the
officer as a military artist and gentleman, nor the variously
directed attitudes toward that conception, were changed
substantially during the war years. This is not to say that
the image was unaffected. It was—and significantly. But the
change amounted more to an adjustment of the model than
an adjustment of the theory. In spite of the North's grudg-
ing admiration for Lee and other soldiers of his style, quite
naturally the Confederates could no longer serve as pro-
totypes for America's military men. They were guilty of
treason. As Hale reminded the North in *The Man Without
a Country*, "The wish of poor Nolan ['Damn the United
States'] . . . was precisely the wish of every Bragg and
Beauregard . . . two years ago."17

Emerson's essay on "American Civilization," published in
1862, is a prize illustration of the bankruptcy of the southerner as a symbol of American leadership. Long before the

war (in 1837), the Concord sage had grumbled in his journal about the bellicosity of the South. "The Southerner asks concerning any man, 'How does he fight?' The Northerner asks, 'What can he do?'" And he added the estimate that the gentlemen of the South were only a bit more civilized than the Seminoles. With the war, he could express this opinion openly. "The war is welcome to the Southerner: a chivalrous sport to him, like hunting, and suits his semicivilized condition. . . . It does not suit us. We are advanced some ages on the war-state,—to trade, art, and general civilization."[18]

Interestingly, it was the southern writers who, long before the war, had prepared the way for anti-cavalier expression. Backing step-by-step into philosophical defensiveness, they began to picture the planter as less a heroic knight of the energetic days of the southern frontier and more a tragic anachronism. As early as the thirties, southern novelists were becoming obsessed by the notion of inevitable decline and were grasping for symbols of traditional order, rank, and stability. The contrast between plantation gentility and Yankee acquisitiveness was increasingly emphasized. While the patroon system was breathing its last in New York, the South was avidly devouring Scott's novels romanticizing feudal nobility. Mark Twain's retrospective charge that Sir Walter undid the American tradition in the South, and thus caused the Civil War, was extreme but not fatuous. The influence was there.

By the 1850s, the mood of decay had deepened substantially. It became the vogue to celebrate the heroes of bygone days rather than those of the present generation or even the recent past. So obvious was this in the works of John Esten Cooke that George W. Bagby, a Virginia humorist, complained in 1858 that "Mr. Cooke's eyes are in the back of his head. I am proud of my granddaddy . . . and deeds of his generation; but I don't want to get so plague-take proud of him and his time to undervalue myself and my time." The protest was in vain. By the eve of the Civil War the southern cavalier in fiction had changed, as Taylor describes him, from a self-confident Hotspur to a Hamlet who was no longer the master of his environment. He was regularly depicted as the son of a declining family, financially irresponsible, and inclined to drink excessively. He possessed a childish pugnaciousness, an arrogant aristocratic manner, and a rapier-like wit. Weak and sensitive heroes and southern hotheads were the order of the day in the novels of Beverly Tucker, Edmond Ruffin, and others.[19]

Sentimental novelists in the North soon picked up the theme. They fixed their long-standing distrust of military libertines on the southern officer and added to his other sins a Legree-like cruelty toward slaves. Susan Warner's *Daisy*, one of her many popular novels, illustrates the point. Daisy can see the difference between southern and northern cadets and officers at West Point even in their posture. The heroine asks her Academy escort (a southern cadet who declares he would not hesitate to shoot an insubordinate slave) why the officer in charge of the parade stands so stiff and awkwardly, for, she says,

> It is ungraceful
> It is military. . . . *He* isn't ungraceful. That is Percival—of South Carolina.
> The officer yesterday stood a great deal better. . . .
> Yesterday? That was Blunt. He's a Yankee . . .
> I despise them.[20]

This change in southern military stereotype—from J. P. Kennedy's graceful and gracious Virginian, Arthur Butler, to the rigid Percival of South Carolina—was significant. It provided both democrats and pacifists with new ammunition. For egalitarian champions of militia forces, the discrediting of the once admired soldier-cavalier gave credence to their charge that America's southern-oriented regular officer corps had always been a European-styled aristocracy at heart. (Soon they would hail the Civil War victory as the triumph of the moral strength of northern democracy over the admittedly superior military artistry of the Confederate commanders.) Likewise, the pacifists, who for years had preached that the military's code of honor was a major cause of war, now had—as they saw it—an entire society as proof of their point.

★

Those more sympathetic to the profession of arms did not, however, lose their faith in the military gentleman, Northern-style. While plantation gentility and polite learning were put aside as prerequisites for officership, devotion to duty, restraint and obedience, and the rewards of "soldiering" were increasingly stressed in their place. Charles Eliot Norton's experience sums up the change. Four war years after his sophomoric adulations of chivalresque warriors of the past, he had altered his emphasis considerably. In an article simply but expressively entitled "Our Soldiers," he wrote, "No other career offers such a field as that of arms for the exercise of the virtue of obedience. . . ." He praised military manliness and self-sacrifice, but "the love of glory," Norton had by now decided, "is the infirmity of noble minds. . . . With the good soldier . . . [the] strongest motive is duty." Rather than a Lancelot, he now took as his model self-effacing contemporary professionals like General Reynolds, "bred to arms, modest, reticent, studious, and brave." To Norton, military leaders were still a class apart from the enlisted man, but "the rank and file," he at least took time to declare, "have shown themselves worthy of the most distinguished officers."[21]

Soldiers all, and better men for it, was the new theme—and the military gentleman would never again be quite the same. The northern McClellans as well as the southern Beauregards had been rejected. Regard for such virtues as sacrifice, honesty, and above all, duty increased while glory, honor (in the sense of personal repute), and polish were less admired. The officer-and-gentleman in fiction, history, or real life who lingered in the leisured atmosphere of a Revolutionary drawing room or an antebellum plantation was recognized as a relic from the past. The new military ideal would be more like the cavalry officer of the New West than the cavalier of the Old South: educated but not too intellectual, courteous but not too smooth, cultivated but physically more rugged than his predecessor. He was a compromise between Sergeant Horseshoe Robinson and Major Arthur Butler, between Sam Grant and Robert E. Lee.

But that is a matter for later discussion. For the moment, it is sufficient to realize that the crisis beginning in the 1850s and culminating in the Civil War did not destroy the concept of the officer-and-gentleman. It only modified the Union's prototype.

SECTION FOUR

A NEW PROTOTYPE AND A SUPERIMPOSITION OF PATTERNS, 1865-1898

Oddly, it was between the Civil and Spanish Wars, America's period of longest and most profound peace, that military professionalization took root in this country. In those years the officer would become less an artist operating from battlefield instinct and more a systematic practitioner of modern military science. He would be less expected to be French or British in style than Prussian, and his assumed social characteristics would have decreasing resemblances to those of an antebellum gentleman. In short, the new professional would be marked more and more by his calling and less and less by his class.

The change, both in fact and image, it should be stressed, was gradual. It was not fully completed until World War I, if then. For more than a generation, military gentlemen and professionals were intermingled in American thought, at times fused. And this is not to suggest that there were no dedicated, full-time "professionals" in the U.S. Army before the Civil War. There had been, of course, as far back as Anthony Wayne's rigorously trained units two decades before the War of 1812. It was, however, only as the nation, including the officer corps itself, gradually digested the military lessons of the Civil War and simultaneously became aware of new developments in European military theory, that it began to consider officership as a profession in the modern sense of the word.

As the new image developed, it was at once colored by profound changes in the nation's culture. The United States was undergoing a transformation that was obvious even to superficial view. The ascendance of a new business elite, the creation of vast industrial complexes, the phenomenal growth of great cities, an increasing stream of immigrants, the appearance of a modern working class, the addition of new states, and the eventual closing of the frontier—all were outward demonstrations that the entire demographic and sociological structure of the nation was shifting ground.

With the theories of warfare also undergoing mutation,

the result was another period of transition in which new military images were superimposed on those of the past, and new lines of criticism and new shadings of defense were developed. In the meantime, the army returned to its frontier and coastal defense posts, once again separated physically and intellectually from the nation.

Chapter Nine

A Growing Awareness Of Military Professionalism: The Basis For New Images Of Officership[1]

The commander who does not do his utmost to prepare all of the factors . . . but trusts only to the inspirations of his genius . . . will surely be defeated.
—Captain Zalinski in **North American Review**[2]

Eminent practitioners and military teachers [hold] that there is no art of war; . . . what is known as the strategy and tactics of war, vary as the conditions and the commanders vary.
—C. E. Munroe in **The Chautauquan**[3]

Modern military professionalism was very much a product of the first important revisions in Western military theory since the days of Napoleon. It was an adjustment demanded by a brand of warfare that was quite different from that of the eighteenth century. The commander who had held within his gaze an entire battlefield of massed troops, the man who had in a single engagement won or lost some national prize of territory and honor was, after Waterloo, a figure of the past. And with the American Civil War the idea that battlefield artistry could alone achieve final victory was finally put to rest. Ultimate military success, the world was gradually coming to realize, now depended much more on strategic considerations involving massive supply requirements and the deployment of huge armies conscripted from the total populace.

In the United States Army, such lessons were absorbed during the Civil War, but they were slow to be formalized into new doctrine. Americans were by nature doers rather than theorists, and the military men were no exception. Changes in strategy, organization, and methods of operation were formulated more from trial than from conceptual thought. Although the Union eventually put together a military system capable of winning "the first modern war," it was German theory, not American, which very soon became preeminent in the western world. It was Prussian doctrine—long in development but not fully displayed until five years after Appomattox—that became the keystone of Western military thought. With the astonishingly easy German victory in the Franco-Prussian War (1870-1871), even the militarily proud English revamped their thinking to such an extent that old-guard tacticians complained bitterly, as one did, about "Our Art of War as 'Made in Germany.'" He was totally upset about the "extraordinary perversity of pedantry which has substituted one campaign of six months' duration of one foreign race . . . for the brilliant records of our people . . . since the glorious days of great Elizabeth."[4]

This "art of war as made in Germany" was really more a social-military science than an art. It tended to be absolutistic in essence. With Clausewitz as its guiding light, it declared that armies are an extension of their particular society and wars total engagements. Victory was for the side which was best prepared to utilize the total military capabilities of its nation. Moderation in warfare was, the Prussians determined, a hopelessly antique notion. They reasoned that, since a country could not remain fully at arms at all times, it was as important to be able to mount an army for combat expeditiously as to lead it skillfully in battle; and greater attention than ever before was given to routine details of preparatory planning and training. Prussian doctrine thus recognized two major leadership requirements among others: a cadre capable of quickly shaping an army in time of need, and a tightly controlled general staff which could prepare contingency war plans in peacetime and direct huge conscripted armies in wartime.

All of this demanded revisions in the prerequisites for officership. Officers of the line were less expected to be cavaliers leading their forces by gallant example and inborn instinct. They were to be proficient members of an efficient machine, meticulous students of the enemy, and accomplished manipulators of thoroughly trained units and carefully calculated supplies. And the high staff officers, also unlike their military predecessors, now expressed a determination to remain aloof from political affairs. In theory at least, the practitioners of modern military science were to be the tools of, not part of, the government.[5]

★

American spokesmen warmly welcomed the new Germany, and especially its military professionals, into the community of Western nations. Most reacted with initial favor to the German victory over France, seeing it as the triumph of an emerging liberal culture in Europe. They were quick to point out that the war was won by an army of the people in the fashion of democratic nations. "While the ephemeral supremacy of Napoleon . . . shrank within fifteen years back into the limits with which the arch-traitor to liberty received it, . . . the Prussia of Frederic the Great has grown into a power," exalted one writer. According to E. L. Godkin and *The Nation*, the Prussian army was "fighting for a free press, a free parliament, popular education . . . supremacy of reason over brute force, of the citizen over the soldier."[6]

Enthusiastic acceptance of Prussia as a progressive world power had long been in preparation. For years there had been a growing school of thought that proudly proclaimed America's Anglo-Saxon origins. As early as 1834, one writer had predicted, "When [the] emancipating cry is heard among the nations, where is the leader to be found . . . to guide the liberals of all Europe to a permanent, reasonable, and constitutional freedom? PRUSSIA IS THAT LEADER. Start not, gentle reader! ponder the subject well, and you will perhaps agree that this answer is neither unreasonable nor visionary."[7] O. W. Long's study of *Early American Explorers of European Culture* provides under single cover copious illustration of the extensive foundation for the postbellum wave of Germanism, a foundation established by such intellectual leaders as Ticknor, Everett, Cogswell, Longfellow, and others.

By the 1870s, the Germanophiles were in full voice. Bancroft was comparing von Moltke to Washington; and while serving in the United States diplomatic corps he so openly favored the Germans in the Franco-Prussian War as to cause embarrassment to the State Department. John Motley's close friendship with Bismarck was probably unique in history. Between them it was a matter of personal affection, with Bismarck writing, "Jack, my Dear—Where the devil are you. . . ?" and Motley replying to "My dear Old Bismarck" that he would come to Berlin to see him as soon as possible.[8] The idea of Germany as the new America of Europe came easily in such a climate, and a whole Anglo-Saxon school of historians traced America's democratic institutions back to primitive German tribes. As Henry Adams later admitted, "I flung myself obediently into the arms of the Anglo-Saxons in history."[9]

Meanwhile, Commanding General Sherman, working to update America's military thinking and particularly its schooling system, was busy encouraging the study of foreign armies. Emory Upton, a West Point lieutenant of 1861 who came out of the Civil War with general's rank and an abiding disgust for the undue cost in lives and resources expended by the Union's haphazard military system, led the move toward Prussian methods. For better and for worse, it was Upton, sent by Sherman to study the Prussian system firsthand, who became the army's postbellum intellectual leader, and his influence continued well into the twentieth century.[10]

National interest in Prussia's army and its leaders prevailed for a quarter of a century. As late as 1895, *The Chautauquan* featured a sketch of von Moltke in which the writer observed a "chivalrous trait—so typical of high-class Prussians . . . [and] so refreshing in contrast to the eternally petty views of everyday mankind—the impartiality, the tone of high respect [for] a possible antagonist."[11] America's military journals were marked by such articles as "The Prussian General Staff and What it Contains That is Practical from an American Viewpoint," while highly regarded civilian publications like *Atlantic Monthly, North American Review*, and *Harper's Monthly* ran features acclaiming the new paragons of disciplined efficiency. Three years after the German victory over France, *Harper's* carried such a piece by General McClellan (still respected in spite of his tarnished Civil War fame). McClellan, who in 1862 had been a supreme example of the posturing military "genius," was now endorsing the systematic Prussian military machine. "The German empire," he asserted, "possesses the best organization and the best army in the world; . . . so perfect in discipline and instruction, so well officered and handled throughout, from the renowned von Moltke down to the youngest corporal."[12]

To appreciate the degree of change in military thought that a few years had made, we need only to contrast McClellan's article in 1874 to a review of Duparcq's *Elements of Military Arts* appearing in *Atlantic Monthly* during the Civil War. The reviewer, in 1863, quite accurately observed that "enlightened men of all nations concede to the French school of soldiers and military authors a certain preeminence. . . ."[13] Within a decade that faith in the eighteenth-century French-led school of military art was nearly gone. As Commanding General Schofield later phrased it, "The genius of great commanders in the field [has] been compelled to yield . . . to the scientific skill and wisdom in finance which are able and willing to prepare in advance the most powerful engines of war."[14]

★

As the "genius of great commanders" yielded to "powerful engines of war," so in the nation's mind did the figure of the military gentleman begin to yield to the military professional. The process was gradual and the product of many factors. The change came in part as America slowly absorbed the military experience of the Civil War put forth in journals, biographies, memoirs, and political debates. Thirteen years after Appomattox, former General James A. Garfield was still trying to convince his fellow congressmen that warfare had indeed changed and that "an effective army-staff is [now] a work of years. It cannot be . . . sent at once to the field, ready for efficient work."[15] And the change in military image came in part with the anticipated and eventual closing of the frontier territories. As one officer told the readers of *The North American Review*, "The army which for a century guarded the frontier [has] passed away, . . . the chase and Indian combat . . . all given way to a new field of duty."[16] And the change in image came as the Military Academy abdicated its leadership in engineering science to civilian schools. In the last quarter of the century, West Point, "the first school of technology in an English speaking country," began to "emphasize the 'professional' aspects of a military career and to dignify the systematic, scholarly study of military affairs."[17]

For a generation or more, the new professionals and old patrician types were mixed in America's impression of officership. The military gentleman in his various guises gradually became only a myth from the past found lingering in second-rate novels and outdated histories. War as a science, the nation was coming to realize, was fundamentally incompatible with gentlemanship and part-time officership. There was a growing recognition that "nothing but the most careful study and preparation to meet the complex character of all . . . contingencies in future warfare can give any reasonable assurance of success. . . . Genius alone will not conquer an opponent whose officers and men have had superior training. . . ."[18]

The question now at hand is: "During this period, how did America react to this new military man, part eighteenth-century gentleman and part modern professional?"

Chapter Ten

Gentlemen-Professionals As Social Parasites: A Convergence Of Evolutionary Theories And Postbellum Business Thought[1]

Industrialism builds up; militancy wastes.
—William Graham Sumner, "War"[2]

The Republic wants neither standing army nor navy. In this lies her chief glory and her strength.
—Andrew Carnegie, **Triumphant Democracy**[3]

America's worship of free enterprise in a burgeoning industrial nation was central to its changing outlooks. The theme of the Gilded Age was success, financial success in an open and highly competitive system, and by almost any of its basic tenets, the army officer had to be a misfit. He declined to compete; he was "given" his commissioned rank; he advanced by longevity; he was a member of a regulated and closed organization contributing nothing to the capitalist system; he lived on a fixed government stipend; and he remained in a service offering low pay and a ridiculously slow rate of promotion. He was, it seemed, the opposite of the Horatio Alger hero, the very antithesis of rugged American individualism and ambition.

Although criticisms of this nature had been heard before, there were decided changes both in emphasis and underlying rationale. A distinctive school of sociological thought was developing that consciously juxtaposed productive and peaceful industrialists, representatives of America's present and future, and destructive and bellicose militarists, artifacts from a primitive age. Much as the Enlightenment disciples of progress had envisioned mankind's newfound power of Reason doing away with irrational and inhumane warfare, this latter-day faith in evolutionary progress through commercial interdependence foresaw the same end. Anglo-American industrial methods and economic systems applied worldwide were expected to make armies obsolete. Just two years before the Spanish War, a writer for the *North American Review* surveyed "The Natural History of Warfare" and concluded, "So long as the control of the government was in the . . . classes of men who had naught to lose and much to gain by war, the influences were overwhelmingly for its continuance; now that the business people are gaining control of the world's affairs there is reason to hope that the cure is about to come to this ancient and enduring ill."[4]

Behind such attitudes were the postulations of the newly developing sciences of society. Spokesmen like William Graham Sumner would assert for thirty years that, "a peace-

ful society must be industrial because it must produce
instead of plundering; it is for this reason that the industrial
type of society is the opposite of the militant type. . . . On
the continent of Europe today these two types of societal
organization may be seen interwoven . . . and fighting each
other."[5]

Evolutionary interpretations of social development,
prompted by Darwin's breakthrough in biological science,
were basic to this sort of thinking. To understand the point,
however, it should be remembered that, with the notable
exception of the "little imperialists" of the late 1880s and
1890s, the social Darwinism accepted by postbellum industrial America did not pose a survival-of-the-fittest struggle
between national forces. The opposition in America to such
interpretations was, in fact, often almost violent. In 1889,
for example, one author moaned that "since the theory of
evolution has been promulgated, [war-promoting milita-
rists] can cover their natural barbarism with the name of
Darwin and proclaim the sanguinary instinct of their inmost
parts as the last word of science."[6]

The evolutionary theory preferred by America was that
of Herbert Spencer and industrial England. The competition it recognized was individualistic by nature, economic
in form, and frequently pacifist in spirit. The "fittest" who
would survive were not those strongest militarily, but those
most productively efficient. Where the Jacksonians had seen
wars as problems for the future to be met not by professionals but by citizen-soldiers rallying to arms, the new social
theorists saw war as a thing of the past, and no army was
needed at all. As Huntington observes, they argued that
"armaments were the cause of wars and the military profession a useless and vestigial remnant of a previous irrational
age; [thus,] the standing army and the regular officer were
the natural instruments of [outdated] aggression."

Spencer's theories—like the man himself—remained
exceptionally popular in America's intellectual circles for
twenty years, and Hofstadter's study of *Social Darwinism in*

America confirms that "most writers on war seem to agree with Spencer that military conflict had been highly useful in developing primitive civilization but had long outlived its value as an instrument of progress." There is ample proof of this general outlook. One finds it, for example, as a major theme of Lewis Henry Morgan's new science of anthropology.[7]

What we tend to overlook, however, is that the leading social theorists themselves were often anxious to retain what they considered to be worthwhile features from past military codes. When writing as a social philosopher, John Fiske might express a Spencerian, almost Condorcet-like optimism that the "ever-increasing interdependence of human interests, itself both the cause and effect of industrial progress, is ever making warfare less and less indurable"; when writing as a historian, however, he took care to show his continuing respect for traditional military values and those who personified them. Interestingly, opportunistic General Charles Lee (the Revolutionary soldier-of-fortune whom Washington eventually relieved of command) was more contemptible to Fiske than "aristocratic" Benedict Arnold, so detested by the Jacksonian era. Arnold, said Fiske almost sympathetically, tragically lacked the strength of character to stand up to the abuses and ingratitudes which he met; hence he fell victim to temptations which stronger soldiers were able to resist. Lee, whose extreme ambition should have recommended him to the age of Horatio Alger, was in Fiske's view the very opposite of worthy soldiership, as represented by patrician Washington, Quaker-soldier Nathaniel Greene, and the European aristocratic professionals.[8]

But while he admired soldiers of the past and the soldiers' code, Fiske was certain the profession of arms would soon be obsolete. "The very heterogeneity of the military art, the increasing complication both of the implements and of the methods of warfare, . . . renders war ever more costly, and makes the community less willing to engage in it," he theorized. The end result would, he predicted, be a happy one. "These cooperating processes must go on until—probably at no very distant period—warfare shall have become extinct in all the civilized portions of the globe."[9]

Professor Sumner, the Episcopalian rector turned economist, was considerably more pessimistic; yet he was even more explicit in proclaiming both the positive contributions made by military institutions in the past and the military's incompatibility with industrial societies of the present. Like other evolutionists, Sumner counterposed productive industrialism and wasteful militarism. Still, he was not ready to concede that laissez-faire capitalism could bring world peace. To him there were always two forces at work. There was the struggle with nature conducted by internally cooperative societies; but there was also "the competition of life [between societies] . . . which make war, and that is why war has always existed and always will." "The modern world," he was still complaining in 1903, "is saturated with humanitarianism and flabby sentimentalism. . . . The public is led to suppose that the world is advancing along some line . . . toward peace and brotherly love. Nothing could be more mistaken. . . ." Abhorring war as both inhumane and nonproductive, Sumner was too much a realist to presume it would soon go away.

He was even less inclined than the optimistic Fiske to discard the "military virtues" developed through the ages. In an essay in praise of "Discipline," written in the 1880s, the Yale professor explained, "Responsibility to self we call honor, and it is one of the highest fruits of discipline. . . . We laugh at the artificial honor of the Middle Ages . . . but let us not throw away the kernel with the shell." And he added, "It is the highest achievement of educational discipline to produce this sense of honor in the minds of young men . . . at a time when all codes and standards seem to be a matter of opinion." No superintendent of West Point argued that point more forcefully.

Sumner's view of the military was consistent over the years. It can be summed up in his declaration that "institutions and customs in human society are never either all good or all bad." If the industrial society was an evolutionary advancement over the military, evolution was also a painfully slow process; as he pointed out, "there is a code and standard of mercantile honor which is quite as pure and grand as any military code . . . but it has never yet been established and defined by long usage." Even after the war with Spain—which thoroughly revolted him and moved him to damn America's actions in his famous essay entitled, ironically, "The Conquest of the United States by Spain"—he would argue that "we cannot adopt either peacefulness or warlikeness as a sole true philosophy; military discipline educates; military interest awakens all the powers of men. . . ."[10]

★

Not then without personal respect for certain virtues of officership, the new social scientists nevertheless provided an intellectual foundation for much more sweeping, if usually less profound, attacks by others—notably in business and politics. In American business thought, evolutionary concepts were still strongly re-enforced with interlacing Christian and nationalistic fibers. The survival-of-the-most-productive idea was buttressed by (to use the common tags) the doctrine-of-work and the gospel-of-wealth. Whether proclaimed from pulpit or mahogany desk, the duty of the good citizen and Christian was to "Work for the Night is Coming" and, as lay minister Russell Conway preached thousands of times across the nation, "Get rich, get rich!" Rockefeller, like others, could find many sympathetic ears to his assertion that "in the long run, it is only to the man of mortality that wealth comes. . . ." The negative corollary, as Conway often proclaimed with evangelical fervor, was equally obvious: those who refused to compete were some-how not living up to the moral spirit of the nation.[11]

When such thinking was beamed on the military careerist, the features it highlighted were less than flattering. To the spokesmen for big business, the professional soldier was not only nonproductive, he was a social parasite draining life-blood from America. Andrew Carnegie was the most influential of the business critics. An ardent nationalist and racist, he could at times find warm things to say of individual military professionals like Grant, in whom he saw a prime illustration of the strength of Anglo-American blood lines. "There came in the Scotch blood . . . that tena-cious, self-contained stubborn force. . . . His very nature forbade retreat. Thus stood the sturdy, moody Scotch-American of steady purpose, fighting . . . as that English-American Lincoln did—for Uncle Abe's family came from Norfolk. . . ." But when considering standing armies as a whole, Carnegie found them worse than useless. If wars had to be fought, it was patriotic citizen-soldiers and not cold-hearted professionals who should do it.

In his *Triumphant Democracy*, the industrialist-pacifist thanked God that America's navy "is as nothing" and the regular army impotent and "scattered all over the continent in companies of fifty or a hundred." But in the next breath, he proudly recalled that in 1860, "at the blast of trumpet, [America] called into action two millions of armed men . . . to defend the unity of the nation, and who, when the task was done . . . returned to the avocations of peace."[12] Historical events to the contrary—such as the Union's diffi-culty in raising volunteers, the common practice of hiring substitutes, and instances in which entire units left the scene of impending battle because their enlistment period had terminated—did not dissuade him from this view.[13] Reinforc-ing his distaste for career soldiers was his violent disagree-ment with modern military scientism that refused to get itself involved in extramilitary decisions. "To Carnegie, the military professional was virtually criminal in his denial of conscience, . . . in refusing to evaluate the rightness or wrongness of the course for which he fought."[14]

The events leading into the Spanish War confirmed for Carnegie his opinion that the professional soldier could never be representative of triumphant America, in patriotism, efficiency, or morality. In 1898 and 1899, he published essays in the *North American Review* that gained considerable notice and presented once again his basic argument: it is regular armies which are the forces behind imperialism; our army is weak and ineffectual and should be kept that way; professional soldiers are not missionaries for good but the opposite.[15]

This brand of business-pacifism at times drifted far from the views of the social theorists from whom it took its philosophical lead. Carnegie's idealized image of America's minutemen rallying to arms, for example, stands in sharp contrast to Sumner's blunt opinion of nonregular troops about whom, he complained, "a great deal of nonsense has been written and spoken." "Such troops," Sumner insisted, "are always insubordinate and homesick." General Jackson, Sumner judged, was a successful leader only because he knew how to be severe, enforcing "discipline and obedience by measures which . . . no other frontier commander would have dared to use." Indeed, the army in the Mexican War was "corrupted by swagger and . . . methods of which Jackson had set the example." (For support, Sumner cited the case of a court-martialed officer whose defense consisted of an elaborate comparison of his own case and Jackson's actions in Florida; but who was cashiered, nonetheless.)

In Sumner's view, part-time soldiers at any level were likely to corrupt military efficiency and justice.[16] Not so in Carnegie's way of thinking. It was the career soldiers, and especially the professional officers, who were to be despised and feared. One of the blessings of America, the Scotsman claimed, was that she had never bred those "strong military classes, to whom . . . peaceful avocations are discreditable."[17]

★

The question necessarily arises, "At what point and why did the newly powerful voice of business become openly opposed, if only temporarily, to officership?" After all, America's military and business leaders had long had certain interests in common and, by experience and necessity, had often been allied. Our nineteenth-century geographical separation had provided national security without the usual sort of military barriers to create serious commercial limitations.[18] As one consequence, after 1815 the mission of our armed forces was more to protect the nation's commercial interests than to defend the country itself. The military team—especially the navy, but the army as well —was perforce closely associated with business interests.

The army's requirements to control labor riots in the cities and to protect railroad construction teams on the frontier were postbellum continuations of this alliance. And those associations were not just external or casual. The Union Pacific's chief engineer was, for example, a retired general who, with the aid and protection of regular army units, pushed the railroad through Indian country using military organizations and techniques. The chief of his track-laying force was a former general and according to his supervisor, "It was the best organized, best equipped and best disciplined track force I have ever seen. I think every chief . . . had been an officer of the army."[19]

Nor had the integration of military and business efforts been particularly strained by any strongly opposed set of ethics. The officer corps and the first-generation giants of business and industry had outlooks very much in common. Both groups tended to be stoutly Protestant and inner-directed by nature; both placed greater trust in practical, often technical, training than in broad intellectual development; both admired ruggedness, physical and moral. The parallelism of their views is evident in the favor with which the early business titans looked at the military academies.

Academies by nature appealed to self-made men who sus-
pected that the collegiate atmosphere was morally debilitat-
ing. Since many had risen without much education (Van-
derbilt's illiteracy being only the most famous illustration),
they were inclined to believe that higher education under-
mined industry and self-discipline. They praised schools
devoted to building character, denounced the fleshpots of
college life, and scorned "impractical knowledge" as a burden. To the business elite, as with much of the officer corps,
success was the product of "the power from within"; and
military-like fortitude and obedience were considered to be
far more important than a liberal education.[20]

But for all their similarities, the military and business
ethics were beginning to cross points openly by the mid-
1880s. A clue to the cause lies in Professor Ralph Gabriel's
observation that at about that time "success literature"
reached a crossroads. In the biographies and popular fiction promoting America's cult of success, naturalism and
Darwinism were replacing supernaturalism; and an undis-
guised admiration of shrewdness and the determination to
"get ahead" in the competition of life had become predominant themes.[21] By contrast, the literature championing
military figures continued to stress unblinking reliability
rather than Yankee sharpness, disciplined teamwork rather
than competitive individualism, and unimpeachable integ-
rity rather than *caveat emptor*. Even if it had been said in
jest, the officers could not have accepted Gould's quip, "I
had nothing to lose save honor." To an officer corps led
by Civil War veterans, frontier-styled initiative was fine, but
free-swinging competition was contrary to team effort—and
in combat dangerous to the point of being immoral.

Harmony between business and military thought ran
counter to postbellum America's very definition of success.
As a perceptive English observer wrote in 1885, "Analyse
the elements of it and you will see that success [in industrial
America] is identified to some extent with fame; still more
with power; most of all, with wealth."[22] Members of the

officer corps of this period were not likely to achieve any of the three; moreover, the day in which sons of the power-ful or the well-to-do frequented United States military ranks was passing. Princeton's team of Masland and Radway, who in 1957 did the first comprehensive study of *Military Educa-tion in America*, summed it up: "After the Civil War a nation heavily preoccupied with industrial development and hap-pily remote from the quarrels of Europe gave its soldiers neither attention nor social status nor money."[23]

Common now was the case of John Pershing, who can-didly admitted that he attended West Point because it offered him a better education than he could otherwise afford. Later, as a lieutenant in an army in which most cap-tains were over forty, he came close to resigning to go into law. Anything but successful by the reigning standards, the officers found themselves with an intense need to justify their profession—to themselves at least. Certainly they took more pains to defend their commitment to military service than had their predecessors. The military journals of the period repeatedly proclaimed the satisfaction of unheralded service over wealth—even as they complained of too little pay and governmental attention.

Nor could the officers share the business apologists' optimistic estimate of the contributions to peace to be derived from modern commercialism. The reverse, they felt, was true. "It is barely possible," *United Services* editorialized, "that our country may for many years to come enjoy the same freedom from war's alarms that she does now, but it is not probable, and it should ever be borne in mind that business prosperity and the amassing of wealth are not in themselves any protection to a nation, but rather the contrary." To the professional soldier, riches amassed by parvenues both weakened the nation's character and made it a target for aggressors.[24]

Thus, for a generation or more, America's military philosophy moved in a direction nearly opposite to one main thrust of national thought. The officers themselves were caught straddling eighteenth-century notions of *noblesse oblige* and modern military professionalism, neither of which were compatible with postbellum business ideals. Viewing themselves as defenders of threatened republican and Christian virtues, they went into a sort of ascetic seclusion to wait until the materialistic madness had spent itself. West Point became more monastic than ever, and cadets were forbidden to use money, the symbol of American capitalism. Looking back in 1906, a retired general expressed the philosophy of his military generation when he asserted, "The satisfaction to be derived from the social successes of the idle rich is as naught compared to the pride which comes from having rendered the state some gallant or useful service."[25]

No matter how they rationalized it, however, the officer corps of the postbellum era was finding itself uncomfortably out of tune with *Triumphant Democracy*.

Chapter Eleven

Gentlemen-Professionals As Opponents Of "The People": Blending Of Jacksonianism Into Populist Views[1]

Privilege uses the soldiers of the Republic as it uses the courts—for itself and in violation, in abrogation, of the rights of the body of the people.

—Henry George[2]

We are asking the public to condemn the government for its action in sending troops to protect capitalists and their property against the just demands of railway men.

—Working Men's Party pamphlet[3]

The rift between business and military ideals that developed in the postbellum period did not portend any increasing congeniality on the part of labor. Quite the opposite. The nation's wage earners, who for half a century had been expressing their opposition to the "military elite," adjusted their view of the military leader somewhat; but their enmity, if anything, became deeper. They began to see officers as more Junker than Old Regime, but a dangerous and un-American caste, no matter.

With time their particular portrait of the officer corps became increasingly different from that of the business critics. While Spencerians like Carnegie were belittling military men as a dying race and thanking God that America "has never bred strong military classes," labor sympathizers were fabricating spectres of ever-stronger, all-powerful class opponents. While the business ethic was scorning military vocationists for ideals contrary to New World capitalism, labor was protesting that the military professionals were protecting the capitalists and perpetuating an unjust accumulation of riches. When businessmen spoke as pacifists, they portrayed officers as warmongers seeking personal aggrandizement; but when labor leaders spoke as pacifists they characterized military men as the handmaidens of the plutocrats who were inciting war for financial profit.

After the Civil War, the workers' criticism remained for a time essentially Jacksonian. Urban-centered wage earners, who had long voiced their opposition to taxes for the support of a "commissioned class", soon took up that cry again. The National Labor Union protested a proposed military pension system on the grounds that "patriotism is in the people, ambition and plunder in the officers. . . ."[4]

But it was the strikes which erupted in 1877 and boiled for twenty years that put uniformed men in direct, physical opposition to the workers. The impairment of military-labor relationships was profound and long-lasting, and labor's side of the story was widely enunciated for the first time.

With ever-stronger unions and more skillful essayists, the workers' attitudes on nearly all subjects were being broadcast more forcibly than ever before. The rapid growth of the Knights of Labor was soon followed by the American Federation of Labor; and the combined voices of men like Henry George, Adam Hewitt, Samuel Gompers, and Eugene Debs became a real influence. Despite their other differences, the labor leaders were all quick to damn the army's role in the strikes and demonstrations, and they characterized the professional soldiers as dedicated enemies of the working class.

There was certainly ample opportunity for such censure. Prior to the '70s, regular army units had rarely been called upon to quell civil disorders. But between the first great wave of protests in 1877 and the Pullman strike of 1894, they were used repeatedly—in more than three hundred separate labor disputes, according to most accounts. State militias, immediately available to the governors, were employed even more. One contemporary observer counted 328 different instances in which National Guard troops took part in riot control duty in less than one decade (between 1886 and 1895).[5]

The type of military forces employed in riot control was, as far as the friends of labor were concerned, not of first importance. To them, anyone who put on a uniform, whether a regular or not, was a hired gunman for a business-controlled government. Henry George summed it up when he described General Bell, a National Guard officer, as "one of the kind of men who forget the rights and duties of the civilian when they don soldier clothes. Their first duty, they say, is to obey."

Even so, it was the regular officers for whom labor spokesmen reserved their fullest contempt. Echoing the cries of antebellum democrats, George contended that the regular army made "mere machines of men of the line, to move at the command of officers risen, not out of the ranks in a democratic way, but educated apart, at the manner of

old European nobility. And from that exclusive rearing possessed of the aristocratic idea that those who have power
are those who are born to rule and must be upheld." As
a liberal journalist put it, "Regulars . . . [the mob] knows
to be a machine, the most terrible of all the machines
invented by man. . . . [It] strikes like the flail of destiny,
without remorse, or pity, or misgiving."[6]

★

As the century moved toward its close, labor's critique was
increasingly colored by European theories of class warfare
and its language. New waves of immigrants, coming largely
from impoverished and politically suppressed elements of
southern European monarchies, swelled the workers' ranks,
and they brought with them socialist theories and memories
of officers' braid as symbolic of enforced political oppression. Marxist lexicon posing capitalist-controlled tyrants
against the proletariat became commonplace—and not
merely among the most radical groups. Samuel Gompers
stated flatly, "Standing armies are always used to exercise
tyranny over people." After federal troops had been called
in to restore order in the Idaho mining strikes of 1892, an
A.F. of L. organizer reported that "the arbitrary and mendacious conduct of some of the U.S. Army officers was
never equaled in Russia, Siberia, or by a plantation Slave-
Driver for cruelty towards those arrested or [those who]
came under the displeasure of the mine-owners."[7]

The envisioned coalition between robber barons, political
bosses, and military leaders was, no doubt, a kind of useful
labor-populist political demonology. It is, nevertheless, a
gross mistake to dismiss such views as only proletarian prop-
aganda without basis in fact. The regular officer corps of
the time was hardly egalitarian in outlook. The army's
century-long experience of having its peacetime rosters
filled during times of economic depression with unem-
ployed laborers and foreign immigrants, and its ranks

promptly depleted by their wholesale desertions in better days, left the military leaders with little sympathy for European outcasts and labor insurrectionists. They often evidenced no more understanding of the workers' plight in the cities than labor leaders did of the military's problems and privations on the frontier.

The writings of the military men clearly reveal the mixed tensions created within a traditionally hierarchal order that was operating in a theoretically classless society, but one torn in fact by class division. On the one hand, the officer corps showed decidedly progressive attitudes compared to those of other western armies. They harangued Congress for better educational and recreational facilities for their troops and struggled to dispel the idea that their enlisted regulars were worthless and unthinking derelicts. In 1881, *United Services* magazine, spokespiece for the army, editorialized, "Time was when the soldier, both in fact and in the contemplation of his officers, was little less than a machine. . . . Times now have changed. . . . The soldier has ceased to be the wooden man of former days, and has become a reasoning and intelligent factor. . . ." About the same time, General McClellan was telling readers of *Atlantic Monthly* that, unlike other nations, "with such men as those who compose our armies . . . discipline is best established through a kind and considerate but perfectly firm and just conduct." General Schofield (who commanded the troops in the Idaho mine strike) would say it better. "The discipline which makes soldiers of a free nation reliable in battle is not to be gained by harsh or tyrannical treatment." And a regular army captain, writing to the public about "The Future of Warfare," pointed out that "successful action will in the future rest more than heretofore on . . . noncommissioned officers. . . . To them must be given a greater degree of consideration and authority."[8]

Officers were also becoming sufficiently concerned about the deterioration of their relations with the American people to take collective action. The Military Services

Institution was formed partly because a substantial segment of the army's intellectual leaders recognized that "in order that the army should be maintained in anything like a satisfactory or efficient state, it is essential that its relations to the people and the government should be made closer and more harmonious." To stimulate thought on this matter, the institute offered a prize for the best essay on the subject "The Necessity for Closer Relations Between the Army and the People, and the Best Method to Accomplish the Result."[9]

Ironically, the results of the contest illustrate best the very attitudes that labor spokesmen were so bitterly denouncing. The winning essay, written by a regular captain, concerned itself not at all with "the people" in a liberal's sense of the term. There was no suggestion that military men pay any particular heed to the concerns of the laboring populace. Instead the captain's main recommendations were: (1) that the regular army work more closely with the militia in putting down labor strikes, and (2) that officers should continue to be detailed to colleges "to impart military knowledge to the young men of the country"—the *important* young men being clearly implied. The author theorized quite bluntly that "there is not to-day any responsible social element in the country that wishes, in the light of current events, to weaken . . . the safeguards of law and order. . . . The privilege of general suffrage . . . has been advanced . . . until now the criminal and ignorant classes are as powerful, man for man, at the polls as the law-abiding and intelligent classes."[10]

It is instructive to note that the judges who selected this essay were Senator Robert T. Lincoln and the army quartermaster general, a career bureaucrat whose permanent station was in Washington, D.C. Voting *against* it was a line officer in Colorado. Their views point up the larger fact that the captain's candid disdain for "general suffrage" and for the "ignorant classes" was certainly neither totally representative of, nor peculiar to, the officer corps and military publications. It was common to much of the American scene. The New York *Tribune* characterized the strikers of 1877 as an "ignorant rabble." The *Times* called them "hoodlums, looters, blacklegs, thieves, tramps, ruffians, incendiaries, enemies of society, brigands, rapscallions, riff-raff, felons, and idiots." The *Herald* said the mob was "a wild beast and needs to be shot down."[11] Indeed, a much more harshly phrased article than the captain's had appeared just a few years before in the *Contemporary Review*, printed with apparently full editorial sanction and without rebuttal. In it, the author, a Britisher, argued for professional rather than volunteer armies because "military service," he said, "offers the most obvious and effectual method in which [the able-bodied unemployed] can be made useful to that country to which they are only a nuisance and a burden. The discipline of the army is needed. . . . They are men . . . with terrible proclivities toward evil—almost certain to be criminals if they are not made soldiers. . . ."[12]

Twenty years of labor foment only exposed and deepened an already existing philosophical and social gulf. The officers assigned to strike-control duties were directed to maintain order, but in labor's eyes "that elastic something called 'preserving order,' . . . is the favorite explanation for arbitrary acts on the part of the military army."[13] A lawyer in a letter to the *Journal of the Military Service Institution* summed up the dilemma. He reminded the nation's soldiers that "the distrust of a standing army in times of peace is almost universal, and . . . this feeling is not likely to decrease in the minds of the masses in such times of general corruption and perversion and selfish ends." He went on to point out that, "in the impending crisis between capital and labor . . . the army, regardless of the social, moral and economic questions involved, must be the conservator of the existing order of things, and therefore handicapping still further the masses in their struggle against the influences that they consider so oppressive."[14]

★

The enmity between labor and capital, the Prussianistic overtones of the military's growing professionalism, the importation of European class theories—these and other forces had, by the end of the century, redirected the worker's critique of the military. When the Civil War ended, labor was still picturing the officer much as had the Jacksonians, as a member of a privileged class detrimental to America's competitive economy as a whole, including business as well as labor interests. The National Labor Union stated as part of its 1870 platform, "Standing armies are dangerous to the liberties of the people; . . . they entail heavy and unnecessary burdens on the productive industries and should be reduced to the lowest standards."[15] But as the split between big business and organized labor developed in the Gilded Age, that attitude changed. American army officers became in the worker's eye the Prussianized tools of rampant capitalism. The image changed from aristocrat to dupe, and the hostility deepened.

Chapter Twelve

Gentlemen-Professionals As A Congeries Of Mercenaries, Aristocrats, And Bureaucrats: Post-Bellum Political Censure[1]

The debates in Congress have been interesting . . . for the picture they present of Congressional feeling about the army . . . There is no sign anywhere of a strong public desire that the army should be dismissed or even reorganized. . . . The hostility . . . seems to be confined to a class known as "politicians."

—[E. L. Godkin] in **The Nation**[2]

The postbellum era has been tagged by military historians as "the dark ages" of the United States Army. Considering political-military relations, there is little wonder. Criticisms from business apologists, labor antagonists, and rededicated pacifists converged on Washington; and what one finds in the Congressional records is a conglomerate of unappealing sketches of the army and its leaders.

There were still Jacksonian overtones, but the political attack was becoming noticeably more heterogeneous than in prewar days. Much as the Jacksonians had broadened the earlier critique of the Federalist era, postbellum politicians in turn presented yet more varied—and contradictory—arguments. Where post-Revolution political hostility had focused on the standing army as a threat to republican government, Jacksonian opposition was widened to view the regular officer corps as an antidemocratic military caste. That image remained very much alive in political rhetoric following the Civil War. Such leading figures as John A. Logan (former Union general and founder of the powerful veteran's organization, The Grand Army of the Republic) told the nation that "the boys who carried muskets so gallantly . . . made all these [generals] who now hold themselves so high." And he pledged grandly, "I shall stand up here as the defender of these boys . . . against all the generals, or marshals . . . or potentates, regardless of whatever aristocracy may be attempted to be set up in this land."[3]

But the lingering Jacksonian view was by now only one element in a still more diversified critique that portrayed the officer corps as everything from potential dictators to hapless ne'er-do-wells. And if no more vocal than the shrill monotones of the Jacksonian opposition, the postwar political hostility was of more real consequence, for in showing its disapproval Congress frequently turned its financial back on the military services. As Leonard White succinctly stated it, "The military policy of Congress from 1865 to 1898 was to support an army at the minimum strength to fulfill its minimum missions."[4]

It did not take long after the Civil War for this situation to develop. The guns were hardly still when congressmen were complaining that "our avenues are filled with generals . . . and colonels drawing full pay, while the poor tax-payer is overburdened . . . supporting these idle vagabonds who are well paid and doing nothing." By the '70s, these cries were commonplace. The Democratic leader of the House warned that in view of growing labor unrest, the burden of a large army could lead to revolution and communism. Another representative declared himself willing "to put West Point up to the highest bidder, or to give it away."

By 1878, Congressman James A. Garfield was protesting that "during the last three years there has been manifested in Congress a growing spirit of unfriendliness if not positive hostility toward the army." Agitation for reductions in military pay and manpower (40 percent of the officer corps and 20 percent of the enlisted strength) was running strong. Garfield carried his counterarguments to the public in two issues of the *North American Review*, drawing some detailed comparisons to illustrate the severity of the reduction proposals. "It would be better," he concluded, "so far as pay is concerned, to be a door keeper in the House . . . than a senior captain of infantry; better to be the locksmith . . . than a second lieutenant of the line!"[5] But the low point had already come in 1877 when Congress neglected to make its annual appropriations for military expenses. As a result, many of the soldiers were forced to borrow funds for most of a year to meet their living costs until Congress reconvened. (The enlisted men did receive rations, but both officers and enlisted soldiers had to depend on loans, frequently from usurious bankers, to meet their personal expenses.)[6]

The cycle was vicious. As the war receded, the army became increasingly unpopular in Congress and the legislators gave it less and less support; in return, the army became more hostile, archaic, and inefficient. Cartoonist Thomas Nast characterized the whole sad situation with a shabby Uncle Sam threatening two skeletons, representing the army and navy, with a branding iron marked "further reductions." Signs in the background of his cartoon read: "Treason is a virtue," "Patriotism is a crime," and "More Congressmen wanted."

★

Without doubt, Congress had cause for disapproval. The War Department, after finally hammering out a workable staff organization in the Civil War, had unfortunately returned to the antebellum bureau system, and with it returned the permanently appointed bureau chiefs. Thus, while it was ignoring the frontier soldiers, Congress had a ringside seat for viewing the jealousies, ineptitudes, and feathering of nests that became steadily worse within the War Department. Leonard D. White explains the consequences. "An unpopular [Department], lacking a compelling purpose, facing an indifferent Congress, deprived of funds, and without an affirmative policy that could command public interest was almost certain to deteriorate."[7]

It did. Military men recognized the trend and complained bitterly. The army's brooding intellectual leader, General Upton, denounced the entire War Department system. As an example, he pointed out that under the protection of the secretary of war, the separate branch chiefs had "withdrawn the operation of their departments from the control and even inspection of the general in chief. . . ." As a result, "the Ordnance . . . manufactures our guns. . . , the Engineers build the fortifications on which the guns are mounted, and both are turned over to the Army to be tested in war without an opportunity for . . . the officers who may die in their defense, to make the slightest suggestion." The problem became progressively more acute. In 1893, General Gibbons was again warning the nation that "the control of all details of army matters is rapidly passing into the hands of two or three staff departments, . . . themselves not being under control of the Commanding General of the Army." The process, he feared, was "rapidly transforming our army into a mere *paper* machine. . . . Of all useless things in the world the *paper* soldier is the most useless."[8] But Congress was not inclined to distinguish between bureaucrats and line officers. It was more likely to agree with congressmen like Logan who argued that the entire army was "over-officered and inefficient" and suggested that the head of the Commissary Department be entitled Brigadier General of Beansoup.[9]

In the line units, the downward spiral continued for over twenty years. Duties were uninspiring and promotions almost nonexistent. By 1891, there was not a single artillery captain under forty and the average age was over fifty. Garrison life in the seacoast forts was monotonous and, worse, a sham. Without funds to replace the guns, the batteries became worthless as foreign navies began to mount longer range weapons. At the frontier garrisons, with their privations and isolation, only grueling marches and nasty Indian skirmishes broke the monotony of what one military historian called "the most provincial garrison life into which any government ever forced an army."[10]

The army was righteously angry about the whole western situation. Ignored themselves by Congress, they saw the Indians being sold arms and sheltered on safe-haven reservations during the winter only to sally forth on raids the following spring. Members of the Bureau of Indian Affairs had a different view. They were picturing the regular troops as the lowest kind of hired killers. One employee of the Indian Service published a series of articles entitled "Abolish the Army," in which he charged that "professional soldiers do not want peace. War is their opportunity, fighting their only business."[11]

The mutual distrust between army and government representatives, the penury of congressional authorizations, and the growing inefficiency and corruption in the War Department could only lead to wounds that would rankle for decades. Congressional hostility was matched by that of the officers. "Isolated from the civilians and contemptuous of them as soldiers, the professional officer corps was not inclined to accept the highest military direction from citizens who impressed them as military incompetents." Many reached the conclusion that professional soldiers should be the definers of military policy, and otherwise there was little need of intellectual interchange between them and their government.[12]

★

It is grossly erroneous, of course, to picture the federal government as totally hostile to the professional soldiers or vice versa. Bills against the military failed; officers repeatedly enjoined their colleagues to remain in tune with the nation; leaders in both parties paid tributes to the regulars; and beginning with the Arthur administration there was a gradual but steady renewal of interest in military affairs. While he lived, Garfield was only the most prominent of many defenders of the regular army; and the addresses delivered by government leaders at the Military Academy continued to go far beyond the pleasantries required.

But, for the most part, the military images radiating from Washington were unattractive creations produced by a convergence of critical views that agreed on at least one point. The regular officer—whether bureaucrat, aristocrat, or mercenary—was no longer a leader of, but a misfit in, the American society.

Chapter Thirteen

Gentlemen-Professionals As Proficient National Servants: Utilitarian Appreciation[1]

The solemn fact is that to know much of the science of war the cleverest man needs years of study and experience; and another solemn fact is that in such a momentous business we had better look for supreme guidance to experts and experts alone.

—John William DeForest[2]

As a soldier, General Grant combined inventive genius with relentless determination.

—Reverend P. W. Lyman[3]

Although postbellum criticism of officership was considerable, respect for the profession of arms remained firm and outspoken in important areas of American society. Influential voices frequently, publicly, and enthusiastically declared their appreciation for the military leaders. In doing so, they extended, with modifications, some already well-established patterns of expression. From the nation's birth, support for the profession of arms had derived largely from two sources: an inherited admiration for military men as exemplars of knightly attributes (loyalty, reverence, bravery, obedience, honesty, et al.) and a more pragmatic regard for their immediately useful professional services.

America's military favorite was a gentleman, but always a worthwhile one—even when not at war. If for many he exemplified high ideals, he was most admired when also "contributing": building roads, mapping the West, and protecting the railroads. Similarly, during the Civil War, the ideal army chieftain became a kind of imaginary blend of types: courtly but unyielding, bold but reliable, brilliant but diligent, gracious but above all a winner.

This bifocular standard continued after the war. Many of those who endorsed the military professionals in the 1870s and 1880s were clearly moved by a practical-minded conviction that viable nations must remain strong. Trained soldiers and well-cultivated military expertise were, they reasoned, necessary American commodities. Both major party presidential candidates in 1880 agreed. "The preservation of liberty and peace depends on the . . . science and art of war [acquired by] thorough and patient study," said one. "[Our] small standing army . . . is expected to keep pace with the progress of the profession," echoed his opponent.[4] Others who supported the army and its leaders were still moved not so much by what the military man could offer professionally as by what he represented. They held up the traditional codes of the serviceman for comparison with the devious ways of unscrupulous materialists in the Gilded Age. As Francis Wayland, Jr., told a West Point audience in 1874, "I rejoice [that] topics . . . urged upon [other] collegiate graduating classes need not occupy our attention [for] . . . you have acquired those habits of truthfulness, trustworthiness, and personal honor . . ." that are lacking elsewhere.[5]

The distinction made here is, of course, a matter of degree only. Most of the army's supporters continued to look to military leaders for professional utility *and* social example. Yet there was a difference in emphasis, and realizing it contributes to our understanding of some of the separately distinguishable forces which over the years have shaped the military image in the United States.

★

Those of the postbellum era who pictured military careerists as necessary, competent, and dedicated practitioners continued to assume that wars are, and would for a while continue to be, almost inevitable recurrences. They took the essentially Christian and pessimistic view that man is inherently sinful and bellicose. War should be avoided, but endless peace is a pipe dream. The clergy themselves helped set that tone, often arguing that war is a divinely ordered, recurring life test. Military experience, some felt, was destined by God to put steel in the nation's blood—just as some northern clergymen also took the retrospective view that the painfully drawn out Union victory was one of God's ways of punishing the South for its past sins. Reverend P. W. Lyman, in his eulogy for General Grant, declared that "the unbroken sunshine of plenty and prosperity brings selfishness. . . . Suffering [as in war] is needed to purify nations as well as individuals."

Reverend Lyman's oration demonstrates how tough-minded the Christian defense of the armed services and the military professional could be. Recognizing that the ability to marshal great force and the determination to apply it are characteristics that win modern wars, the clergy praised the men who embodied those traits. In Lyman's words, "No . . . out-flanking of armies would have annihilated the Confederacy. It had to be stamped out. . . . Its resources . . . destroyed; . . . its soldiers killed. . . . Grant's greatness lay in the fact that he perceived the situation and . . . [attacked] with relentless determination." So said the man of the cloth. Since "sheer force of character" was a basic military requisite, greatest admiration was reserved for self-made commanders, men like Grant who had clearly advanced on the strength of their own achievements. "Let it be noted," Lyman cried, "that [Grant's] position does not rest on birth, or on official antecedents."[6]

Strong-willed, proven professionals—that was the new model. America's educators seconded that view. They often saw army men as necessary defenders against both foreign and domestic foes and admired their mental discipline and dedication. Francis A. Walker, president of Massachusetts Institute of Technology, gave a classic description of the devoted military craftsman at his best in a paper entitled "Hancock in the War of the Rebellion." The general, Walker said, bore himself "knightly and heroically," but his real forte was as "the greatest hand at 'papers' that the army ever knew. . . ." While so-called military artists were ignoring regulations, Hancock studied "the state of his command through the morning reports." The general won his victories, Walker contended, by just such meticulous preparations. "No commander ever prepared more carefully in camp for success in the field. [Most] think of him as a kind of meteor on the battlefield . . . achieving his triumph by sheer brilliancy [and] intuition. In fact it was with infinite labor that he forged the weapons his hand was to wield with effect."[7]

Where religious spokesmen saw man's sinful nature making war inevitable and experts on war indispensable, post-Darwinian educators—strongly Christian themselves —agreed, but also added mankind's basic animalism as a factor perpetuating conflict. That view became stronger as the century progressed. Early academicians (Horace Mann, for example) were inclined to take an optimistic, Enlightenment outlook, postulating that education would eventually eliminate international conflict by reshaping man's perfectible nature. With the Mexican and Civil Wars, the educators apparently became convinced that mankind's pugnaciousness was here to stay. In the postbellum era they turned their attention to channeling this inherent combative spirit to better ends. As late as 1903, pragmatist William James (and after him, E. L. Thorndike) was still seeking "A Moral Equivalent for War," i.e., a useful outlet for youth's natural belligerency.[8]

The educators' appreciation of the army also stemmed from their own involvement in the nation's readiness plans. The Morrill Land Grant Act of 1862 extended military education into civilian institutions by requiring that courses in military arts and sciences be offered in colleges accepting government grants. In 1868, the act was extended and the president empowered to assign up to twenty officers to schools with more than 150 male students. The German victory over the French in 1871, attributable in large degree to their broadly based conscription and training, gave renewed vigor to proposals for compulsory training throughout America's school system. Though some educators wanted no part of it, others took the attitude that the country's future battles would be won in the classroom and they intended that the educational system should do its part in keeping the nation strong. Soldier-editor-author, Theophilus Rodenbough argued for them. "We are told by those who would depreciate the value of a military education, of men who are 'born generals'. . . . But the most practical men . . . now admit, that an academic preparation is essential to a fully-equipped officer." He proposed that each state have an academy that would serve it as Annapolis and West Point served the nation.[9]

There was an inertia factor involved as well. Postbellum educational thought remained, as it had been since Puritan times, more moralistic than intellectual, and decidedly reluctant of innovation until late in the century. Academicians, following Horace Mann's lead, were inclined to think of learning as a hedge against extremism and accordingly looked upon attacks on "proven" institutions as unlicensed radicalism. In 1875, the same year he accepted the presidency of the progressive, new Johns Hopkins University, D. C. Gilman warned the country that "we must protect by our good words this school of the nation" [the Military Academy].[10]

A turning point in the educators' attitudes took place around 1885, however. After a generation of peace, general interest in the military was waning and younger leaders were showing noticeably little enthusiasm for German-inspired professionalism. The shift was slight at first, but apparent. The new lines of criticism were signaled in the reports by the annual Boards of Visitors to the Military Academy. The 1883 Board, as a writer for *Lippincott's Magazine* reported, was "impressed with the perfection of everything, and had nothing to suggest." Likewise, the Board of 1884, he noted, was almost "petrified at the accomplishments of the cadets" and even suggested that West Point might be too efficient. The Board said, "it may by some be questioned if it is necessary, in order that a young man become a good officer, that he should know as much or be able to do as much as he is made to do and is taught at West Point."

Subsequent Boards, however, were at times sharply critical, and in the tone of one about to tread on hallowed ground, our reporter prophetically concluded, "it may be almost impious to suggest it, but . . . there are [now] people who question whether the Academy has proved itself eminent as a school of engineering."[11] By the end of the century, as Masland and Radway confirm, "criticism of the Academy, particularly of the alleged narrowness of its program and the authoritarianism of its methods, was common."[12]

So too, we should add, was a growing disaffection in educational circles toward the profession of arms in general. Harvard's pioneer, Charles Eliot, is a case in point. His admiration for the country's patrician soldiers of the past was unhedged. He praised Washington as a military man, pointing out that at twenty-three he "was a skillful and experienced fighter, and a colonel in the Virginia service. What a contrast to our college undergraduates of to-day. . . ." Where Washington had been a "land-owner, magistrate, and soldier . . . our modern rich man is apt to possess no one of these functions. . . . It is a grave misfortune for our country." The national father, Eliot proudly went on, was a stern diciplinarian. "If he could not shoot deserters he wanted them 'stoutly whipped.' He thought that army officers should be of different class from their men, and should never put themselves on equality with their men."

But Washington, Eliot finally decided, belonged to a different age, and modern soldiers are nothing much better than hired killers. In a tribute to "Heroes of the Civil War" delivered in Harvard's Memorial Hall in 1896, he stated, "The service these [civilian-soldiers] rendered to their country was absolutely disinterested. No professional interest in war, . . . no mercenary motive can be attributed to any of them. . . . The world has long since determined the limits of its occasional respect for mercenary soldiers. It admires in such only the faithful fulfillment of an immoral contract." Quite obviously, Eliot considered any "professional interest in war" in the modern age "immoral" or at best synonymous with "mercenary motives."[13]

The tide of educational opinion in the late nineteenth century was turning, but it was still in. Only after the Spanish-American War, and especially after the Philippine episode, did men like Eliot and David Starr Jordan become outspokenly antimilitary. (By 1913, Eliot was conducting a full-scale attack against the military profession in general and the Military Academy in particular.) Most educators, like most of the country, strongly supported the country's military actions. In 1898, the National Education Association resolved: "The teachers of the U. S. recognize that [the war with Spain] has been entered upon in the loftiest motives. The cause of freedom and humanity, and the solidarity of both the American people and the Anglo-Saxon races is vastly increased by such an armed contest."[14] That WASPish and nationalistic position was hardly a platform for criticism of military professionalism.

★

Commonplace and "unmilitary" in his personal mode, yet highly professional and eventually victorious in his military endeavors, Ulysses S. Grant symbolized for millions of pragmatic, Christian, and republican-minded Americans, officership at its best. With little retouching, his life epitomized those features of doggedly acquired skill, courage, and the will to win that were so appreciated by many in the late nineteenth century. Even after his less than inspiring efforts as president, those soldierly qualities appealed to a remarkable range of people, including some of the period's leading humanitarian champions.

New England's liberal reformer and minister, Thomas Wentworth Higginson, is a good example. In his review of the general's memoirs (1886), Higginson said that Grant "is the first great and conquering commander developed by modern republican institutions"; therefore, he was able to see things that "Wellington or von Moltke might very probably have missed." For semipacifist Colonel Higginson (who commanded America's first negro regiment during the Civil War), "Grant's early . . . non-preparation for military life inspires [a] . . . feeling of gratified surprise. . . . So much stronger is the republican instinct than any professional feeling which even West Point can create that Grant, though trained in the pursuit of arms, never looked at things for a moment merely from the soldier's point of view. This was the key to his military successes. . . ."

For all his qualifying statements, however, Higginson respected Grant most as a "great and conquering commander" whose military management rated him a better general than even Lee. "It is possible that Lee might have commanded a million men as effectively as Grant did, but we shall never know, for that brilliant general had no opportunity to make the experiment." And patriot Higginson found satisfaction in observing "that the most willing European critic can impair the fame of one great American soldier [Grant] only by setting up that of another [Lee]. In the next national war—may it be distant—our Grants and our Lees will form part of one army."[15]

The appeal of Grant seems much the same wherever we look. Though philosophically quite removed from Higginson, literary naturalist Hamlin Garland likewise esteemed the dedicated but unpolished soldier. In a serialized biography for *McClure's Magazine* in 1896 and 1897, Garland presented Grant as a simple, sincere man who had made mistakes but whose basic goodness and strength prevailed. Like Higginson, Garland warmly commended his subject's "unmilitary nature," yet made much of the soldier's devotion and professional skills. Most revealing is Garland's chapter contrasting "Captain Grant and the Political Colonels." In it he details how Grant, with relentless efficiency, straightened out an Illinois regiment suffering from the bunglings of "political officers." It was under his professional hand that, "the picnic, the filibustering expedition, [became] a military regiment under military discipline. A man of action, of discipline, of war, of experience had assumed command. His lightest word was to be considered. He did not threaten, or wheedle, or persuade; he commanded. . . . He was never angry, never vindictive, but he was the master." The reason? "Grant was a West Pointer and a veteran, and knew his duties. Everything he did was done without hesitation." As a result "the regiment became proud of him well knowing they had the best commander and best regiment in the state."[16]

To political and moral "realists"—whether educators, ministers, or men of letters—who were inclined to see wars as recurring events in America's development, the true military professional was a trained expert and devoted man of service. As Higginson said, in the next national war—may it be distant—it would be the Grants and the Lees again leading the fight.

Chapter Fourteen

Gentlemen-Professionals As Paragons Of Virtue: Guardians Of Threatened Values[1]

We civilians talk, we almost talk solely, of our rights, but in the army, it seems that men talk chiefly of their duties, . . . and never of their rights. . . . It seems to correct all the mistaken tendencies of the time before they became soldiers.
—William Dean Howells[2]

It is, of course, your duty to be patriotic and brave, courteous and truthful, honest and honorable for . . . it is the law of your profession that he is no longer entitled to hold a commission . . . in the Army . . . **who ceases to be a gentleman**.
—Hon. George W. Houk[3]

The image of the patrician soldier had less currency after the Civil War, but the military gentleman was far from dead. For many Americans, he lived on as an exemplar of established values. As such, he could be found in contemporary novels, plays, histories, in endless reminiscences of the Civil War, mixed—or fused—with the new Prussian types at West Point, in the social circles of Washington, and even on the frontier. He might be modernized and professionalized, but his essential role was to serve as a guardian of threatened ethical and social ideals.

Like the more pragmatically-tinted picture of the officer as an essential national defender, this man too had a fierce sense of duty and the professional know-how to direct a modern army. Still, he was more genteel by nature and his military ventures were marked with a flair which suggested that military science had not fully replaced military art after all. His distinguishing characteristics were closer to the mythology surrounding Robert E. Lee than William Tecumseh Sherman or Ulysses S. Grant.

This image of officership was envisioned largely by spokesmen more immediately concerned with America's changing mores than any external armed threat. They feared rampant materialism more than the inevitability of war. To their way of thinking, the officer was an all-too-rare combination of good rearing and strength of character—and he had fortunately been spared from the corrupting influences of great wealth, especially new wealth.

The models ranged from Revolutionary War leaders to up-to-date professionals. Those who most persistently exhumed military patricians from a century past were also the most outspoken critics of the *nouveau riche*. At their extreme, they spoke as voices from another age, favoring a genteel aristocracy and doting on the vulgarity of new-found wealth.* Their military ideal matched the elder

---

*Mark Twain and C. D. Warner lampooned this situation in *The Gilded Age*. The heroine discovers distinct "aristocracies" in

Holmes' reaction, in 1871, to a portrait of Major Andre: "a face of great delicacy and refinement, . . . a man with the best instincts of the scholar, the finest feelings and manners of a gentleman."[4]

Nostalgic affection for eighteenth-century patricians was not, however, the main thrust behind the virtuous gentleman-professional image as it was perpetuated after the Civil War. Less antique critics of the Gilded Age also refused to admire plutocratic businessmen and the business ethic, and they often chose to hold up military values in comparison. Garfield spoke for them when he said, "A republic, however free, requires the services of a certain number of men whose ambition is higher than mere private gain." Visiting speakers at West Point dwelt at length on this point. As one senator happily observed, "The influence of the rapid and vast accumulation of individual wealth that has so powerfully tended . . . to the establishment of a false standard in our political and social life, . . . has been unable as yet to effect any lodgement here." And he found it "difficult to estimate the beneficent influence of such an institution . . . upon the country at large."[5]

★

It is in American letters (in novels, in periodical pieces, in drama, and in literary criticism) that one finds the fullest expression of this attitude. Remarkably, in all of nineteenth-century writing, one of the most explicit defenses of the

---

Washington. At one pole is the aristocracy of the Antiques "of cultivated, highly bred old families . . . that had been always great in the nation's councils and its wars. . . ." At the other extreme was the aristocracy of the Parvenues. "Official position . . . entitled a man a place in it. . . . Great wealth gave a man a still higher and nobler place. . . . The aristocracy of the Antiques ignored the aristocracy of the Parvenues; the Parvenues laughed at the Antiques (and secretly envied them)."

profession of arms comes from the pens of our postbellum literary critics. Their thesis: modern officers are deserving of the time-honored title of gentlemen not because of wealth, station, or family, but because of their consistent devotion to "higher ideals."

William Dean Howells, "dean of American letters" and early leader of the realistic movement in literature, is the best illustration of the point. Because of his great influence on the contemporary intellectual scene, it is well for us to dwell a bit on his commentary. He argued repeatedly that the nation needed to emulate its military men, especially their selfless sense of service and unblinking loyalty. "In the army," he wrote, "with its few and distant rewards, . . . there is no competition for place and money as there is in civilian life; . . . the performance of duty seems sufficient. . . ." He felt that the great value in novels about the frontier, "which in such singular degree acquaint us with the intimate life of the army, is the lesson in conduct which they teach."[6]

Howells' reviews, written for *The Atlantic Monthly* and later as occupant of the "Editor's Chair" with *Harper's Monthly*, demonstrate the consistency of his attitude during his forty years of preeminence in American letters. In 1881, he sketched his own model of officership with a glowing description of Revolutionary General Nathaniel Greene, whom he saw as a New World gentleman. "His family, though eminently respectable, was not aristocratic; yet he was always prompt to assert the rights of military rank and to repel encroachments upon it. In fact, he was instinctively a soldier, as only Americans can be soldiers,—ambitious but unselfish. . . ." And, as would become his habit, Howells held up the soldier's devotion to service as a lesson to his readers. Greene, he said, demanded of the country "something of the devotion of the army."[7]

Howells' respect for military leaders was not confined to those long dead and past. Of George Custer, whose actions leading to the Little Big Horn massacre made him highly vulnerable to postmortem charges of reckless adventurism,

Harper's editor said simply, "He ought to be known by every grateful American." His only reluctance in praising military professionals came with the southerners. He could admire their soldierly attributes but he disliked their "false gentility" and could never forgive their "disloyalty." General Pettigrew was "a man whom (apart from his error) we should all have found praiseworthy for noble qualities and abilities." General George H. Thomas was the greater man because, although also a southerner, he "rose to the conception of national duty." It was not the military orientation of the South that America's foremost literary critic found at fault; it was their "local patriotism" he condemned.

Apparently, he sensed no conflict between his personal campaign for realism in fictional literature and his own idealized notions of officership. He did, however, have special praise for J. W. DeForest's novel, *Miss Ravenel's Conversion*, as the first to treat the war "really and artistically." DeForest's "soldiers are the soldiers we actually know," he said. "Throughout we admire, as the author intends, [Colonel] Carter's thorough and enthusiastic soldiership, and we perceive the ruins of a generous nature in his aristocratic Virginia pride, his Virginia profusion, his imperfect Virginia sense of honor." Here was Howells' picture of American officership in a nutshell. Eliminate Carter's faulty (Southern) traits of aristocratic pride, profusion, and imperfect honor, and there would remain the perfect military man: a professional of thorough and enthusiastic soldiership, yet a gentleman of humility, honesty, and generous nature.[8]

Fellow literary critics struck the same note. *Atlantic's* staff reviewer, Harriet Preston, was even more outspoken. She praised one book for "the fine and just picture which it presents of . . . the American regular army; of the strict honor, simple bravery, patience under poverty and exile, . . . which have characterized its officers as a class." There is, she asserted, "no other school, North or South, which so regularly and effectively as West Point has made its pupils *gentlemen* in the plainest, soundest, and proudest sense of that term; and it is very well worthwhile to have our memories refreshed about this matter now that the army . . . [is] being made the object of insidious attack by unscrupulous civilians."[9]

★

It is well to remember that much of what Howells and his colleagues were reviewing in those days were novels and plays still heavily marked by traits of literary romanticism: a propensity for heroic figures and stirring plots, an interest in past glories, and a tendency to sentimentality. The protagonists, when soldiers, were almost invariably officers rather than enlisted men, and paragons of virtue as well. Such works often employed formula plots and were at best of marginal literary quality. Yet some, like Captain Charles King's many stories about the community of frontier officers, were of sufficient worth to attract more than dime novel readers and to draw favorable reviews in leading periodicals.[10]

Military men as pictured by the postbellum southern writers were even less real. Hollow personifications of past customs and courtesies, they were no longer, as Lucy Hazard put it, "of the glorious victories that attended colonial and Revolutionary campaigns but of the glorious failures that attended the Confederate cause." Simms and Kennedy may have revived "the audacious young warriors of the empire-building period, [but] Thomas Nelson Page, James Lane Allen, . . . and a host of lesser luminaries dwelt lovingly on the gentle and pathetic figure of the Civil War Colonel with his faded dignity, his quixotic honor, [and] his pathetic impracticality."[11]

Officer types were equally prevalent, but no more convincing, in the still highly contrived postbellum melodramas. They remained the central figures in works like "Belle Lamar" (produced in 1874 and considered "the first creditable play about the Civil War"), Bronson Howard's "Shenandoah" (1888), David Bellasco's "Heart of Maryland" (1894), and William Gillette's "Secret Service" (1898). These morality-type plays continued to pit courageous, Christian, and honorable officers against evil, slick, and traitorous ones. In "Belle Lamar," for example, Stonewall Jackson always graciously gives his outclassed enemies time to surrender before he attacks, and Colonel West in "Shenandoah" nobly leaves his sick bed to lead his regiment into battle.

Of all the literary forms, nineteenth-century drama was the least responsive to new trends, and it was not until well beyond the turn of the century that any strong forces of realism came to the American stage. In much the same way as Cooper's *The Spy* had treated the Revolution a half century earlier, dramas about the Civil War focused on bittersweet struggles created by opposed allegiances between friends, lovers, and members of the same family. A common scheme (in "Heart of Maryland," for example) was to have the heroine's fiance fighting against her brothers and father, and former West Point roommates opposing each other in deadly but graciously conducted combat. The side the hero represented was not usually of importance. It was his fidelity to his cause and to codes that counted. In short, the postbellum stage portrayals of officership changed the old romanticized military gentleman image very little. Proof enough is the fact that Dunlap's post-Revolution classic, *Andre*, was revived in 1887, and was more highly praised than it had been in 1798.[12]

★

A less varnished picture of the military professional began to take form in fiction near the end of the century. While Howells and other novelists were practicing a sort of "smiling realism," a second generation of tougher minded authors was leaning toward philosophical naturalism. Life to the naturalists was a confusion of events whose outcome was more likely to be determined by environmental forces and brooding Fate than by either personal will and talents or by any God immediately responsive to one's prayers.[13] So it was on their fictional battlefields.

As elsewhere, the turning point again seems to have come about the mid-'80s. In 1885, E. L. Scudder, an experienced literary critic, perceptively observed, "It is pretty clear that we are entering on a period of our literature when the war of the Union is to play a highly interesting part. Until lately . . . there has been plenty of cheap use of martial material. . . ."[14] Scudder's forecast was right; and the first clear-cut realistic image of the modern military professional in literature appears at about that time—as the "cheap use of martial material" began to lose its appeal.*

The most apparent link between the old and the new is the work of Ambrose Bierce. In the '80s and '90s "bitter Bierce" produced a number of short stories about the Civil War that show an unusual combination of realistic detail, great sentimentality, and unalloyed cynicism. He pictured the battlefield as a place of stinking death, yet somehow he did not eradicate its glamour; his military characterizations show the effects of this polarity. The younger officers are knightly figures, though tragically so. His lieutenants and captains are often unbelievably brave, gallant, and physically attractive men. Without adjustments, they could gallop onto the pages of Kennedy or Simms—or the Arthuriad for that matter. One is described as having "a gentleman's manners, a scholar's head, and a lion's heart." Another, facing death, "stands erect, motionless, holding his saber in his right hand straight above his head. . . . It is a hero's salute to death and history."

---

*DeForest's attempt at "veritism" in *Miss Ravenel's Conversion* in 1876 was only a precursor of things to come. DeForest himself turned back to more romanticized fiction when he found realism was not yet financially profitable.

The senior officers (and Bierce did not distinguish between regulars and nonregulars) show most of the features of the new military professionals. They are military managers, businesslike manipulators of masses of humanity and seemingly intent upon only one goal, winning the battle. If not indifferent to human life, they subordinate their emotions to the requirements of the job at hand. When at their worst, they are not depraved but brutally insensitive, as in this vignette: "A little apart stood General Masterson addressing another officer and gesticulating with a cigar. He was saying: 'It was the beautifulest fight ever made—by God, sir, it was great!' The beauty and greatness," Bierce drily adds, "were attested by a row of dead, trimly disposed. . . ."

"A Son of the Gods" probably demonstrates best the contrary roles played by Bierce's young gallants and his machinelike senior militarists. A young Union officer deliberately rides to the crest of a hill held by the Confederates, inviting his own death in order to force the enemy to disclose their positions. That he is allowed to do so is the result of his own insistent request; but it is also with the approval of his commander, who would apparently rather sacrifice one life than risk many in testing the enemy's dispositions. As the lieutenant rides back and forth across the face of the hill drawing hostile fire, until eventually killed, the colonel impassively calculates the enemy forces. "The commander has not moved. He now removes his fieldglasses from his eyes. . . . Not a sign of feeling in his face; he is thinking." The final irony is that the heroic act backfires, for the lieutenant's death so inflames the Union troops that they rush forward, taking needless casualties as they do so. In the end, neither the cold professionalism of the colonel nor the gallantry of the lieutenant has saved any lives.

But Bierce did not belittle the profession of arms—only some of its less competent practitioners. He implied that senior officers must be mentally tough to accomplish their tasks. He himself had every intention of staying on as a regular officer after the war. As Marcus Cunliffe reports: "Soldiering still was for him a complete and in an odd way satisfying existence, with its own code and skills, and even its splendors." In his published reminiscenses, Bierce made explicit his respect for officership and his willingness to judge each representative on his own merits. He roundly condemned Bible-quoting General O. O. Howard for causing a Union slaughter which he (Bierce) termed "the crime at Pickett's Mill." On the other hand, he obviously admired General Thomas, both as a man and soldier, and appreciated Sherman's vast military skill. But his ideal was General W. B. Hazen, "a born fighter [and] an educated soldier." "He was aggressive, arrogant, tyrannical, honorable, truthful, courageous—a skillful soldier, a faithful friend and one of the most exasperating of men. Duty was his religion. . . ." When Howard made his blunder, Hazen "uttered never a word, rode to the head of his feeble brigade and patiently awaited the command to go." To Bierce, Hazen's devotion to duty epitomized military professionalism at its best and overrode the faults of his less than genial nature.[15]

Stephen Crane was a more profound and more consistently skillful author than Bierce. In 1893, working from knowledge derived from accounts like *Century* magazine's *Battles and Leaders of the Civil War*, Crane (who had never seen war) wrote his celebrated *Red Badge of Courage*. Published in 1895, it has been generally considered the first successful attempt at a truly realistic war novel.[16]

Crane's attitude toward the army came under attack immediately. Because he chose to center his story on an enlisted man, a radical departure in itself, the officers are simply shadows in the background. When seen at all, the higher ranking ones are often the seemingly insensitive types pictured by Bierce. Like the protagonist, Private Henry Fleming, they too are caught in the tumult of war, but this book was not about them. Some readers presumed that the author was intentionally besmirching America's military leadership. One wrote bitterly to the editors of *Dial* magazine. " 'The young lieutenant,' 'the mounted officer,' even 'the general,' are all utterly demented beings," he complained, "raving and talking alike in an unintelligible and hitherto unheard-of jargon, rushing about in a very delirium of madness. . . . Nowhere are seen the quiet, manly, self-respecting, and patriotic men, influenced by the highest sense of duty, who in reality fought our battles."[17]

But Crane, even before he had any firsthand experience, somehow understood warfare's participants in a deeper way than such critics. In *Red Badge* and subsequent short stories, he pictured a mélange of military figures and established no stereotypes. He admired the soldier of any rank who proved himself to himself, his unit, and his cause—as Henry Fleming's own struggle for self-redemption demonstrated.

Any notion that Crane had a consuming contempt for military professionals should have been fully dispelled by his several stories coming out of his work as a correspondent in the Spanish-American War. "Virtue in War," published in *Leslie's Magazine* in 1899, tells of a regular officer who has left the army only because he is sure that he will never gain a command until too old to be fit. With the approach of the Spanish War, he gives up an excellent business position to command an untrained militia battalion. Like Garland's Grant and Bierce's W. B. Hazen, Crane's Major Gates is a schooled leader whose discipline and training are unappreciated until the payoff in battle. When in the heat of combat other militia units fail to deploy under fire and thus place his own men as well as themselves in danger, "Gates, the excellent Gates, the highly educated and strictly military Gates, grew rankly insubordinate." He quickly forces a solution upon an inept militia colonel, and in his men there was "born a swift feeling that the unpopular Gates knew everything, and they followed the trained soldier."

Crane's conception of the military commander at his best

is a dispassionate professional. As personified by Major Gates and others, he is not an especially attractive person. His is no "face of great delicacy and refinement" to excite, as Andre's portrait could, the admiration of latter-day Brahmins; nor are his manners those of the scholar and gentleman. Aloof and seemingly impersonal, he is in fact fiercely devoted to his troops; and his victory comes not in heroic conquest but in death. Gates' chief antagonist, a previously chafing subordinate, stops to aid his mortally wounded commander and stays on to keep a devoted watch of death even under artillery fire. With Crane and the close of the century, war in literature became real and military gentlemen became, for better and worse, completely professional.[18]

★

But it is Howells—not the die-hard genteelists, nor the writers of the frontier West, nor the southerners, nor the playwrights, nor the new realists—who stands at the center of attitudes expressed by the men of letters in the period between the Civil and Spanish Wars. To him, as to the others, officers were, in one way or another, a blend of gentlemanship and soldiership, and their way of life was yet worthy of emulation. As Howells summed it up, "If, as Ruskin has fancied, the army should ever serve us as the norm of the civil state . . . it might not be long before we should be told that it was against human nature to act selfishly, and that to be recreant to the general welfare . . . was to be guilty of conduct unbecoming a citizen and a gentleman."[19]

SECTION FIVE

FIN DE SIECLE AND BEYOND

Reviewing the intellectual developments of the turn of the century, Alfred Kazin wrote, "By the late 90's strange new currents were in the air. Somewhere between Haymarket [the riot of 1886] and the Columbian Exposition of 1893, which proclaimed America's rising industrial and commercial power, the modern soul had emerged in America." Or maybe Henry May's explanation of *The End of American Innocence* is more accurate. The ingredients of a new age, he tells us, were taking form before the turn of the century, but the modern temper did not fully surface until those unusually invigorating years between 1912 and 1917. Henry Steele Commager chooses the late '80s and the '90s as "the watershed of American thought," and Arthur Link begins *The American Epoch* with the last decade of the nineteenth century. However figured, there is general agreement among the surveyors of our history that the turn of the century was a time of considerable intellectual and social ferment.[1]

The characteristic spirit was a willingness—indeed, a determination—to question and reexamine previous assumptions and values, no matter how sacred or how deeply entrenched. This was more than just the social scientists' conscious rejection of *a priori* thinking and the studious application of empirical methods to sociological analysis. There was that, but there was also a strong emotional, as well as rational, impulse to presume that what had been said in the past was false until proven true—an impulse not unlike that seen in recent times. With it went an urge toward revisionism in all disciplines of thought. "Why should we take our values from the past?" the president of the American Historical Society would ask appropriately.[2]

In this skeptical atmosphere, the military professional was once again reconsidered, reevaluated. The results were generally wounding. It was not so much that the new generation of American spokesmen disagreed with the emerging picture of officers-as-professionals: thoroughly trained, highly dedicated, fundamentally honest and disciplined protectors of the nation and its traditional values. It was precisely this image that they now began to accept and to fault. That style of "military mind," they were sure, was antipathetic to much of what, they were equally sure, liberal-oriented America stood for most.

Just beginning to achieve a degree of cohesiveness, the growing American intellectual community, including social analysts, journalists, editors, academicians, and others, was striving to be progressive, open-minded, and especially tolerant of previously disdained voices—as their affection for the populist movement illustrates. These spokesmen were more inclined to be cosmopolitan than nationalistic and more concerned with freedom of thought than the maintenance of established codes. Relatively liberal in religious outlook as well, they were becoming more fearful of puritanical rigidity, hypocrisy, and zeal in any form or field than of fracturing old loyalties. They would, when convenient, agree with the business community's disapproval of the army's inefficiencies and weaknesses. But, aspiring to be humanitarian champions of the oppressed, they were more inclined to envision the profession of arms from the populist-labor perspective, and to see the United States officer corps as misplaced European junkers.

At the focus of such thinking was a deep concern with militarism as a modern-day ideology. The military professional in national service was becoming, in the eyes of his most influential critics, a professional militarist dedicated *first and above all else* to his profession and its way of life. The shift was subtle, but profound. It undid the record of the past, without acknowledging that fact. Where the founding fathers, for example, had feared military power as a tool for despots, the new intellectuals feared the military ethic itself. They saw militarism diluting and corrupting, rather than physically overwhelming, liberal thought. And where the Jacksonians had thumped the regulars for military incompetence, physical softness, pale patriotism, and lack of mental and moral discipline, the new school turned that formula almost around. They were inclined to worry about an army that was too proficient, too tough, too moralistic, too patriotic, and too disciplined. They feared the triumph of supernationalism, regimentation, and organized mediocrity.

All of this is not to suggest that the professional-as-a-militarist idea became predominant before the turn of the century. But the trend was clearly established and eventually it would do much to redirect the nation's conception of its military leaders in the twentieth century. In this regard, as in so many other areas, the turn of the century was, indeed, a watershed in American thought.

Chapter Fifteen

Military Professionals As Professional Militarists: A New Emphasis Amid Crosscurrents Of Intellectualism And Imperialism[1]

Very few appreciate the fact that in all ages it is disobedience rather than obedience to existing laws which has made progress possible. . . . What must we expect, then, when every one shall have been trained into a military—that is, blind—obedience?

—A. B. Ronne[2]

Patriotism is being carried to insane excess. I know men who do not love God because He is a foreigner.

—Mark Twain[3]

In 1896, addressing the question "What is the Use of a Regular Army?," a troubled career officer commented sadly, "There is [still] an undercurrent of respect. . . , but the army has no active or powerful friends."[4] Even before the Spanish War and its aftereffects on the military image, army leaders were finding themselves with ever fewer champions willing to speak their case publicly. Closely associated with no particular interest-group, they were becoming convenient targets to be lumped with everybody's special enemy.

If one seeks a point in time (or, more exactly, a locus of points) that marks the break, somewhere around 1885 seems the best choice. Before then—for all the virulent attacks from one quarter or another—middle-class, Christian, business-oriented America and its military men were essentially in tune. And when civilian and military modes of life were in open contradiction, there were many in the civilian community who preferred the soldier's ethic and said so. Admiration for Germany's newly famous military professionals was still running high in the '80s and was still rubbing off on America's attitudes toward its own officer corps. More important, reconstruction was ended, and after twenty years of mellowing tempers the entire nation was enthusiastically, even studiously, reviewing the details of the Civil War as never before—and largely in a mood of appreciation for the more skillful practitioners of military science on either side. *Century* magazine's monumental *Battles and Leaders of the Civil War*, which began as a serial in 1884, was published three years later in four folio volumes to meet the great national demand. Similar, if lesser, works flooded that decade. They included the inevitable post-event bickerings, cloudy memories, name-callings, and wounded prides; yet one message was eminently clear. The most successful military men, North and South, were career soldiers and admired for it.

On the political scene, military service remained almost a prerequisite for presidential candidacy until the mid-'80s, and a reputation for the managerial skills acquired in the army was clearly an asset at the polls. Hancock, the Democratic candidate in 1880, was acclaimed for his thorough military efficiency, and if his West Point background was used with some effect against him in the campaign by followers of citizen-soldier Garfield, Congressman Garfield himself was on record as the regular army's staunchest defender. E. L. Godkin's *The Nation* reflected the prevailing respect for professional military skills even as it argued in 1881 against a belated movement to return Grant to office for a third term. "We admit," *The Nation* editorialized, "that it is fair enough to infer that because a man has commanded an army well he will probably rule a state well, . . . [but] after the experiment has upset it, it is very odd to go on talking as if there had been no experiment at all."[5]

As the '80s faded, however, the critical climate began to change noticeably. More and more, the military code was pointed to not as an example for social conduct, but as a danger to beware. We have already seen, piecemeal, some of the contributing forces. By the early '80s social evolutionists were positing theories that demoted the long admired military statesman to the role of an outdated relic. Industrialists, the new scientists of society were saying, would replace the semicivilized warriors as leaders of the world. In the religious field, young ministers were turning their attention to correcting the ills of the social environment rather than saving individual souls; and the "social gospel" of a W. D. Bliss or Walter Rauschenbusch could never see military experience as an ordained testing ground for men and nations, but only as a transitory evil to be eradicated as soon as possible. Progressive educators like Eliot and Francis Parker were expressing the view that the military commission was *per se* an "immoral contract"; and, where the Military Academy at West Point had for nearly a century been a source of obvious pride to the American educational community, liberal-minded young academicians were now foremost among its critics. Even in imaginative litera-

ture the picture was changing. War was becoming the hell
Sherman insisted it was, and its participants, whether wearing epaulettes or not, were no longer unalloyed heroes but
very fallible individuals.

What happened to the image of the military leader at the
hands of progressive-minded scholars, essayists, and
authors during the last ten or fifteen years of the century
is well illustrated in America's historical writings. George
Bancroft died in 1891, Parkman in 1893, and, like Lowell
and Longfellow in literature, with them went the last symbolic, if already faded, leadership of the previous era. A
new school was forming and the change in outlook toward
the military was considerable.[6]

There were, to be sure, postbellum historians who,
although adopting the new evolutionary approach and
empirical methodology, did not discard the earlier American concept of history as a review of providentially determined political and military events. Accordingly, they also
did not drastically alter previously established portraits of
the nation's military heroes. John Fiske, as noted earlier,
is an excellent example. The most popular historian of his
day, he managed to be at once an evolutionist and a fol-
lower of Bancroft, and he continued writing nationalistic
histories in which officers were praised for their military
achievements as well as their military-bred strength of
character.

But even the most conventional historians made adjustments in their military portrayals. Seeing the soldiers of the
past through the eyes of a new age of professionalism, they
evidenced a greater appreciation for the soldier *qua* soldier.
Typically, John Esten Cooke in his *Virginia, A History of the
People* (1883) berated one French colonial commander's
"profuse courtesies," but quickly forgave the fault because
"under the courtier . . . was a soldier." And while old villain
Braddock was, in Cooke's judgment, still "a very bad selec-
tion of leader," it was now due more to Braddock's military

deficiencies than his characterological shortcomings. "Brave as his sword, [poor Braddock] wanted the brain of an army-leader." Conversely, Washington epitomized "the firm soldier-hand [which] was felt throughout the whole army." Under such sympathetic pens, military leaders of the American past were becoming more professional as soldiers while yet remaining men of strong moral fiber, worthy of high admiration.[7]

It was the younger, revision-minded historians who most changed the military image. Their evaluation of officership was clearly a byproduct of their mounting criticism of the nation's past foreign policy, its capitalist system, and its self-congratulatory nationalism. Spurred by their distaste for the growing spirit of imperialism, they increasingly associated the military leader with various shibboleths which they were determined to eliminate. Their oft-expressed opinion was that conventional histories of the past had had a "disproportionate fondness of political and military affairs."[8]

Consider the new historians' treatment of the American Revolution. Prior to the 1880s, the Revolution was the dominant event in our historical writings, and the chroniclers' attitudes toward it were almost universally pro-American and anti-British. By the '90s, opinions and interpretations were changing sharply. Moses Coit Tyler went so far as to defend the British-American Loyalists as sensible moderates who "would have given us political reform and political safety, but without civil war and without an angry disruption of the English races. . . ." Others were taking a similar line, and the overblown image of the nation's first soldiers suffered in the process. Their military skill was questioned; even the sainted Washington's generalship was belittled and his ultimate victory credited more to foreign assistance than to inspired tactical leadership. Soldierly virtues were deemphasized; the loyalty of the Continental Line was at times questioned; and the Cincinnati Society again became almost a dirty word, after having been nearly forgotten by mid-century writers. (In 1853, the *North American Review* ran an article on the society treating it as an historical curio and telling its story in complimentary terms.)[9]

In like manner, the events of the War of 1812 and the Mexican War were presented in a new light. The failures of the militia forces were played down and Jackson's triumph at New Orleans became, more than ever before, proof of the superiority of the "unprofessional" soldier. The Mexican War was becoming a deliberate land grab on the part of "mendacious Polk" and his followers, including high military leaders who were linked with southern territorial ambitions and slave-holding interests.

John Bach McMaster's *A History of the People of the United States* is a fair representation of the changing tone. Read today, McMaster's pioneering attempt at a "social history" does not appear especially damning to the military, but how derogatory his views seemed at the time is made clear by a bitter rebuttal appearing in the *Journal of the Military Institution of the United States*. The reviewer took strong exception to the idea that Washington was "cold and forbidding" and "not the greatest of generals." He was revolted by McMaster's claim that the Continental Army was "in 1783, mutinous and rebellious," a statement which he said was "misleading and if Mr. McMaster had been old enough to serve in [the Civil War] . . . to preserve that union which our ancestors fought to secure, we venture to say he would have refrained from libeling so intensely and nationally patriotic a body as the Continental Line of the Revolution." He noted, quite accurately, that McMaster had cordial expression for only one military man, Andrew Jackson, "whose intrepidity, whose energy, whose fiery temper, and intense love for right made him in after years, the most remarkable man the Republic had yet produced."[10]

McMaster's scholarship, later works have shown, was justifiably questioned. Regardless, his more scholarly colleagues reflected much the same distaste for military careerists. To Professor Woodrow Wilson, Winfield Scott seems to have been the embodiment of un-American and dangerous "militarism." Where previous historians had recognized the man's vanity and antagonistic nature, Wilson refused to grant even his professional achievements. The president-to-be's account of the Mexican campaign has General Scott choosing "a hard road to the Mexican capital, but the dogged valor and the alert sagacity of his men made everything possible. . . . They were most of them only volunteers. . . . Their success was due to their moral qualities—to their steady pluck and self-confidence, their cool intelligence, their indomitable purpose, their equal endowments of patience and dash." In short, it was the volunteers, with little or no help from their commander or the regulars, who won the war.* In similar language, Wilson called Sherman's "terrible march through Georgia . . . almost unprecedented in modern warfare for its pitiless . . . destruction and devastation."[11]

Carried to an extreme, this picture of the military leader became the complete caricature of the brutal, narrow-minded, arrogant militarist who lacked the enduring qualities of "true" Americans. Julian Hawthorne, cashing in on his father's literary fame, became a late-century Parson Weems, writing "history" as he wanted to see it. In doing so he played at a higher pitch many of the same tunes of the more notable liberal historians. With Hawthorne, patrician Colonel Washington becomes a democrat who travels through the back country with a good native American "Kit Gist, a hunter and trapper of the Natty Bumppo order, [who] was his guide." Braddock, of course, is the "obstinent,

---

*For several reasons the terms "regular" and "volunteer" are ambiguous in this case. Regardless, Scott had borrowed heavily from Taylor's seasoned troops, volunteers and regulars, to make his invasion; and later he had to halt his campaign to await replacements for several precarious months in hostile territory because 3,000 volunteers "of indomitable purpose" went home when their enlistment ran out.

ruffiany, stupid martinette," and Hawthorne (like Wilson with Scott) strips the general of even his previously uncontested courage. "Braddock has been called brave; but the term is inappropriate; he could fly into a rage when his brutal or tyrannical instincts were questioned or thwarted, and become insensible, for a time, even to physical danger. Ignorance, folly, and self-conceit," Hawthorne explained, "not inseldom make a man seem fearless who is a poltroon at heart." In the fashion of the new historians, Scott is contrasted to good, common Zachary Taylor. "Scott was a martinette . . . fond of dress and display, arrogant and domineering. . . . Taylor, on the contrary, [was] kindly and democratic. . . ." On the battlefield, Taylor "was a great fighter and absolutely free from fear; he would loll in his saddle and crack jokes, in the midst of a rain of bullets and cannon balls. . . . Scott was brave enough . . . but his ideas of military propriety kept him from needlessly exposing himself; he remained grandly in reserve, and sent his subordinates to the front. . . ."

Here for the anti-military idealist was the epitome of militarism neatly juxtaposed with "a true American type of the good old simple sort; unpretending, sagacious, humorous, and grit all the way through."[12] As America's new generation of progressive-minded writers reviewed the past, it was the Scott rather than the Taylor image that represented military regulars. And, as they looked to the future, they could agree with those less critical that the officer was a professional, but they were less inclined to admire his military professionalism than to fear his professional militarism.

★

The mounting surge of imperialism through the '90s confirmed the humanistic intellectuals' worst suspicions. Seeing the involvement of prominent military men, they were quick to sweep the officer corps *in toto* into the expansionist camp. To them, the soldier was devoted not to keeping the peace but to making war, and the "military mind" was an interchangeable part in all the regimented automatons.

Certain contemporary military writers gave ample basis for such opinions by publicly proclaiming that "war is one of the great agencies by which human progress is effected"; and "the instinct of conquest is in the Anglo-Saxon blood. . . ." Their voices blended with that group including Brooks Adams, Homer Lea, Henry Cabot Lodge, Theodore Roosevelt, and Herbert Croly who espoused the strenuous life, a muscular kind of Christianity, the beneficent effects of national adventure and the necessity of the "big stick."[13]

Given the country's geographical circumstances, more of the key figures among the imperialists were navalists, in and out of the service, than army boosters. But even though they supported the navy's long-standing plea for modernization, they did not represent the views of most of its officers. Naval Captain Alfred T. Mahan's *The Influence of Sea Power Upon History 1660-1783*, published in 1890, soon became a basic text of political-military thought here and abroad. But by going beyond professional boundaries, Mahan alienated himself from much of the officer corps —the "shellbacks" as they were sometimes disdainfully called by more energetic expansionists.

Quite opposite from General Upton, the postbellum army's intellectual leader who devised military theory in a political-social vacuum, Mahan justified strength on non-military—economic and political—grounds. By urging officers to become statesmen as well as military operators, he took a position contrary to the professionals' inbred dedication to serve as directed but to remain outside political involvement. Mahan admitted that by the '90s his personal interests and talents were more directed to literary pursuits than his naval career. He requested relief from a final sea tour and was denied, partly on the grounds that "it is not the business of a naval officer to write books." A subsequent efficiency report on Mahan noted that his "interests are entirely outside the Services for which . . . he cares but little and is therefore not a good officer."

Even so, Mahan had willing supporters within both serv- ices and much of what he and his associates wrote for broad consumption was unquestionably part and parcel of the cur- rent military ethic. They took the Clausewitzian position that nations must deal diplomatically from strength; thus, even in peace, strong military forces serve the nation. They readily agreed with Roosevelt, who told the officers attend- ing the Naval War College, "Those who wish to see this country at peace . . . will be wise if they place their reliance on a first-class fleet of battleships, rather than upon any arbitration treaty. . . . Diplomacy is utterly useless." "So it is," echoed an army lieutenant. "All human government rests untimately on force. Behind the diplomat . . . is the military power of the nation he represents."[14]

When arguing from religious grounds—which they fre- quently did—the expansionists contended that "war is an ordinance of God." Admiral Luce told the readers of *North American Review*, "The flaming sword will continue to pre- vail, until man enters once more into that peace which pas- seth all understanding. . . . But mortal man cannot yet dis- cern the coming of that day." If less fervent in expression, there were army officers on record with the same philosophy. (As a matter of fact, so was a good part of the nation.) "Peace is a dream", wrote one soldier, quoting von Moltke. And he added, "Human nature must change before war shall cease. . . . Oppression and misrule must pass away; the spirit, not the professions of Christianity must reign uni- versal, before man shall cease to war upon his kind." Prepa- ration for war was therefore not merely justifiable on politi- cal grounds, but of moral urgency. "Heaven forbid," Luce wrote with all apparent sincerity, "that we should ever seem to be an advocate of war. . . . But this is not a question of what one could wish: it is . . . a great fundamental truth."

As did the Spencerian pacifists, the expansionists too proclaimed evolution as the overall pattern of history—but with a major difference. The imperialists saw history as a continuing power struggle, not between individuals, but between racial and national forces. America's manifest destiny could therefore be advanced only to the degree she could compete, militarily and otherwise. Mahan was only one of several prominent spokesmen of the day who was picturing war as a vehicle for the spread of Christianity and democracy. By 1897, Roosevelt was hoping aloud for a war in Cuba for "humanity and self-interest," not only for the opportunity to free the Cubans, but also for "trying both the Army and the Navy in actual practice."[15]

★

What were the effects of the jingoistic '90s on America's conception of the military leader? In the immediate sense, not particularly great. For many, the events leading to the Spanish War seem only to have confirmed their already set impressions. The military professional was a worthless parasite, an indispensable national servant, an enemy of the workers, a bungling bureaucrat, a paragon of gentleman-hood, or a ruthless mercenary—and usually some combination of these—depending on the particular spokesman's point of view. In short, the habit of judging the military man through the eyes and mind of one's primary allegiance (to capitalism, to labor, to pacifism, etc.) continued. At the same time, although not yet in great numbers, there was a perceptible and significant shift among some of the nation's most influential writers which would, with time, have great effect.

Consider *The Nation's* noted editor. Acknowledged by William James to have been a "towering" influence on him and his generation, Edwin L. Godkin was anything but consistent in his opinions on war and military figures. On one occasion, he admitted that "killing enemies is a legitimate calling" but felt that it was, nonetheless, the "meanest office in any state after that of the public executioner." At another time, he contradicted himself saying, "It will be a sorrowful day . . . when those who stay at home have neither gratitude nor admiration for those who shoulder the musket. . . ." And he considered the Spanish people so debauched that "they have lost the capacity for combined and protracted effort even in military enterprises which is one of the highest marks of civilization."

For all these inconsistencies, Godkin's view of professional soldiers became measurably more severe with the mounting wave of chauvinism that he so detested. Military leaders were guilty by association. In 1896, he could pay warm tribute to General of the Army Nelson A. Miles, who had recently made "a most impressive protest against the barbarity of war. Like most men," Godkin wrote, "who have done their fighting on the field, not on paper, [Miles] has only words of reprobation for those who are crying 'On to war!'" Yet, in only three years, Godkin had fully reversed himself and given a perfect summation of the liberal intellectuals' conception of the militaristic mind. In an article titled "Military Morality," he wrote, "The truth is, that when military men turn casuists, and talk of moral responsibility, they enter on a trackless wilderness. There is no rarer qualification among those who either direct or conduct or love wars than moral responsibility." Godkin apparently overlooked, or chose to ignore, his own argument of not long before that the experienced soldier has only reprobation for those urging war.[16]

Mark Twain seems a similar case. A long-time defender of U. S. Grant (from Matthew Arnold in one notable and heated exchange), and a favorite at West Point where he delighted in coming to wisecrack with the cadets on informal occasions, his outlook on the military grew darker as the Spanish War approached. He began to see patriotism as only a blind force followed by people who "wrap themselves in the flag." His darkening view of mankind in general and the soldier in particular was deepened by his contempt for Roosevelt, which reached the boiling point when the Rough Rider bragged about his San Juan Hill exploits. Later in the war, Twain would write his bitterly satiric attack, "The Defense of General Funston," in which he condemned Funston for accepting help when dying from the Filipino Aguinaldo and, when recovered, killing his guard and capturing the enemy leader. The "defense" Twain ironically put forth was that "it was not the General's doing, but his innate disposition that was to blame."[17]

The reputation of the officer corps at the century's turn did not fare well even at the hands of the imperialists themselves. There was little doubt what the expansionists *wished* the officer to be. Henry Cabot Lodge presented that picture in his enthusiastic historical portrait of the young Colonel Washington who "comes before us, as, above all things, the fighting man, hot blooded and fierce in action, and utterly indifferent to the danger which excited and delighted him." Moreover, Lodge goes on, Washington was "plainly one of those who could learn . . . [what] he had been taught in a series of fresh and valuable [combat] lessons."[18] A hot-blooded fighting man, but a calculating perfectionist educated in the school of battle: that was the expansionist model of soldiership.

The contemporary crop did not measure up. Indeed, to the more aggressive imperialists, America's military leaders were bureaucrats, shellbacks, or foot-draggers. Especially disappointing was the army which had, in its not-so-splendid isolation of three decades, grown archaic in its logistical system, its leadership, and its staff organization. By 1899, Roosevelt was actively supporting Secretary of War Elihu Root's plans for reform of the War Department. Speaking through *The Outlook* magazine, the vice president urged Root's proposed changes and warned that "not merely inertia, but the malign influence of officers who have procured soft places at Washington will be against [the] Secretary. . . ."[19]

There is no doubt that America's military machinery was rusty. But the friction between the romantic expansionists and the more realistically-inclined officer corps was a deeper matter, one of contrary philosophies. Although influential officers from Upton and Sherman to Schofield and Miles sought a stronger standing army, they were notoriously reluctant to commit it to battle. As Huntington says, "For the military the fundamental aim was national security. For the Neo-Hamiltonians, it was national assertion and national adventure." Or, as one military writer of the day put it, "The political agitator . . . would forever keep down the military . . . [while] constantly endeavoring to foment international trouble by appealing to the prejudice of the masses by every means of jingoism."[20]

★

The images that loom out of the '90s are as contradictory as any in our history. Conquering heroes to much of the nation, the military leaders were reluctant fighters and soft bureaucrats to the imperialists. And, from quite an opposite point of view, they were iron-heeled monsters to the growing school of progressive idealists. As A. B. Roone complained, "The business of the professional soldier being to kill, it also becomes part of his business to find or devise new occasions for the exercise of his professional duties."[21] But, however received, America's military professionals were more than ever before considered professional militarists, and an increasing alienation between the soldier and America's liberal-oriented intellectual spokesmen was henceforth inevitable.

Chapter Sixteen

An Epilogue: Some Prominent Twentieth-Century Patterns[1]

The eighteenth and nineteenth centuries fixed in American thought our basic conceptions of the military leader. The impact of the twentieth century on the image of the professional soldier has been more a matter of modification than mutation. The cumulative effects have, nonetheless, been formidable. Although this century has spawned few, if any, fundamentally new military stereotypes, it has seen some remarkable realignments of military sympathizers and critics.

In a century where new "generational outlooks" seem to come along every decade or so, the frequent shifts in ideological loyalties have caused repeated blurrings of our already confused attitudes toward the military. A full appraisal of the situation needs a volume to itself, and such a work (although in progress) is not completed. Still, to suspend this story at 1900 has one unacceptable drawback. Unless we make at least some of the connections between the earlier attitudes and images we have just examined and our notions of the military man today, it is difficult for us to appreciate the very strong residual influences of those previous patterns of thought.

Hence, in quest of that modern grail called "relevance," this extension, or epilogue, to the basic study is offered. It is an overview based on tentative findings, and it outlines only some of the broader developments that came about during the first half of the twentieth century. This kind of epilogizing will not substitute for the fuller examination called for, but for the time being it should help put the preceding material into more current and concrete perspective.

★

It was between the war with Spain and World War I that America began to realize that she had lost much of her nineteenth-century innocence. An agrarian nation had become industrial. The country had engaged in overseas conquests. Reaction to laissez-faire tenets was setting in and defenders of the old idealities were losing their hold in philosophy, history, and literature. Attacks on the "genteel tradition" reached full voice, and even staid old periodicals like the *North American Review, Harper's,* and *Atlantic* found themselves adjusting to the competition of outspoken new journals. Reform from the top, to borrow Eric Goldman's description, was converging with reform from the bottom as upper-class crusaders took up lower-class grievances and began to formulate twentieth-century liberal theories.[2]

As the national mood was changing, the officer-and-gentleman figure, like other superceded patricians, was at long last fading away. "The old order of service in the army . . . [had] given way to new fields of duty," as one retired general observed sentimentally.[3] Gone with the passing of the frontier and with the Philippine occupation was the army's century-long focus on the North American continent. Gone with Elihu Root's reform of the War Department was the old Calhoun bureau system. And gone forever with World War I—a dreary, static war of attrition with muddy trenches, incessant artillery barrages, sweeping automatic fire, and lung-blistering poison gases—was the old "heroic" mode of warfare and leadership. The Marquis of Queensbury fair play and the grand courtesy that had accompanied the carnage and terrors of the Civil War seemed quaintly foolish in a day of depersonalized combat and calculated psychological warfare. Withall, the role and image of the army officer completed a transfiguration begun fifty years before. The gentleman soldier of the nineteenth century was fully converted to the military professionalist of the twentieth century.

Realignments in America's military critique proved equally far-reaching. Reform-minded social commentators from various persuasions took up the cry against modern-day "militarism," and the literati, in sharp contrast to their pro-military nineteenth-century predecessors, became before long the most aciduously demeaning of all the twentieth-century critics. Labor's complaint, on the other hand, would gradually lose its heat, until by mid-century blue collar workers were among the military careerists' stoutest, if somewhat silent, supporters. Spokesmen for big business, also at philosophical odds with the profession of arms just before the turn of the century, were soon (almost by default) again allies of the armed forces as they found themselves the twin target for the progressives' attack on the business-military complex. In short, America's oft-proclaimed "traditional" attitudes toward its professional soldiers proved to be no more stable in the twentieth century than before.

Military-Industrial Conspirators

The vision, so prominent today, of the army officer as a member of a business-military conspiracy overtaxing the civilian economy while encouraging "financially profitable" wars had its roots, as we have already seen, in nineteenth-century pro-labor thought. That picture was made indelible a few years later with the reform liberals' reaction to the Spanish-American War and the Philippine Insurrection. To understand that situation, we need to recall that at that time some of America's most articulate commentators were not only aligning themselves with the growing populist-progressive movement, they were also increasingly inclined to be economic determinists in their interpretations of events past and present. As both social-economic theorists and champions of humanistic causes, the new liberals found it easy, in their retrospective analyses, to blame the Spanish War on the industrialists and their "military henchmen." It was, so their arguments ran, the business tycoons controlling the government and seeking broader markets who had dictated the war; ergo, America's military professionals were, much as they had been characterized in the labor strikes, the hired gunmen of big business.

There was truth to that line of argument. Prominent

military as well as business figures were among those who counseled that trade follows the flag and advised that the United States was in need of more commercial outlets. Even after the Spanish had capitulated, and while Congress was debating the disposition of the captured Philippines, respected congressional spokesmen, like Carl Shurz, felt obliged to warn again and again that "the greed of the speculators . . . will push us from one point to another, and we shall have [more] conflicts, . . . [requiring] more and more soldiers, ships and guns."[4] Despite such advice, the United States did annex the islands; and, predictably, during the postwar critiques, the causal relationship between the mercenary "greed of speculators" and "more and more soldiers" was vociferously rehearsed by writers far more outspoken than the rational Shurz.

The historical record, now many times reviewed, shows the charge to be a half-truth, however. Many, probably most, of the conservatively-inclined business and military men were reluctant to involve the United States in an unnecessary war fought for vague idealistic purposes on behalf of Spanish-speaking, Catholic Cubans. Not unusual had been the military writers' prewar complaints that the political jingoists were overheating the populace while suppressing necessary military improvements. On the other hand, once the war had run its short course and the tempting Philippine prize had fallen into the national lap, the business men and military advisors did generally endorse annexation. They saw little reason not to accept whatever national advantages had come out of the conflict.

The reverse seems close to true in the case of the populist-progressives. As political idealists, they were eager "to free the oppressed Cubans from the Spanish yoke"—and by force, if necessary. But they were far less anxious to extend United States commercial influences into the Pacific. That was an entirely different matter. It worked not to the advantage of populist causes and progressive goals, but to the apparent gain of their capitalistic and more conservative opponents. Richard Hofstadter spelled out this "curiously ambiguous" aspect of populism. "On the surface," he explained, "there was a strong note of antimilitarism and anti-imperialism. . . . . [The populists] looked upon the military as a threat to democracy, upon imperialist acquisitions as gains only to financeers. . . . But what they chiefly objected to was institutional militarism rather than war itself. . . . Under a patina of pacifist rhetoric they were profoundly nationalistic and bellicose."[5]

The resulting philosophical cross-currents were plainly evident. The opportunistic Samuel Gompers, shortly after branding all armies "tools of tyranny," urged labor's support for the invasion of Cuba; but William Dean Howells, who so admired the officer's sense of service, became an active supporter of the Anti-Imperialist League. (So too, to Teddy Roosevelt's disgust, did the Army's Chief of Staff, General Miles.) Ignoring such revealing contradictions, the postwar progressive historians and political theorists by and large found it to their advantage to picture the Spanish-American War as the inevitable product of a sinister business-military collusion.[6]

The military-industrial conspiracy idea surfaced again a few years later with the liberals' reactions to World War I, both before and after America's involvement. The first winds of the European conflict brought the by now familiar picture of the officer corps as saber-rattling allies of business profiteers back in vogue. Again, there were sufficient examples to feed the fire. Leonard Wood, the politically ambitious medical officer who became Chief of Staff (and caused stricter professionals considerable heartburn) became the nation's most outspoken preparedness advocate. Although with only limited success, Wood and his followers preached the gospel of readiness throughout the land. Still damning in anti-military eyes were the open friendships between such high-ranking army officers as Wood and blatant advocates of large-scale armament, like explosives manufacturer Hudson Maxim.

Again ignored by many critics were the more moderate

military views. Walter Millis, retracing the *Road to War*, discovered (to his own surprise) that reporters found military men on the whole more sober and realistic than the impassioned "civilians now rushing into print." Even General Wood was somewhat misread. Frederick Palmer was amazed to find the General and his staff, in 1916, reworking U.S. coastal defenses rather than thinking about overseas commitments. As Palmer stated, "Even the strongest advocate of a large army never breathed a word that a single soldier should ever be sent to Europe."[7]

The initial wave of military criticism was quickly reversed when America decided to enter the conflict. Because the business-military complex was suddenly and sorely needed to win the idealists' "war to end all wars," previous differences were suspended. Once the fighting was over, however, postwar disarmament advocates picked up where pre-war anti-preparedness spokesmen had left off. Capitalizing on the nation's realization that it had, to some degree, been seduced into a European power struggle, the disarmament school soon revived the business-military warmonger image. Their 1920 version was, nevertheless, by necessity somewhat retouched. The officer of the '20s was no longer a mere tool of the financiers as in the 1880 to 1914 version. He was now promoted to co-equal in the alleged collusion. "The business mind," as one critic explained it, "has taken [the military mind] into double harness."[8]

This "promotion" from gunman to co-conspirator was a byproduct of a two-step adjustment in America's social theory. Back in the 1870s and 1880s, early disciples of Spencerian Darwinism had pictured the business leader as the cultural hero of a dawning industrial age and welcomed him as a replacement for "the outmoded military chieftain." To the social Darwinists, in fact, the cooperative force of international commercialism was the world's best hope for lasting peace. By 1900, that rosy estimate was changing as welfare-minded social scientists identified the business titan as the chief represser of the working man.

By the 1920s the switch was complete. The capitalist had

become the intellectuals' anti-hero, and commercialism and militarism were simply twin diseases. Typically, when economic theorist Stuart Chase (leaning heavily on John Ruskin's and Thorstein Veblen's earlier postulates) set out to expose the worst "wastes of consumption," he classified *all* military expenditures as "illth" (Ruskin's famous term), along with the costs of crime, drug traffic, super-luxuries, and prostitution. To Chase, military service accomplished only one end; it kept a million American workers from "productive occupations."[9]

In the depression '30s that style of criticism of the army waned somewhat, quantitatively speaking, but the basic charge of military-industrial repression continued to be pressed by some writers with almost feverish contempt. Young Lewis Mumford, in his brilliantly provocative, sweeping interpretations of the entire history of mankind, embellished Chase's approach with a combination of sociological and psychological premises. Mumford agreed with Chase that "an army is a body of pure consumers" producing "illth . . . instead of wealth—misery, mutilation, physical destruction, terror, starvation and death. . . ." Then, shifting roles to Freudian analyst, he condescendingly illuminated the military psychosis. "When a child is intolerably balked by another person. . . , he wishes the other person were dead. The soldier, a slave to the child's ignorance and the child's wish, differs from him only by his ability to effect . . . [murderous] action." Indeed, Mumford decided, it is a good thing that "the army has usually been a refuge of third-rate minds, . . . [otherwise] civilization might easily have been annihilated long ago." But his chief lament remained: "the alliance of mechanization and militarization" has "encouraged the rough-and-ready tactics of the militarist in industry."[10]

In such fashion, the picture of the shallow-minded, overzealous military officer working in double harness with the acquisitive, self-seeking business magnate became a deeply rooted stereotype in intellectual—particularly academic

—circles well before World War II. We shall not detail here the further popularization of that image, which has burgeoned during the cold war. In an unfortunate age where the bulk of our national budget has gone into defense technology for nearly a generation—and frequently not well spent—wide criticism of the military-industrial complex comes as no surprise. In the '50s, C. Wright Mills' theory of *The Power Elite* became the new standard text.[11] It was, in fact, only the logical extension, with broader basis, of the fears expressed by a whole school of military critics since 1890. Today, Lewis Mumford continues to damn such ventures as the first moon landing as "a symbolic act of war" which, he says, was deliberately planned "to support on a more exorbitant scale than ever the military-industrial-scientific establishment. . . ."[12] (Scientists, it seems, are the newest addition to the conspiracy.)

The point of emphasis here is that we tend to believe, erroneously, that the present times created the current conception of the military-industrial conspirator. In fact, that image came ready-made to our times.

Fascist Sadists

Today's military-industrial conspiracy idea is essentially an extension of the Jacksonian-populist-progressive strand of criticism which has, in one form or another, always been suspicious of "power elites," whether aristocratic, plutocratic, or bureaucratic. Through the years, this line of argument has consistently aimed its censure at class divisions and economic matters. (A recent example has been the complaint against U.S. military commitments in southeast Asia, based not so much on moral grounds as on the premise that those commitments drew needed money from social reform programs.)

A parallel critique, since the early Quakers and especially since 1815, has concerned itself less with the military establishment's influence on economic and social reform and more with its deleterious impact on America's humanitarian spirit. The roots of that concern lie not so much in political-economic liberalism as in pacifist idealism. Seen through pacifists' fears, the officer figure has been less a member of a power elite lavishly wasting the nation's money in simple-minded zeal for military preparedness, and more a fascist megalomaniac anxious to exercise the authoritarian-ism permitted by his rank and always eager to engage in blood-letting games of war. He is dangerous not because he is shallow and inanely bureaucratic, but because he is shrewd, ruthless and coldly efficient.

A rather commonplace conception in the first half of the nineteenth century, the officer-tyrant image lost a good deal of its currency after the Civil War, in spite of occasional charges of military despotism from Indian welfare agencies and labor strikers. The Civil War experience itself did much to dispel the notion that America's professional officers were, as a group, heartless and tyrannical men. On the whole, the nation's conclusions, clearly recorded in twenty years of postbellum reflections, were quite the reverse. At the same time, pacifist convictions about the immorality of all warfare and warriors were, in large measure, discredited when many compromised their own position. Suspending their beliefs for "a greater cause," they urged invasion of the South and after Appomatox demanded, in less than humanitarian fashion, harsh reconstruction measures. Charles Sumner, for one, adjusted his prewar pacifist pre-cepts to such a degree that, following the war, he felt obliged to rewrite his earlier works. And as chairman of the Senate's Foreign Affairs Committee in the late '60s, Sumner, who in the '40s and '50s had so bitterly berated military pride and honor as a major cause of war, belliger-ently demanded Great Britain give Canada to the United States in compensation for having supported the South. Hardly a pacifist-like position.

The pacifist-moralists were taken to task in the postbel-lum period for refusing to defend their nation while being quick to claim advantages gained by the blood of others. E. L. Godkin for one ridiculed their lack of realistic insight, and neither the press nor the clergy were particularly sympathetic organs for their views. By 1887, one pacifist leader estimated that there were "no more than 400 active members in all the peace organizations in the country."

Even when given the new rallying cause of anti-imperialism, pacifist unity at the turn of the century was split by factions. The humanitarian-pacifist reformers of the populist-progressive era were caught in a dilemma. As a rule, they were in sympathy with labor's grievances and therefore philosophically opposed to capitalist doctrine. Yet some of the leading pacifists of the day were business tycoons, and the pacifist organizations could not—or would not—refuse the enormous financial support proferred by moguls like Andrew Carnegie and Edward Guinn. Paradoxically, Carnegie was attacked in Congress for twenty years as a typical warmongering industrialist pushing the nation into armed conflict with Spain, and later Germany, while, at the same time, the Endowment for International Peace was operating largely on money he had donated. (Much of that money, ironically, had been earned through the manufacture of armor plate for naval vessels. Nor did the Endowment complain when its ten million dollar stockholding was substantially increased by the excellent performance of U. S. Steel stock during World War I.)[13]

All in all, pacifist-oriented military criticism between 1850 and World War I was neither unified nor notably effective. It was the neo-pacifist spokesmen of the 1920s who regained national prominence and brought back to full life an image of the army officer every bit as dictatorial and arrogant as the prototype developed by their spiritual forebears a full century before. There was one essential difference. Now the regular officer was a Prussianistic professional, trained to his tyrannical ways, rather than an ersatz aristocrat, despotic by class instinct. "The West Point, or Prussian idea of army caste," post-World War I critics liked to explain, "is [designed] . . . to hold the men down while in idleness, [using] repressive, harsh discipline."

Like their forebears, the new pacifist idealists rarely qualified their condemnations. The military man, wherever found, was *all* bad, they bluntly asserted, as in a 1925 article in the *New Republic*. "All militarists in every country proclaim the same doctrines. . . . All of them, everywhere, pretend to enormous solicitude over the preservation of existing institutions. . . . All of them, everywhere, are profoundly convinced that every foreign state is a potential enemy." And so on. Once a man donned a uniform, all humanitarian factors in his makeup, the "humanitarian" critics felt sure, were subverted. The theme that the military profession necessarily brutalizes everyone it touches was given unqualified expression, even by some usually objective and scholarly writers. In 1933, with typical authoritative tone and no cited factual support, historian Mary Beard wrote along with the others, "The soldier demobilized . . . is a different man. . . . His finger finds the trigger quickly. He was trained to kill. . . . In short, he is lawless as well as slothful."[14]

But it was the writers of imaginative literature who most effectively propagated the modern image of the brutal militarist. Dos Passos' *Three Soldiers*, written in 1920, became a model for half a century of anti-war novels whose apparent mission has been (as a character in Herman Wouk's *The Caine Mutiny* would later explain it) "to expose war in all its grim futility and waste, and [show] up the military men for the stupid, Fascist-minded sadists they are. . . . I like novels where the author proves how terrible the military guys are, and how superior sensitive civilians are."

John Andrews, the protagonist in *Three Soldiers*, became the prototype of the "superior, sensitive civilian," the college (Harvard) educated, artistically-inclined intellectual who is crushed "under the [Establishment] wheel." "Life is very ugly in America," Andrews decides, but Europe has "a sappy richness." Being vaguely socialistic, he dreams of starting a mutiny and is "proud" to have deserted from the army and "military slavery." He loves people of the good, simple variety and hates all the officers, sergeants, and MPs who represent authority. Dos Passos' officers are not characters in the true sense, but symbols seen only in very brief but revealing poses. ("A staff car shot by, splashing [the soldiers] with mud, leaving them a glimpse of officers leaning back into the deep cushions.") They seem always to be haughty, sallow-faced, shouting and cruel. A captain orders a dying soldier to stand at attention; an MP lieutenant has Andrews severely beaten for not saluting him; a major in the medical service threatens "to chuck" badly wounded soldiers from his hospital for singing when they learn of the armistice. In 500 pages, only one officer speaks civilly to Andrews and then only when he learns that Andrews has already graduated from Harvard where the lieutenant is still an undergraduate. (The top grade sergeants are equally evil and it is, predictably, the very worst of the lot who wins an officer's commission.) Private Andrews sums up the pacifist-socialist viewpoint when his French lover asks him, "You are so well educated. . . . How is it you are only an ordinary soldier?" "Good God," Andrews replies, "I wouldn't be an officer."[15]

The fascist-sadist portrait prevailed to the very eve of World War II. Often, of course, it was founded on deeply intelligent concern. In 1938, Pearl Buck, in eloquent passion, took to task blind militarists of *all* nations while she berated a Japanese pilot who had boasted of bombing Chinese cities. "I recognize it. It is the mind of the militarist. . . . It destroys ideals of mercy and understanding and cooperation. . . ." And, with uncommon insight, she added, "This animal spirit of ruthless, selfish conquests [is] . . . so dangerous [because] it is possible in any of us."[16]

At other times, however, the attacks were simply the most vicious sort of intellectualized slander. In 1939, Mauritz Hallgren (in Harold Stearn's widely hailed *America Now*) raved that America's "semi-Fascist" military leaders were

planning "a dictatorship far more sweeping" than Mus-
solini's or Hitler's. Nothing, he stated flatly, "could be more
certain. . . . [Our] professional warriors envisage defense
of the nation in terms of . . . Napoleonic slaughter and suppression of democracy."[17] This at a time when the patheti-
cally weak U.S. Army was training with wooden guns.

World War II confirmed, if anything, that the nation's
professional soldiers represented a remarkable range of
personalities and philosophical outlooks, but few budding
dictators. By then the fascist stereotype had, however,
become another standardized image and very soon he too
would be back at center stage. In the war's aftermath,
America's novelists, with a few notable exceptions, missed
another golden opportunity to probe with perception the
profoundly different effects that modern warfare has on its
participants—including the diverse band of American military careerists. Seldom did the novels about World War II
present a cast of believable individuals, men possessed of
their own particular psychologies and inner dimensions.
Instead they were largely formula pieces whose two-
dimensional characters could, as literary critic Henry Siedel
Canby observed, be easily interchanged.[18]

William Saroyon's *Wesley Jackson* is only a later-day John
Andrews, and the novelist sternly warns us, "You don't put
a man like that in the army. . . . You put a bullet in his
head and be done with it." One of Norman Mailer's civilian
draftees in *The Naked and the Dead* swears—along with his
creator—that after the war "I'm gonna walk up to every
sonfabitch officer in uniform and say 'Sucker' . . . and I'm
gonna expose the goddamn army." Mailer's characterization
of the West Point general is, as expected, an overly ambitious, power-mad tyrant who forces his aide-de-camp (again
the sensitive Harvard man) to pick up the general's cigarette
butts and generally grovel. "The Army functions best," the
general growls, "when you are frightened of the man above
you and contemptuous of your subordinates." Likewise
General Marvin in John Hersey's *A Bell for Adano* is

described by one observer as worse than the fascists the
Allies drove out of Italy. He is given to repeated childish
tantrums during which he callously destroys beautiful
antique furniture and upsets the town's economy by order-
ing all its bothersome mule carts off the road.[19]

In 1951, George MacMillian, reviewing "A Decade of War
Novels" for *The New York Times*, concluded that "the figures
are all alike. . . . The officer caste in World War II fietion
fulfills a symbolic function; in these anti-fascist novels the
[American] officer is the Fascist. . . ."[20] Indeed, since World
War I, the officer corps, in fact as well as fiction, has fulfilled for many a similar symbolic function; in anti-fascist
expression the army officer has been America's fascist in
residence. To that point of view, the My Lai massacre was
not an aberration but proof positive of the true character
of all military professionals.

Modernized National Defenders

While the voices of military criticism gained depth and
strength in the twentieth century, the range and vigor of
the defense declined appreciably. The pessimistic estimate
made in 1896 by one depressed soldier-commentator that
"The Army has no active or powerful friends"[21] was then
still very much an overstatement. But, if exaggerated, that
appraisal was in a sense prophetic. During the next century,
in spite of the boosts in esteem brought by two generally
"popular" world war crusades, the officer corps gradually
lost the "active and powerful" support of many of the
nation's most influential opinion-makers.

As the writings of the 1880s and 1890s had portended,
this crucial shift came about not so much as the result of
any real changes in the philosophic position of the military
leaders, but more from within the critics themselves. The
officer corps, so admired from John Marshall to William
Dean Howells, began to lose the championship of the
nation's leading intellectual spokesmen when those spokes-

men modernized—liberalized—their own social, moral, and
political outlooks, and did so much more rapidly than either
the army or the general public. In the new century, the
social commentators' repugnance for America's military
establishment would grow apace with the mounting destruc-
tiveness of warfare and the threat it posed to mankind, and
their expressed respect for career soldiers as a class waned
proportionally.

In the face of that drift of intellectual alienation, public
support for the military leader became steadily more anti-
intellectual, moralizing, and defensive in nature. The picture of the military leader projected by his defenders soon
began to reflect such changes in tone and rationale. The
ideal officer of the twentieth century became a kind of combination military manager, father image, and Eagle Scout.
He represented trustworthiness, obedience, cooperation,
efficiency, manliness, and reverence. The urbane, sophis-
ticated, and colorful figure who had dominated pro-military
characterizations before the Civil War (and who later had
stood side-by-side with the earthy yet gracious Grant-like
type in the postbellum period) was going out of vogue.
Those highly individualistic nineteenth-century types were
being eclipsed by a straightforward, straightshooting,
straightthinking, and straightliving middle American soldier. The likes of Douglas MacArthur, Billy Mitchell, and
George Patton were the exceptions that confirmed the rule.

Contrasting the styles of military tribute during the
Spanish-American War and World War I, a span of only
two decades, indicates the general trend. During the former
there were still—in the "better" magazines, for example—
strong overtones of the fading genteel tradition and
nineteenth-century military romance. *Harper's Weekly* came
out with a resplendent *Pictorial History of the War with Spain*.
The cover, like something from the French Revolution, has
a toga clad Miss Liberty clutching the flag in one hand and
brandishing a sword in the other. Within, detailed accounts
of "glorious victories" are interspersed with full-page color

portraits of horse-mounted generals and gold braided admirals.[22] While much of that same flavor was, of course, still evident during World War I, the typical tributes of 1917 to 1919 tended to be more "realistic" and democratic in tone. They often focused, for example, on the day-by-day endeavors of small units, companies and platoons, rather than the "grander" exploits of the higher command.

While scores of writers turned out lavish tributes to Pershing, MacArthur and other generals of World War I, the perfect hero of the war "to save the world for democracy" was unquestionably Sergeant York—a backwoods, semi-pacifist amateur who beat the professionals at their own game. In doing so, he became a model citizen-soldier for the nation's "unmilitary" liberal school of writers. York epitomized President Wilson's point-of-view. "America," the president had proclaimed at the war's start, "is the prize amateur nation of the world. Germany is the prize professional nation of the world. Now when it comes to doing new things, and doing them well, I will back the amateur against the professional every time." As the regular army well knew, that kind of amateurism was as old as the anti-intellectual Jacksonians—but now it was being espoused by the new breed of intellectual progressives.

The emphasis in World War I was more upon the whole team. For those who chose to read them—and the sales records indicate that millions did—a flood of varied wartime and postwar publications created a grand mosaic of the great American military machine which "tipped the scales of battle" in favor of the forces of good. There was high praise for all, including the previously ignored basic soldiers, America's enduring yeomen in khaki. As Sergeant York was proudly quoted, "A right-smart lot of them boozed, gambled, cursed and went AWOL. But once they got into it . . . they always kept on a-going. Most . . . died like men, with their faces to the enemy." There were multi-volume tributes to *The Armies of Industry* which "ensured victory by ensuring the timely arrival of the overwhelming force of . . . America's munitions." There were the self-congratulatory publications of major army units like the Rainbow, the First, and the Yankee Divisions and such special outfits as the Lafayette Flying Corps.[23] There were mutually complimentary memoirs of corporals and generals, regulars and non-regulars. And there were histories of the United States during the Great War in which such previously demeaning critics as John Bach McMaster would celebrate September 12, 1918, as a date "memorable in our history, for then it was our army struck [at St. Mihiel] its first great blow." America's military prowess, McMaster joyfully observed, was thereby demonstrated unmistakably to the enemy and to our doubting Allies alike by "this splendid victory."[24]

In short, the pro-military message of the First World War was that an unbeatable—if somewhat mundane—American battle-team, welded from a determined populace, from Yankee industrial genius, and from expert professional military leadership had responded valiantly and effectively to President Wilson's lofty call for "force, force to the utmost, force without stint or limit, the righteous and triumphant force which shall make right the law of the world."[25]

For all that wartime encomia, congratulations for the professional soldiers got lost soon after the armistice in heated debate over proposals for compulsory peacetime military training and the attendant threats of militarization of the country's youth. In the magazines of the '20s, there were, it is true, many articles which asserted the positive benefits of ROTC and similar military-educational programs. Under such typical titles as "Making a Man of Him" and "Army of Men Without Hate," they strove to demonstrate (sometimes by citing the statistical results of physical and mental examinations taken before and after military training) that America's young men were *not* being brutalized in the army; that they were instead physically and morally strengthened by their experience, and their ideals of liberty and democracy reinforced. In the process, the pro-army writers of the post World War I years standardized the familiar poster-like portrait of the modern American military man: sturdy, clear-eyed, determined, and disciplined. Rather than refinement or brilliance, his hallmarks had become steadfastness and durability. These rebuttals to the anti-militarists' attacks of the interwar years appeared most often in educational and professional journals, like *Educational Review* and *School and Society*. But wherever they appeared, they were just that: they were rebuttals. They were defensive replies to free-swinging indictments (e.g., "Our Brutal Soldiery" and "Are Militarists Feeble-Minded?") offered up regularly in broadly circulated magazines like *Nation, New Republic, Literary Digest, Outlook* and *American Mercury*.[26]

With the depression, the situation, if not the basic pro-military model, changed somewhat. The army was largely ignored by the public, while the attention of reform-oriented crusaders turned to more pressing economic and domestic problems. In fact, the image of the physically fit and dutiful serviceman was even given a minor boost by the political progressives' tributes to their own uniformed, para-military Civilian Conservation Corps. Along with their endorsements of the CCC for providing food and shelter to those in need, and useful manpower for engineering and forestry projects, advocates for the New Deal program liked to point out its military-like benefits: the sense of camaraderie, the teamwork, and the self-discipline developed in the cleansing atmosphere of a rugged, wholesome, outdoor life. In general, however, the nation forgot the regular army in the 1930s, or at least preferred to keep the professional soldier once again at arms length from the civil scene.

World War II, of course, brought a dramatic reversal. Its impact on the reputation of the military leader was enorm-

ous and overwhelmingly in his favor. The influences of
those years are only now fading; yet the results might well
prove to be less significant in the long-term, historical
development of the military image than events of more
recent times. That question, however, cannot now be
answered. Whatever its eventual effect in this regard, World
War II—because it was a declared and an "unlimited" war,
a unified nation-wide endeavor in behalf of a clearly justifiable cause—brought the soldier general respect. The military establishment of the United States had not enjoyed that
position since the last year of the Civil War, almost a century before. The World War II years saw (along with occasional criticism of controversial figures like "Yoo-Hoo"
Lear, impetuous George Patton and imperious Douglas
MacArthur) exceptional credits for the conventional types
in the armed forces. The roster of widely admired
"standard-American" soldiers, professional and otherwise,
ran from generals like Marshall, Eisenhower, Bradley,
Ridgeway, and Gavin to Lieutenant Colin Kelly and Private
Audie Murphy and thousands of men of less lasting notoriety whose devotion to national service was poignantly if
unceremoniously recorded by equally devoted writers like
Ernie Pyle.

When the war was over, Harry Hopkins, among other
prominent figures, was wondering aloud about the "one
miracle" he could not explain: "how did . . . an unwarlike
and unprepared country . . . [suddenly] produce so large
and so brilliant a group of military leaders. . . ? What had
they been doing during all those twenty years when . . .
our army had been kicked around like 'a mangy, old dog'?"
That sort of compliment was common for a while. A grateful Henry Stimpson sketched modern democracy's ideal
military leader when he told the regular officer corps, "You
have shown yourselves brave but not brutal, self-confident,
but not arrogant, and [have] . . . wielded the mighty power
of this country to another victory without . . . usurpation
of any power."

The critics were soon back on the attack, and before long direct support of the professional soldier began to thin. Even in the self-congratulatory atmosphere of the war's aftermath, only a few widely respected civilian spokesmen felt constrained to take up their pens, as did John J. McCloy, "In Defense of the Military Mind." McCloy wrote, "I have found the general level of brain-power and character of all ranks at least as high among the professional officers as among the representative cross section of lawyers, businessmen, and educators with whom I have been thrown into contact in civilian life."[27] Except for ceremonial occasions, such judgments were discreetly avoided by most of America's political and social pundits, and then very seldom put in writing.

Open support of the military operators by those with no vested interest became cautiously selective. There were, to be sure, certain elements within the service ranks that could be comfortably admired by even the more liberal commentators. The Berlin commander and his air lift crews (preserving freedom in the face of threatened aggression), the U.N. forces in Korea and the border patrols in Germany (repelling or preventing incursions on friendly territories), the United States military advisors in communist-threatened Greece (protecting the birthplace of democracy) and, later, the spacemen (representing the old Jeffersonian ideal of the peacetime soldier-scientist-explorer)—all these *special* types were subjects for congratulation. But not the military in general. If reassigned to the bureaucratic Pentagon, or if spending the nation's money in costly military research and development tests, or if leading troops in a limited and unwanted war far from the United States, the "brass" was not to be championed by America's formulators of opinion.

In turn, the officer corps began to resume its old defensive pose of maligned and martyred servants dutifully doing the bidding of their presidential commander-in-chief in the face of denigration, whether enforcing school integration or engaging in distasteful guerrilla warfare. Sadly, the dialogue between the professional soldier and a large portion of his critics once again became strained, often beyond constructive exchange.

Chapter Seventeen

Some Conclusions And An Afterword

What [one] finds at the very beginning of his research is not a world of physical objects but a symbolic universe—a world of symbols.

—Ernst Cassirer

All of these you are, and each is partly you,
And none is wholly false, and none is wholly true.

—Stephen Vincent Benet

When we take the time to go back and look, it turns out that America's view of the army officer is not, and never has been, represented by a single image at all, but rather by several diverse, if related, figures. In overview what should strike us most is the very complexity of the total picture. On that score the figure of the military leader is probably unmatched in our cultural history. From our nation's birth, certainly since the 1820s, he has consistently evoked a greater range (if not volume) of responses than any other familiar "type" that comes to mind: the Puritan, the Catholic, the southerner, the Mason, the frontiersman, the Indian, the immigrant, the Negro, the farmer, the small-town Babbitt, the big city laborer, or who-have-you. Each of these types has experienced periods when his very mention created controversy, but such has always been the case with the army officer in this nation. Even when Americans have wanted to ignore their armed forces (as they often have), their military representatives have been continually before them in one pose or another: in history texts, in pacifist literature, on the stage, in congressional appropriation debates, in novels, in the White House, or at the picket line.

Pick any point in the nation's past and one can find a full spectrum of military images. At one end there will be an almost impossible creature who somehow combines all the unbecoming, though incongruous, features contributed by every school of criticism from every period up to that date. At the other is a glamorized yet sanitized Galahad who gradually takes on more realistic traits but never quite reaches reality. And if our picture of the soldier has always been contradictory and usually unreal, it has been equally unstable. Even during the nineteenth century, with the country's geographically assured security and relatively stable social order, and the army by and large out of public sight, change, as we have seen in this study, was basic to the military image.

If there is a single historical lesson to be drawn, it should be that any so-called "traditionally American" view of the military profession is a home-made myth. For writers and speakers to declare the "Americanism" of any particular attitude toward the soldier is clearly and simply unfounded in fact. Furthermore, for commentators and scholars to presume, as they too often do, that they can divine the complex national view of the military man by sampling the voices of one or two elements alone (the opinion of the journalists or the academicians, for example) is an additional self-deception. The soldier's image has been, and quite obviously continues to be, as many-faceted as the American mind itself.

To begin with, every age looks at its military men through the lens of its contemporary life style, military tensions, and value system. Yet, every age has its several factions as well, all of which, it seems, have a decided inclination to shape their own stereotype of the military careerist according to *their*, not his, particular social and ethical allegiances. So there is constantly at work a set of generalizing period influences and a spectrum of particularizing genre attitudes that have perpetuated themselves from generation to generation. Expressed as a kind of historical formula, it may be said that the state of the art of warfare, along with the military-social situation of the times, very much determine fundamental *styles* of soldiership (the gentleman-soldier, the western constabulary type, the Prussian-like professional, the Pentagon bureaucrat, et al.), but *attitudes* toward the careerists are more strongly affected by trends in *nonmilitary* matters. Thus, the patrician-officer figure of the eighteenth century, because he was clearly a man for his times, enjoyed wide respect in the Federalist era but came under severe political attack in the subsequent Jacksonian years, even though the army *per se* was of little interest to Jacksonian America. Thus, the postbellum professional type, a manipulator of enormous armies and supplies, was admired in the afterglow of the Civil and Franco-Prussian Wars along with other titans of the early Industrial Age but faced growing censure as reactions to the Gilded Age set in, even though the military itself was at the time out of tune with big business. Similarly, attitudes toward the military today are probably, at bottom, less the immediate results of the Vietnam War than of certain adjustments in our national life style and hero-figures that have been evolving for many years.

Which brings us to a related matter. It has not been our major military involvements that have marked the turning points in our attitudes toward the military. When seeking historical benchmarks, we would do much better to study the broad changes in the social-philosophical atmosphere. This is especially true of developments within the liberal persuasion. This is not to say that the progressive view has been the only determining factor in the civil-military equations, but it has been the chief variable and therefore the most visibly consequential element. As we have seen in the preceding chapters, two of those adjustments were especially influential. A quick review should demonstrate how important they are to our current understanding of civil-military relationships. The first came when Federalist and Enlightenment thought began to recede and blend into Jacksonian ideas, and faith in the *aristoi* gave way to faith in the common man. In the process the rather singular conception of officership common in the eighteenth century was refracted into a number of sub-types, and the liberal critique of the military became essentially egalitarian, anti-intellectual, nationalistic, and amateuristic. By that light, the army was a decadent Old World institution. Regular officers were accordingly accused of being overly intellectual and lacking in common sense, unmanly and excessively refined, undisciplined and unreliable, unpatriotic, and profligate. The consistent focus of the Jacksonian outlook (which is still with us to some extent today*) was not on *what* it opposed, but on *whom*: polished military aristocrats.

The second major adjustment in the liberal military critique began to take form in the last quarter of the nineteenth century. The change came when Jacksonian thinking was redirected, first by Spencerian theories of social evolution and later by a developing intellectual insurgency that tended to be collectivist, cosmopolitan, and humanistic in outlook. The resulting estimate was no less severe than the Jacksonian critique had been, but its conception of the officer corps was reversed: military leaders were not overly intellectual and refined, but dull and compensatingly systematic; not soft and frail but excessively tough and insensitive; not undisciplined and unreliable but overly disciplined and blindly responsive; not unpatriotic but chauvinistic; not profligate but puritanical. No longer was it a question of to *whom* our liberal spokesmen were opposed, but to *what*: militarism and the military mind. Coming late in the nineteenth century, that rationale established the foundation for what has become the most influential force in military criticism today.

In short, the liberal-oriented critique has been consistent in attitude (between suspicious and hostile) but often additive and, perforce, self-contradictory in argument. On the other hand, the defense of the military has been much more constant in its rationale but far less responsive to intellectual and philosophic trends. Even so, the defense of the soldier

---

*Congressmen like Edward Hebert and the late Mendel Rivers, as supporters of the armed forces, have worried aloud that the service academies are becoming too intellectual and hence soft. Elements of the national press rejoiced recently when the army demonstrated that it could still appoint a general who did *not* have a college education. And it was not so many years ago that *Time* magazine was concerned that a two-fisted, uncomplicated fighter like Curtis LeMay would be denied appointment as Air Force Chief of Staff by the "super smooth" West Pointers.

in America has not, generally speaking, denied the nation's fundamental liberal theories. It has instead struggled to blend New World ways and traditional "military virtues," seeing them as not only compatible but mutually essential to a viable republic. In the antebellum days, for instance, the defenders of the officer corps unashamedly placed their faith in the better educated classes who, in Cooper's words, were "the natural repository of manners, taste, tone, and, to certain extent, of the principles of the country." Eventually that model evolved into a sort of Emersonian gentleman, a man of inner strength who was an officer-and-gentleman not because of wealth, leisure, and cultivation, but in spite of privations, low pay, and arduous duties. Regardless, it was his strength of character and the example he set that counted.

Along with this historic belief in the beneficial example of military character there has existed an appreciation of the soldier *qua* soldier and his utility to his country. The Jeffersonian idealist has long preferred the military man of science, courageously and systematically pushing back new frontiers—men such as Zebulon Pike in the old West, George Goethals in Panama, or Frank Borman and Edwin Aldrin in space. "Political realists" from Secretary of War Calhoun to present-day pragmatists have been more interested in military competence, in soldiers who in Garfield's words can, "keep alive the knowledge and practice of military science. . . , preserve inviolate our national boundaries. . . , keep the peace and protect the public property . . . [and] aid the civil States in case of invasion or insurrection. . . ." All that has called for proficient, undistracted, full-time professionals, and that school of observers has tended to see the officer corps in just that way.

★

Such diverging opinions of the military have tended to balance each other out during much of our history, but the general shift in critical weight that began near the end of the nineteenth century has now become crucial. Where the officer earlier found his stoutest allies among the opinion-makers of the intellectual community, the literary field, and the fourth estate, that situation has obviously been fully reversed. During the past few decades the majority of America's most influential scholars and commentators have become generally reformist in outlook and, under the pressure of their faith, have been increasingly quick to criticize and ever more reluctant to speak publicly in defense of the profession of arms.

Today, films, novels, music, and the visual arts are all heavily involved in direct criticism. Military buffoons and sadists are commonplace even on the sports page. A recent *New York Times* sports editorial stated that, "if [baseball umpire Emmett] Ashford were a lummox, rigid and authoritarian, he would thumb men out of the games the way generals would shoot off nuclear weapons for every civil war. But Ashford is a gracious man . . . with three years of college. . . ." And so it goes. The high school student is presented with the doubly involuted sardonic humor of *Catch-22* (which he does not fully understand) and the gleeful sickness of *M*A*S*H**, instead of the tersely realistic *Red Badge of Courage* or the profoundly anti-war *All Quiet on the Western Front* that his parents read. We laugh at the contemporary military caricatures of screen and novel, but they undoubtedly leave lasting marks. One serious high school senior (an honors student competing for advanced college validation) recently wrote on a national exam, "As the plot [of *Catch 22*] progresses the insanity becomes uglier. Where once there were only dumb generals as victims, now beautiful whores are thrown out of windows."

★

The ultimate impact of contemporary attitudes toward the military is highly speculative. Given the factual, as well as fictional, military disgraces, tragedies, and bunglings of recent times, the results are likely to be devastating for more than a generation. Whatever the outcome, it can be stated categorically that our recent experience was, for us, historically unique. Never before had this nation, while faced with an extended and burdensome war, encountered such vigorous, sustained challenges to its value system. In earlier conflicts, war-time was a period for reaffirmation of "basic Americanism" and for pride in the soldier's role in its defense. The appropriate role of the professional soldier in America is surely more confused now than at any previous time. Perhaps confusion is inevitable in a nation which, however reluctantly, has felt obliged, for survival's sake, to continue an enormously taxing arms race that in itself threatens the human race; a nation, which, however altruistically, has attempted to serve as the world's policeman, defending from aggression societies and value systems far different from our own; and a nation which, however sincerely, has clung to its self-appointed role as the international champion of peace in a time of protracted U.S. military involvements. It is small wonder that the soldier struggles with such contradictions, for he himself is part of those contradictions.

Our armed forces today desperately need a sense of *national* direction, and that direction must come from the people as a whole. It cannot come from within the military alone, where philosophical problems are agonized over but get lost in the practical day-by-day process of implementing political-military policy and decisions. Nor should the guidance come solely from official Washington whose short-term goals shift too conveniently with the political winds and with the personalities of appointed and elected officials. Through its government, the United States has told its soldiers for two centuries what it wants them *to do*, but it has seldom, if ever, told them what it wants them *to be*. As a result, the officer corps has largely depended on its own traditional assumptions. And if the old assumptions are wrong, they ask, what takes their place? It would seem that any philosophical redirection of the military must come from open, reasoned, and multi-sided public dialogue.

As a start toward re-establishing this dialogue, we would all do well to learn a good deal more about our past civil-military relationships and about the impressions and distortions they have left. We also need to chart our present position by sociological as well as historical and political triangulation, sighting on as many points as possible. In short, we need to examine the *entire* record.

Even more importantly, we need to examine that record as dispassionately as possible. We have had enough one-sided treatments which relate the glorious and unappreciated efforts of selfless military servants, or which warn against the threats to the American spirit posed by an un-American army. Such polemics aggravate the problem rather than deepen our understanding of the situation. The contrast between the overall military record of the nineteenth century and the military stereotypes it fostered demonstrates this point. During that century, the historical record was quite homogeneous and relatively unexciting. The regular army did not at any time stand alone at an American Thermopylae and save the nation. On the other hand, the closest its leaders came to acting like budding despots was probably McClellan's arrogant discourtesies to Lincoln early in the Civil War—discourtesies matched by members of Lincoln's own cabinet. For the most part, the officer corps served competently and, with a few exceptions, rather quietly. Often strong-willed men, they were seldom fools. If not always brilliant and at times guilty of sizable errors, they generally got their jobs done and with relative humaneness.

By that account, their image should have been fairly tempered. Such was not the case then, nor has it become so now. When not being ignored, career soldiers have been subject to the extremes of hero worship and abuse. For the writer seeking a champion for the destined nation, a foil to the American Adam, a guardian of our borders, a slaughterer of the noble savage, a repository of decorum and honor, a terror to the laboring masses, or whatever, the officer corps has somehow conveniently filled any or all roles.

To a considerable degree, the image of the soldier has been formed by the eye of his multifarious beholders. In that sense, his reputation has been a chip tossed on the tides of America's changing outlooks. Which of his several portraits—past and present—is the most accurate or most deserved has not been the question here. But one thing is apparent. Stereotyping has done no more for our civil-military relations than it has for our racial and religious relationships. Surely, fencing off the military and labeling them "different" is not the solution to the two-fold problem of how to maintain the strength necessary to exist in the world today and how to keep that strength fully attuned with the national will. De Tocqueville, as usual, had a wiser outlook: "The remedy for the vices of the army [of a democracy]," he observed, "is not to be found in the army itself, but in the country. . . , the general spirit of the nation being infused into the spirit peculiar to the army." What de Tocqueville recognized is that, in the final analysis, armies are extensions of their own societies, and the difficulties for a free nation come when the connections break down. Therein lies the not-too-clear but always present danger.

And there is more at stake than keeping the military in step with the nation. Exaggerated and overheated civil-military differences in a very real sense weaken the country, for in the United States the military man's relationship to the people is the very coefficient of his motivation and, hence, his effectiveness. Jefferson's remark of long ago retains its validity today: "A distinction is kept up between the civil and the military, which it is for the happiness of both to obliterate."

Notes

CHAPTER ONE

1. Henry Whiting, "Army of the United States," *North American Review* 23 (October 1826): 245 ff.

2. The views of each of those mentioned here will be developed more fully in subsequent chapters.

3. James Fenimore Cooper, *Notions of the Americans*, 2 vols. (New York: Frederick Unger Publishing Co., 1963), II, pp. 185-197, 289-305; *The Lives of Distinguished Naval Officers* (Philadelphia: Carey and Hart, 1846); *The Cruise of the Somers: Illustrative of the Despotism of the Quarter Deck . . .* (New York: J. Winchester, 1844); Stanley T. Williams, "James Fenimore Cooper," *Literary History of the United States*, ed. Robert E. Spiller, *et al.* (New York: The Macmillan Co., 1965), p. 255; Alexander Cowie, *The Rise of the American Novel* (New York: The American Book Co., 1951), pp. 115-165; Edwin H. Cady, *The Gentleman in America* (Syracuse: Syracuse University Press, 1949), pp. 105 ff.

4. George Bancroft, "Commemoration of Jackson," *Literary and Historical Miscellanies* (New York: Harper and Bros., 1855), pp. 457-458; Russell B. Nye, *George Bancroft, Brahmin Rebel* (New York: Alfred A. Knopf, 1944), pp. 142-146, 149, 303-305; Orie W. Long, *Literary Pioneers, Early American Explorers of European Culture* (Cambridge, Mass.: Harvard University Press, 1935), pp. 157-158.

5. *The Journals of Ralph Waldo Emerson*, ed. E. W. Emerson and W. E. Forbes (Boston: Houghton, Mifflin Co., 1909-1914), 9, pp. 512-516; Marcus Cunliffe, "The American Military Tradition," *British Essays in American History*, ed. H. C. Allen and C. P. Hill (New York: St. Martin's Press, 1951), p. 212; and Hazen C. Carpenter, "Emerson at West Point," *The Pointer* 27 (January 12, 1951): 5, 27.

6. Merle Curti, *American Peace Crusade* (Durham, N. C.: Duke University Press, 1929); Edward M. Burns, *The American Idea of Mission* (New Brunswick, N. J.: Rutgers University Press, 1951), p. 252.

CHAPTER TWO

1. The objective of this chapter is to provide a synthesis of late eighteenth-century views which will serve as a point of departure for an examination of the military image in the nineteenth century. Consequently, this chapter depends less on primary source materials than those which follow. While samplings have been taken from a variety of works, including some not considered in conventional military studies, no exhaustive search of post-Revolutionary writings has been made. The best collection of primary materials available in a single work is Walter Millis, ed., *American Military Thought* (Indianapolis: Bobbs-Merrill, 1966). For a review of the background to and the beginnings of America's military institutions, four excellent discussions, each approached from quite different directions, are: Daniel Boorstin, "A Nation of Minute Men," *The Americans* (New York: Random House, 1958), I, pp. 345-372; Samuel P. Huntington, *The Soldier and the State* (Cambridge, Mass.: Belknap Press, 1957), I, pp. 19-30, 194-195; Walter Millis, *Arms and Men* (New York: G. P. Putnam's Sons, 1956), pp. 1-53; and Russell F. Weigley, *History of the United States Army* (New York: The Macmillan Co., 1967), pp. 1-94.

2. A letter "To the President of Congress," September 24, 1776; in *American Military Thought*, p. 9.

3. Susanna Rowson, *Charlotte Temple* (New York: Optimus Printing Co., n.d.), p. 53.

4. Millis, *Arms and Men*, pp. 17-21; Boorstin, *The Americans*, pp. 345-347; Mark M. Boatner, *The Civil War Dictionary* (New York: David McKay Co., Inc., 1959), p. 313. During 1704, only 2,000 British soldiers and sailors were killed in action (although about 3,000 died of causes related to the war). On December 13, 1862, the Union army lost over 12,000 men at Fredericksburg, 3,000 killed or missing, and 9,500 wounded.

5. Hugo Grotius, *The Law of War and Peace* (Indianapolis: Bobbs-Merrill Co., 1962); Emmerich de Vattel, *The Law of Nations* (Philadelphia: Nicklin Company, 1835); Millis, *Arms and Men*, pp.

13-21; Boorstin, *The Americans*, pp. 345-347; Alfred Vagts, *A History of Militarism* (New York: W. W. Norton, 1937), pp. 45-73.

6. Huntington, *Soldier and the State*, pp. 19-30. See also Vagts, *History of Militarism*, pp. 53-73, 81-88, 101-105.

7. Edwin H. Cady, *The Gentleman in America* (Syracuse: Syracuse University Press, 1949), pp. 16-19. For a balanced treatment of these two strands, see John C. Miller, *The Federalist Era, 1789-1801* (New York: Harper and Brothers, 1960), chapters 3, 5, and 7; or contrast the Jeffersonian bias of Vernon L. Parrington, *Main Currents of American Thought* (New York: Harcourt Brace and Co., 1927) and Nathan Schackner's sympathetic treatment of the Federalists in *The Founding Fathers* (New York: Putnam and Co., 1954).

8. T. Harry Williams, *Americans at War* (New York: Collier Books, 1962), p. 8; James Brown Scott, ed., *The Militia*, Senate Doc. 695, 64th Cong., 2d Sess. (Washington: Government Printing Office, 1917), pp. 61, 73. See also Russell F. Weigley, *Towards an American Army* (New York: Columbia University Press, 1962), pp. 2-6.

9. Washington, "To The President of Congress," in Millis, *American Military Thought*, pp. 9-10; Cady, *Gentleman in America*, p. 18. Of the many early commissions in the archives of the United States Military Academy Library, all include the "special trust and confidence" phrasing.

10. "Claims of Peace on Literary Men," *The Book of Peace* (Boston: George C. Beckwith, 1845), pp. 583-584.

11. Harvey Wish, *The American Historian* (New York: Oxford University Press, 1960), p. 39. See also Hugh H. Bellot, *American History and American Historians* (Norman, Okla.: University of Oklahoma Press, 1952), pp. 57-107.

12. See, e.g., William Gordon, *The History of the Rise, Progress, and Establishment of the Independence of the United States of America. . .* , 4 vols. (London: n.p., 1788), IV, pp. 405-406; David Ramsey, *The History of the American Revolution* (Philadelphia: n.p., 1789), I, pp. 216-217.

13. Perley I. Reed, *American Characters in Native American Plays Prior to 1870* (Columbus: Ohio State University, 1918), pp. 47-70; Arthur Hobson Quinn, *A History of the American Drama* (New York: D. Appleton-Century Co., Inc., 1936), pp. 33-112. See, for example, John Daly Burk, "Bunker Hill, or the Death of General Warren," *Drama from the American Theater, 1607-1909*, ed. Richard Moody (New York: World Publishing Co., 1966), pp. 70-86.

14. Hamilton to Jay, March 14, 1779, as quoted by Millis, *Arms and Men*, p. 21; Washington, "To The President of Congress," p. 12; see also "Sentiments on a Peace Establishment," pp. 17-28; Jefferson to Wirt, 1808, as quoted by Richard Hofstadter, *Anti-Intellectualism in American Life* (New York: A. A. Knopf, 1963), p. 158. See, too, Miller, *Federalist Era*, pp. 108 ff. and Hofstadter, *The American Political Tradition* (New York: A. A. Knopf, 1948), pp. 1-7.

15. Williams, *Americans at War*, p. 9; Vagts, *History of Militarism*, p. 99; Millis, *Arms and Men*, pp. 21-25; Boorstin, *The Americans*, pp. 347-352.

16. Boorstin, "America and the Image of Europe," *Perspective, U.S.A.* 14 (1956): 5-19. Edward M. Burns, *The American Idea of Mission* (New Brunswick, N. J.: Rutgers University Press, 1957), pp. 237-239; Max Lerner, *America as a Civilization* (New York: Simon and Schuster, 1963), pp. 23-28; Arthur A. Ekirch, *The Civilian and the Military* (New York: Oxford University Press, 1956), pp. 22-23. Jefferson is quoted by Ekirch from *Considerations on the Society or Order of Cincinnati* (Philadelphia, [1783], p. 8. For a contemporary view, see Gordon, *History of . . . Independence*, p. 393 ff.

17. Major General O. O. Howard, "The Example of Washington," *United Service*, IV (1881), p. 505; William Alfred Bryan, *George Washington in American Literature*, 1775-1865 (New York: Columbia University Press, 1952), pp. 13-22; Boorstin, "The Mythologizing of George Washington," *The Americans*, II, pp. 337-362.

18. Royall Tyler, "The Contrast," in *Representative American Plays*, ed. Arthur Hobson Quinn (New York: Appleton-Century-Crofts, Inc., 1953), pp. 51-71, and Moody, pp. 27-59.

19. Quinn, *History of Drama*, pp. 52, 86, 126; Reed, *American Characters*, pp. 47-70.

20. Although first published in England, *Charlotte Temple* was written by an American, Susanna Rowson, and according to Edward Wagenknecht, is "rightly characterized as an American novel in view of its enormous vogue." *Amelia, or the Faithless Briton* (Boston: W. Spotswood and C. P. Wayne, 1798); Edward C. Wagenknecht, *Cavalcade of the American Novel* (New York: Henry Holt and Co., 1952), pp. 1-6; Cowie, *The Rise of The American Novel*, pp. 9-21; Quinn, *American Fiction* (NewYork: D. Appleton-

Century Co., Inc., 1936), pp. 15-24; Carl Van Doren, *The American Novel* (New York: The Macmillan Company, 1940), pp. 6-8.

21. Martin, "Social Institutions in the Early American Novel," *American Quarterly* 9 (Spring 1957): 81.

22. Hannah Foster, *The Coquette* (Boston: n.p., 1797); Martin, p. 81ff.; Cowie, p. 22.

23. William Dunlap, *Andre: A Tragedy in Five Acts* (New York: The Dunlap Society, 1887). For a resumé of the plays about Andre to the time of this edition, see Brander Matthews "Introduction."

24. Burk, "Bunker Hill; or the Death of General Warren" in *Drama from the American Theater*.

SECTION TWO

1. Henry Adams, *History of the United States of America*, 9 vols. (New York: C. Scribner's Sons, 1891), III, p. 80.

2. Merle Curti, *The Growth of American Thought* (New York: Harper and Brothers, 1951), p. 233.

CHAPTER THREE

1. The clearest delineation of the Jacksonian democrat's image of the regular officer is found in the political records. The best general sources are Thomas Hart Benton, *Abridgement of the Debates of Congress, from 1789 to 1865*, 16 vols. (New York: D. Appleton and Co., 1857-1861), *Annals of the Congress of the United States . . . March 3, 1789-May 27, 1824* (Washington: Gales and Seaton, 1834-1856), and *American State Papers, Class V, Military Affairs*, 7 vols. (Washington: Gales and Seaton, 1832-1861); Leonard White, *The Jacksonians: A Study in Administrative History, 1829-1861* (New York: The Macmillan Co., 1954), pp. 205-212 gives a clear and balanced summation of the political critique of the army found in the congressional records; and Samuel P. Huntington, *The Soldier and the State* (Cambridge, Mass.: Belknap Press, 1957), pp. 203-211, has an illuminating, if brief, section on the influence of populism on America's civil-military relations.

2. General Truman Seymour, *Military Education* (Williamstown, Mass., 1864), p. 6.

3. Edward C. Wagenknecht, *Cavalcade of the American Novel* (New York: Henry Holt and Co., 1952), p. 9; Alexander Cowie, *The Rise of the American Novel* (New York: The American Book Co., 1951), p. 16.

4. Aedonus Burke as quoted by Arthur A. Ekirch, *The Civilian and the Military* (New York: Oxford University Press, 1956), pp. 22-23; John C. Miller, *The Federalist Era* (New York: Harper and Brothers, 1960), pp. 249-250.

5. *Annals of Congress*, 16th Cong., 1st Sess., 1627, 1630-1632; Edgar Denton, "The Formative Years of the Military Academy" (Ph.D. diss., Department of History, Syracuse University, 1964), p. 207; Ekirch, *Civilian and Military*, p. 69.

6. Major Staunton to Lt. Col. Sylvannus Thayer, 26 January 1822, Ms. in United States Military Academy Library.

7. C. Joseph Bernardo and Eugene H. Bacon, *American Military Policy* (Harrisburg, Pa.; Military Publishing Co., 1961), pp. 148-151; Millis, *Arms and Men*, pp. 82-86; Huntington, *Soldier and the State*, pp. 214-217; Russell F. Weigley, *History of the United States Army* (New York: The Macmillan Co., 1967), pp. 140-141. For a contemporary account, see (anonymous), *Life of John C. Calhoun* (New York: Harper and Brothers, 1843), pp. 7, 25 ff.

8. James Monroe, "Inaugural Address," March 4, 1817, in Walter Millis, ed., *American Military Thought* (Indianapolis: Bobbs-Merrill, 1966), pp. 88-89 ff.; Huntington, *Soldier and the State*, pp. 203-211.

9. George Bancroft, *Literary and Historical Miscellanies* (New York: Harper and Brothers, 1855), pp. 408-435.

10. Alexis de Tocqueville, *Democracy in America*, ed. Richard D. Heffner (New York: Mentor Books, 1956), p. 283.

11. Marvin Meyers, *The Jacksonian Persuasion* (Stanford: Stanford University Press, 1957), p. 24; Richard Hofstadter, *American Political Tradition* (New York: A. A. Knopf, 1948), pp. 45-47; Bancroft, "Commemoration of Jackson," *Miscellanies*, pp. 457-458. See also T.[homas] P. A.[bernathy], "Andrew Jackson," *Dictionary of American Biography*, 21 vols. (New York: Charles Scribner's Sons, 1932), V, pp. 526-533; and Arthur M. Schlesinger, Jr., *The Age of Jackson* (Boston: Little, Brown and Co., 1950), pp. 36-37.

12. Seymour, *Military Education*, p. 4.

13. For the best illustration of the democratic line of attack, see "Report of Select Committee on the United States Military Academy, March 1, 1837," *American State Papers: Military Affairs*, VII, pp. 1-19. Huntington, *Soldier and the State*, pp. 203-207, has an excellent summation, as does John Hope Franklin, *The Militant South* (Cambridge, Mass.: Harvard University Press, 1956), pp. 140-144. See also Sidney Forman, *West Point, A History* . . . (New York: Columbia University Press, 1950), pp. 49-51; and Stephen E. Ambrose, *Duty, Honor, Country: A History of West Point* (Baltimore: John Hopkins Press, 1966), pp. 104-124.

14. [I. J. Austin], "The Military Academy," *North American Review* 57 (October 1843): 283-292.

15. Washington, "Sentiments on a Peace Establishment," p. 27.

16. White, *The Jacksonians*, pp. 205 ff.

17. [Captain Allen Partridge], *The Military Academy at West Point, Unmasked* . . . (Washington, n. p., 1830), p. 6; *Journal of the House of Representatives*, 21st Cong., 1st Sess., p. 343, quoted by Denton, "The Formative Years," p. 246; Benton, *Abridgement of the Debates of Congress*, X, 669-670; Cunliffe, "The American Military Tradition," p. 210-213.

18. Francis Wayland, *Report to the Corporation of Brown University on Changes in the System of Collegiate Education* (Providence: G. H. Whitney, 1850), pp. 15-18, quoted by Forman, *West Point*, p. 88.

19. "Report of Select Committee," pp. 1 ff; Cunliffe, "American Military Tradition," p. 212.

20. Wayland, *The Elements of Moral Science*, ed. Joseph L. Blau (Cambridge, Mass.: Belknap Press, 1963), p. 363; Partridge, *Military Academy Unmasked*.

21. [I. J. Austin], "The Military Academy," pp. 287-288; Boorstin, "America and the Image of Europe"; Cunliffe, "American Military Tradition," p. 211.

22. The literature reflecting the foreigners' views of America's military institutions is remarkably extensive. Francis P. Prucha, "The United States Army as Viewed by British Travellers, 1825-60," *Military Affairs* 17 (Fall 1963): 113-124 is an excellent summation. Quoted here from Prucha are Godfrey Vigne, *Six Months in America* (London, 1832), I, pp. 253-254; Sir James E. Alexander, *Transatlantic Sketches* (London, 1883), II, p. 277; Charles A. Murray, *Travels in North America* . . . (New York, 1839), II, pp. 67-68; Captain Basil Hale, *Travels in North America* . . . (Edin-

burgh, 1829), III, pp. 93-97. For more Enlightenment-oriented views, see Francis Grund, *Americans in Their Moral, Social, and Political Relations* (London: Longmans, et. al., 1827), II, pp. 326-337; and Frances Wright, *Views of Society and Manners in America*, ed. Paul R. Baker (Cambridge, Mass.: Belknap Press, 1936), pp. 79-90.

23. David Brion Davis, *American Quarterly* 15 (Summer 1963): 115-125.

24. Weigley, *Towards an American Army*, pp. 1-9; James Edward Edmonds, *Fighting Fools* (New York: D. Appleton-Century Co., 1938), pp. 82-98; Nathaniel Hawthorne, "The Life of Franklin Pierce," in *Tales, Sketches and Other Papers, The Complete Writings of Nathaniel Hawthorne* (Boston: Houghton, Mifflin and Co., 1883), XII, p. 399. Wilson is quoted by Huntington, *Soldier and the State*, p. 154.

25. Dixon Wecter, *The Hero in America, A Chronicle of Hero-Worship* (New York: C. Scribner's Sons, 1941), p. 12; Frank J. Cavaioli, *West Point and the Presidency: The Voters Attitude Toward the Military Elite* (New York: St. John's University Press, 1962), pp. iii-iv; Eric Bentley, *American Heroes, Myth and Reality* (Washington: J. B. Lippincott Co., 1944); Albert Somit, "The Military Hero as Presidential Candidate," *Public Opinion Quarterly* 12 (Summer 1948): 192-200; Huntington, *Soldier and the State*, pp. 157-162; Curti, *Social Ideas of American Educators* (Paterson, N. J.: Pageant Books, 1959), pp. 161-163; Ralph Gabriel, *The Course of American Democratic Thought* (New York: The Ronald Press Co., 1940), pp. 22, 93-94.

CHAPTER FOUR

1. There are a number of collections of pacifist writings and all give essentially the same picture of military men. Those found most useful here were *The Book of Peace: A Collection of Essays* (Boston: George C. Beckwith, 1845); William Ellery Channing, *Discourses on War* (Boston: Ginn and Co., 1903); and Charles Sumner, *Addresses on War* (Boston: Ginn and Co., 1904). Merle Curti, *The American Peace Crusade* (Durham: Duke University Press, 1929) and *Peace or War: The American Struggle, 1636-1936* (New York: Norton Co., 1936) are still the best histories of the pacifist movement. Arthur A. Ekirch, *The Civilian and the Military*

(New York: Oxford University Press, 1956), makes extensive use of pacifist writings gleaned from the Swarthmore College Peace Collection and elsewhere.

2. Jerrold as quoted in *The Book of Peace*, p. 587.

3. Channing, "Second Discourse on War," *Discourses*, pp. 52-53.

4. Curti, *The Growth of American Thought* (New York: Harper and Brothers, 1951), p. 209; Worcester, *The Friend of Peace*, II (1821), pp. 14-22, as quoted in Ekirch, *Civilian and Military*, p. 66; Channing, "War," *Discourses*, pp. 77-111.

5. James Edward Edmonds, *Fighting Fools* (New York: D. Appleton-Century Co., 1938), pp. 161-162.

6. Burns, *The American Idea of Mission* (New Brunswick, N. J.: Rutgers University Press, 1957), p. 235, quoting from *The Correspondence of John C. Calhoun* (Washington, American Historical Association, 1900), II, p. 692.

7. "Claims of Peace on Literary Men," *The Book of Peace*, p. 580.

8. Channing, "Second Discourse," *Discourses*, pp. 52-53.

9. "Plain Sketches of War," *Book of Peace*, p. 471.

10. Sumner, *The Book of Peace*, pp. 553-576; also found in *Addresses on War*. See also Ekirch, *Civilian and Military*, p. 81.

11. "Insensibility to the Evils of War," *The Book of Peace*, pp. 269-276; also found in "Lecture on War," *Discourses*, pp. 109-110.

12. "Claims of Peace," *The Book of Peace*, p. 580.

13. Charles A. Murray is quoted by Francis P. Prucha, "The United States Army as Viewed by British Travellers, 1825-60," *Military Affairs* 17 (Fall 1963): 116.

14. *Addresses on War*, p. 82.

15. *Washington Daily National Intelligencer* (August 4, 1827), p. 3, quoted in Ekrich, *Civilian and Military*, pp. 75-76.

16. Richard Hofstadter, *Anti-Intellectualism in American Life* (New York: A. A. Knopf, 1963), p. 159.

17. William Graham Sumner, *Andrew Jackson as a Public Man* (Boston: Houghton, Mifflin and Co., 1882), pp. 33-35; Harold Daniel Langley, "The Humanitarians and the United States Navy, 1798-1862," (Ph.D. diss., University of Pennsylvania, 1961).

18. Williams is quoted by Ekirch, *Civilian and Military*, pp. 64-65.

CHAPTER FIVE

1. The most pointed expressions of the Enlightenment conception of officership were centered—like much of the egalitarian critique—on West Point. Just as for some the Academy symbolized "aristocracy," for others it stood for military service at its republican best. Such views are common in the reports of the Annual Boards of Visitors, in graduation addresses, and in essays appearing periodically in well-established magazines, especially the *North American Review*.

2. Iver James Austin, *An Address Delivered Before the Corps of Cadets . . . [June 17, 1842] (New York: Wiley and Putnam, 1842).*

3. Edgar Allan Poe, *Poems* (New York: 1831) as quoted by Sidney Forman, *West Point, A History* . . . (New York: Columbia University Press, 1950), p. 74. The lines quoted are the opening two lines of a sonnet to science in a volume of poems dedicated to the U. S. Corps of Cadets by Poe, who attended the Military Academy for about a year.

4. Walter Millis, *Arms and Men* (New York: G. P. Putnam's Sons, 1956), pp. 61-63.

5. Merle Curti, *The Growth of American Thought* (New York: Harper and Brothers, 1951), pp. 329-330; Daniel Hovey Calhoun, *The American Civil Engineer: Origins and Conflict* (Cambridge, Mass.: Harvard University Press, 1960); Millis, *Arms and Men*, pp. 92-93.

6. Samuel P. Huntington, *The Soldier and the State* (Cambridge, Mass.: Belknap Press, 1957), pp. 198-200; Russell F. Weigley, *History of the United States Army* (New York: The Macmillan Company, 1967), pp. 146-147; Forman, *West Point*, pp. 74-89.

7. Honorable Thomas Buck Reed, *An Address to the Cadets at West Point* . . . (New York: J. Seymour, 1827).

8. Frances Wright, *Views of Society and Manners in America*, ed. Paul R. Baker (Cambridge, Mass.: Belknap Press, 1963), pp. 79-90. See also Francis P. Prucha, "The United States Army as Viewed by British Travellers," *Military Affairs* 17 (Fall 1963): 120-123; and Francis Grund, *The Americans in Their Moral, Social and Political Relations* (London: Longman, et al., 1837), II, pp. 326-327.

9. President John Quincy Adams, in Walter Millis, ed., *American Military Thought* (Indianapolis: Bobbs-Merrill, 1966), pp. 112-113.

10. Jackson, "The First Inaugural Address," in *American Military Thought*, pp. 117-118; John Hope Franklin, The *Militant South* (Cambridge, Mass.: Harvard University Press, 1956), pp. 141-142; Weigley, *History of the Army*, pp. 154-155.

11. Henry Barnard, *Military Schools and Courses of Instruction in the Science and Art of War* . . . (New York: E. Steiger, 1872), p. 723.

12. Horace Mann, *Report of the Annual Board of Visitors* (Washington: Government Printing Office, 1849), Appendix, no page number.

13. James Fenimore Cooper, *Notions of the Americans Picked Up by a Traveling Bachelor* (New York: Frederick Ungar Publishing Co., 1963), I, p. 233.

14. From information provided by William Cullen Bryant, II, based on a letter from William Cullen Bryant to Hon. Lewis Cass, Secretary of War, March 19, 1834, held by Clements Library, Ann Arbor, Michigan, and various other pieces of family correspondence.

15. As quoted by Hazen C. Carpenter, "Emerson at West Point," *The Pointer* 27 (June 12, 1951): 5, 27.

16. Edgar Denton, "The Formative Years of the Military Academy," (Ph.D. diss., Syracuse University, 1964), p. 211.

17. Austin, *An Address Before the Corps*, p. 2.

18. George Ticknor, "West Point in 1826," an unpublished and undated extract of a letter to his wife given to the Military Academy by his daughter and now held in the Academy Library Archives.

19. Emerson as quoted by Carpenter, "Emerson at West Point," pp. 5, 27.

20. Scott is quoted by Captain E. C. Boynton, *History of West Point* . . . (New York: D. van Nostrand, 1863), Frontispiece; and Millis, *Arms and Men*, p. 107.

21. Honorable Samuel J. Bayard, *Address Delivered Before the Graduating Class of Cadets, June 16, 1854* (Camden: Office of the Camden Democrat, 1854), p. 3.

22. Honorable Ashbel Smith, *Address Delivered* . . . *at the United States Military Academy, June 16, 1848* (New York: W. R. Burroughs, 1848), pp. 10-11.

23. Bayard, *Address*, p. 4.

CHAPTER SIX

1. In assessing the impact of three decades of frontier service on the nation's image of the military leader, the most notable bibliographic feature is a negative one. Outside of governmental reports, private accounts, and the like, there was little written about the western army between the War of 1812 and the Mexican War. The paucity of comment reflects the indifference to western military matters attested to by contemporary observers. Congressional debates over Indian affairs and military appropriations found in Thomas Hart Benton, *Abridgement of the Debates in Congress from 1789 to 1865*, 16 vols. (New York: D. Appleton and Co., 1857-1861) and elsewhere are sometimes revealing. So too are the writings of the officers themselves. The most direct commentary on America's view of the frontier officers and men is found in books and articles by articulate world travelers. The richest single source is again Francis Prucha, "The United States Army as Viewed by British Travellers, 1825-1860," *Military Affairs* 17 (Fall 1953): 120-123. For historical background, Prucha, *Broad Ax and Bayonet* (Madison: State Historical Society of Wisconsin, 1953); Russell F. Weigley, *History of the United States Army* (New York: The Macmillan Co., 1967); and Robert Utley, *Frontiersmen in Blue, 1845-1865* (New York: Macmillan and Co., 1967) provide thorough studies, while older histories of the army like William Addleman Ganoe, *The History of the United States Army* (New York: Appleton-Century Co., 1942), pp. 158-195, and Oliver Lyman Spaulding, *The United States Army in Peace and War* (New York: G. P. Putnam's Sons, 1937), pp. 147, 172, 227-242, are still highly useful, if less objective.

2. Capt. Thomas Hamilton, *Men and Manners in America* (London: Blackwood, 1833), I, p. 265.

3. See, e.g., William F. Poole, ed., *Poole's Index to Periodical Literature*, 6 vols. (Gloucester, Mass.: n.p., 1958), I, Part 1, pp. 635-639; I, Part 2, p. 1342; and William Cushing, ed., *Index to North American Review, Volume I-CXXV, 1815-1877* (Cambridge, Mass.: John Wilson and Son, 1878), pp. 6, 53-54.

4. Francis Wyse, *America, Its Realities and Resources*, 3 vols. (London, 1846), II, p. 101, as quoted by Prucha, "British Travellers," p. 118.

5. Richard Hildreth, *The History of The United States of America*, 6 vols. (New York: Harper and Brothers, 1880), II, pp. 308-310.

6. John William Ward, *Andrew Jackson, Symbol for an Age* (New York: Oxford University Press, 1955). The first four chapters examine in detail Jackson's military image; the quoted material is on pp. 47 and 56. For a typical contemporary treatment, see Alexander Walker, *Jackson and New Orleans* (New York: J. C. Derby, 1856).

7. James Fenimore Cooper, *Notions of the Americans. . .* , 2 vols. (New York: Frederick Ungar Publishing Co., 1963), I, pp. 183-184; see also p. 175.

8. Arthur M. Schlesinger, Jr., *The Age of Jackson* (Boston: Little, Brown and Co., 1950), pp. 36-37; Ward, *Andrew Jackson*, pp. 44-45.

9. Quoted by Prucha in *Broad Ax*, pp. 51-52; Cass, "Service of Indians in Civilized Warfare," *North American Review* 24 (April 1827): 365-442; "Removal of the Indians," *North American Review* 30 (January 1830): 62-121.

10. Charles J. Latrobe, *The Rambler in North America*, 2 vols. (New York: Harper and Brothers, 1835), II, pp. 230-231; Prucha, "British Travellers," pp. 115-120; Prucha, *Broad Ax*, pp. 97-103; Weigley, *History of the Army*, pp. 144-172; Fairfax Downey, *Indian Wars of the U. S. Army, 1776-1885* (Garden City, N. Y.: Doubleday and Co., Inc., 1963), pp. 138-148; Ganoe, *History of the Army*, pp. 158-196; Gen. O. O. Howard, "The Example of Washington: An Address Delivered Before the Cadets of the Military Academy at West Point," *United Service*, IV (1881), p. 513.

11. Washington Irving, *The Adventures of Captain Bonneville, U.S.A.* (Norman, Okla.: University of Oklahoma Press, 1961).

12. Daniel C. Gilman, *Address Delivered [at] . . . The United States Military Academy, . . . June 16, 1875* (New York: D. van Nostrand, 1875).

13. Irving, *Bonneville*, pp. 1-li.

14. As quoted by Edgeley W. Todd in "Introduction," *Bonneville*, p. xvii.

15. Hamilton, *Men and Manners*, II, pp. 268-269.

CHAPTER SEVEN

1. Military-gentleman legendry can be found in this period in practically every area of American expression. The most enduring portraitures were penned by men of letters, including our leading

historians, biographers, and novelists; and their writings are vast. Only a few of the most prominent representatives have been used here. I have found no secondary sources that deal directly with the military image in nineteenth-century American literature but, in addition to the standard period histories, William R. Taylor, *Cavalier and Yankee: The Old South and American National Character* (New York: George Braziller, 1961) and Edwin Harrison Cady, *The Gentleman in America* (Syracuse: Syracuse University Press, 1949) are particularly helpful in setting the intellectual background.

2. John Pendleton Kennedy, *Horseshoe Robinson*, Ernest E. Leisy, ed. (New York: Hafner Publishing Co., 1962), pp. 16-17.

3. Walter Millis, *Arms and Men: A Study in American Military History* (New York: G. P. Putnam's Sons, 1956), p. 73; Samuel P. Huntington, *The Soldier and the State* (Cambridge, Mass.: Belknap Press, 1957), pp. 39-50.

4. Taylor, *Cavalier and Yankee*, pp. 96-97; Cady, *Gentleman in America*, p. 18 ff; Francis T. Grund, *Aristocracy in America*, 2 vols. (London: R. Bentley, 1839); and see also Grund, *The Americans in Their Moral, Social and Political Relations*, 2 vols. (London: Longman, et al., 1837), I, pp. 17-33, 66-71; Grimshaw is quoted by J. Merton England, "The Democratic Faith in American Schoolbooks, 1783-1860," *American Quarterly* 15 (Summer 1963): 192-193.

5. Arthur M. Schlesinger, Jr., *The Age of Jackson* (Boston: Little, Brown and Co., 1950), pp. 8-17, 267-282; Merle Curti, *The Growth of American Thought* (New York: Harper and Brothers, 1951), pp. 213-232; Russell B. Nye, *George Bancroft, Brahmin Rebel* (New York: Alfred A. Knopf, 1944), pp. 304-307; Orie William Long, *Literary Pioneers: Early American Explorers of European Culture* (Cambridge, Mass.: Harvard University Press, 1935); Tremaine McDowell, "The Great Experiment" in Spiller, et al., eds., *Literary History of the United States* (New York: The Macmillan Co., 1948), pp. 219-227; Glynden G. Van Deusen, *The Jacksonian Era, 1828-1848* (New York: Harper and Brothers, 1959).

6. John Marshall, *The Life of George Washington* [Philadelphia]: James Crissy and Thomas Couperthwait and Co., 1839), I, pp. 1-34.

7. Mason Locke Weems, *A History of the Life and Death, Virtues and Exploits, of General George Washington* (Philadelphia: J. B. Lippincott Co., 1918), pp. 54-60. See also Michael Kraus, *The Writings*

of American History (Norman, Okla.: University of Oklahoma Press, 1953), pp. 86-88; Harvey Wish, *The American Historian* (New York: Oxford University Press, 1960), pp. 42-44; and William Alfred Bryan, *George Washington in American Literature, 1775-1865* (New York: Columbia University Press, 1952), pp. 92-96.

8. Marshall, *Life of Washington*, I, pp. 10-11.

9. Francis Parkman, *The Conspiracy of Pontiac* (Boston: Little, Brown and Co., 1913), pp. 109-121.

10. Washington Irving, *The Life of George Washington*, 3 vols. (New York: G. P. Putnam and Co., 1855-1859), I, pp. iii-iv, 195-196. The preface explains that the first volume "treats of . . . [Washington's] expedition into the wilderness, his campaigns on the frontier in the old French war, and the other 'experiences' by which his character was formed, and he was gradually trained up and prepared for his great destiny."

11. George Bancroft, *History of the United States of America*, 6 vols. (New York: D. Appleton, 1887), II, pp. 420-424.

12. William Gilmore Simms, *The History of South Carolina* (New York: Redfield, 1860), pp. 343-345.

13. Michael Kraus says that "Hildreth had no love for tales of war, then so frequently the staple of historical writings." Hildreth's dispassionate description of the Monongahela ambush bears out the point. After duly noting Braddock's shortcomings, he quietly gave the Virginia troops and Washington credit as the best of the soldiers on the scene—because they were "acquainted with Indian method of fighting." Later, he roundly criticized the inept soldiership at the opening of the War of 1812, but went on to explain that most of the leaders had "been civilians for more than thirty years, and were indebted for their present appointments rather to political than to military considerations." Kraus, *Writings of American History*, p. 130; and Richard Hildreth, *The History of the United States of America*, 6 vols. (New York: Harper and Brothers, 1880), I, pp. 459-461; II, pp. 308-310.

14. *American Military and Political Biography* (n.p., "printed for subscribers," 1825), pp. 339, 348-349; *Library of American Biography*, ed. Jared Sparks (Boston: Hilliard, Gray and Co., 1834-1848); Cady, *Gentleman in America*, pp. 20-21.

15. Richard Moody, ed., *Dramas from the American Theater, 1762-1909* (New York: World Publishing Co., 1966), p. 66; Arthur Hobson Quinn, ed., *A History of the American Drama*, 2 vols. (New York: Appleton-Century-Crofts, Inc., 1943), I, pp. 151, 157-159,

278; Mordecai M. Noah, "She Would Be a Soldier" in Moody, *Dramas*, p. 638; Isaac Perley Reed, *American Characters in Native American Plays Prior to 1870* (Columbus, O.: Ohio State University Bulletin, 1918), pp. 63-64, 99-105.

16. James Fenimore Cooper, *The Spy* (New York: Dodd, Mead and Co., 1946), p. 53ff.

17. James Fenimore Cooper, *The Last of the Mohicans* in *The Leatherstocking Saga*, ed. Allan Nevins (New York: Pantheon Books, 1954), pp. 281-283, 364-367; Henry Nash Smith, *Virgin Land: The American West as Symbol and Myth* (Cambridge, Mass.: Harvard University Press, 1950), pp. 70-73; Cady, *Gentleman in America*, pp. 105-107. See also Marvin Meyers, *The Jacksonian Persuasion* (Stanford: Stanford University Press, 1957), pp. 57-100; Alexander Cowie, *The Rise of the American Novel* (New York: American Book Co., 1951), pp. 155-158.

18. James Fenimore Cooper, *Notions of the Americans. . .* , 2 vols. (New York: Frederick Ungar Publishing Co., 1963), II, 93; also quoted by Taylor, *Cavalier and Yankee*, pp. 96-97. Grund, *The Americans*, pp. 322-325.

19. James Edward Edmonds, *Fighting Fools* (New York: D. Appleton-Century Co., 1938), p. 178; John Hope Franklin, *The Militant South* (Cambridge, Mass.: Harvard University Press, 1956).

20. Kennedy, *Horseshoe Robinson*, p. 132.

21. Even when not in uniform, fictional heroes were likely to be accredited with attributes gained from previous military service. Roland Forrester in Bird's *Nick of the Woods* "was entitled to superior attention. . . . He was, in reality, the commander of the party, the ostensible leader being . . . entirely wanting in the military reputation and skill which the other had acquired . . . and of which the value was fully appreciated. . . ." Robert Montgomery Bird, *Nick of the Woods* (New York: A. L. Burt Co., n.d.), p. 6. For typical works of the other authors, see Section IB of the Bibliography.

22. Lucy Hazard, *The Frontier in American Literature* (New York: Frederick Ungar Publishing Co., 1961), p. 72.

23. William Gilmore Simms, *The Yemassee* (Boston: Houghton, Mifflin and Co., 1961), pp. 34-35.

24. Kennedy, *Horseshoe Robinson*, p. 17; James Fenimore Cooper, *The Chainbearer or the Littlepage Manuscripts* (New York: Hurd and Houghton, 1866).

25. Cooper, *Notions*, II, pp. 314-315; also quoted by Cady, *Gentleman in America*, p. 107.

26. Robert A. Bone, "Irving's Headless Hessian: Prosperity and the Inner Life," *American Quarterly* 15 (Summer 1963): 167; see also Cady, *Gentleman in America*, pp. 20-21.

27. Honorable Kenneth Rayner, *An Address [at] the United States Military Academy* (New York: John F. Trow, 1853), p. 12; Alexis de Tocqueville, *Democracy in America*, ed., Richard Heffner (New York: Mentor Books, 1956), p. 275.

28. Daniel Pierce Thompson, *The Green Mountain Boys* (Boston: Bazin and Ellsworth, n. d.). See also Cooper, *The Leatherstocking Saga*, pp. 49, 264-265.

29. Kennedy, *Horseshoe Robinson*, pp. 264-266, 306, 484.

CHAPTER EIGHT

1. As with chapter 2, the goal here has been synthesis rather than analysis; and the focus is on the North, for (as Section IV will show) it was northern theories of war and impressions of officership that prevailed in the postbellum age. Although rather extensive samplings were taken, no attempt was made to study fully the immense day-by-day commentary written during the war itself. The monthly periodicals provide a running firsthand view of military men that is, in general, sympathetic and laudatory in tone. T. Harry Williams, "The Attack on West Point During the Civil War," *Mississippi Valley Historical Review* 25 (March 1939): 491-504, is the best single summation of the persisting political criticism of the military careerist.

2. Charles Eliot Norton, "Our Soldiers," *North American Review* 99 (July 1864): 174.

3. Nathaniel Hawthorne, "Chiefly about War Matters," *Atlantic Monthly* 10 (July 1862): 45.

4. [H. T. Tuckerman], "A Review of *The Gentleman* by George H. Calvert," *Atlantic Monthly* 11 (June 1863): 787-788; George H. Calvert, *The Gentleman* (Boston: Ticknor and Fields, 1863).

5. Edward E. Hale, "The Man Without a Country," *Atlantic Monthly* 12 (December 1863): 667.

6. *Harper's Weekly Magazine*, 6 (January 17, 1863): 75-78, as quoted by Stephen Ambrose, *Duty, Honor, Country: A History of West Point* (Baltimore: Johns Hopkins Press, 1966), p. 185. See

also Captain Edward C. Boynton, *History of West Point* . . . (New York: D. van Nostrand, 1863), pp. 238-241; John C. Hurd, "A Review of the *History of West Point* by Captain Edward C. Boynton," *Atlantic Monthly* 13 (February 1864): 260-261; T. Harry Williams, *Americans at War* (New York: Collier Books, 1962), p. 51 ff.

7. Barnard, "Military Systems," p. 790; originally published in *The American Journal of Education* 14 (1864): 109-112, and included in *Henry Barnard on Education*, ed. John S. Brubaker (New York: Russell and Russell, 1965), p. 144.

8. Williams, *Americans At War*, pp. 51-52; Russell F. Weigley, *Towards An American Army* (New York: Columbia University Press, 1962), pp. 79-99.

9. Barnard, *Military Schools and Courses of Instruction in the Science and Art of War* (New York: E. Steiger, 1872); Arthur A. Ekirch, *The Civilian and the Military* (New York: Oxford University Press, 1956), p. 118; Parkman, "To the Editors of the *Boston Daily Advertiser*," *Letters of Francis Parkman*, ed. Wilbur R. Jacobs (Norman, Okla.: University of Oklahoma Press, 1960), I, 156.

10. Holmes is quoted by Edwin H. Cady, *The Gentleman in America* (Syracuse, N. Y.: Syracuse University Press, 1949), p. 157; see also "My Hunt After 'The Captain,' " *Atlantic Monthly* 10 (December 1862): 738-764. Parkman's wartime views are reflected in his several letters to the *Boston Daily Advertiser*. See *Letters*, p. 141 ff.; the quotation is on p. 154.

11. Charles Eliot Norton, "A Review of *Twelve Years of a Soldier's Life in India*. . . ," *Atlantic Monthly* 5 (January 1860): 124-125.

12. Parkman, *Letters*, pp. 159-160.

13. The Newark *Evening Journal* and Simon Cameron as quoted by Ekirch, *Civilian and Military*, pp. 91-93; General Truman Seymour, "Military Education, A Vindication of West Point," Williamstown, Mass., 1864, pp. 3, 6; Boynton, *West Point*, pp. 251-253; Williams, "The Attack on West Point." See Samuel P. Huntington, *The Soldier and the State* (Cambridge, Mass.: Belknap Press, 1957), pp. 212-213; Ekirch, *Civilian and Military*, p. 92; and Weigley, *Towards an American Army*, p. 199, for recent and opposing evaluations of the Southern "defections."

14. Clarence H. Cramer, *Royal Bob: The Life of Robert G. Ingersoll* (New York: Bobbs-Merrill Co., Inc., 1952), pp. 51, 58-59, 249-250.

15. Hawthorne, "The Life of Franklin Pierce," in *Tales, Sketches*

and Other Papers, The Complete Writings of Nathaniel Hawthorne
(Boston: Houghton, Mifflin and Co., 1883), XII, p. 399; Alexan-
der Cowie, *The Rise of the American Novel* (New York: American
Book Co., 1951), pp. 327-363; Robt. G. Spiller, ed., *Literary History
of the United States*, 2 vols. (New York: The Macmillan Co., 1948),
I, pp. 416-440; Newton Arvin, *Hawthorne* (New York: Russell and
Russell, 1961), pp. 269-272; Edward C. Wagenknecht, *Nathaniel
Hawthorne: Man and Writer* (New York: Oxford University Press,
1961), pp. 124-127.

16. Hawthorne, "Chiefly About War Matters By a Peaceable
Man," *Atlantic Monthly* 10 (July 1862): 50-52.

17. Hale, "Man Without a Country," p. 667.

18. Quoted in Wm. R. Taylor, *Cavalier and Yankee* (New York:
George Braziller, 1961), p. 238; Emerson, "American Civilization," *Atlantic Monthly* 9 (April 1862): 502-511.

19. Taylor, *Cavalier and Yankee*, pp. 146 ff., 158, 296; Samuel
L. Clemens, *Life on the Mississippi* (Boston: J. R. Osgood and Co.,
1883), pp. 377-378; John Hope Franklin, *The Militant South* (Cam-
bridge, Mass.: Harvard University Press, 1956), pp. 193-195;
James D. Hart, *The Popular Book: A History of America's Literary
Taste* (Berkley: University of California Press, 1963), pp. 76-77;
Bagby is quoted by Richard Harwell in "Introduction" to John
Esten Cooke, *Outlines from the Outpost* (Chicago: Lakeside Press,
1961), p. xv.

20. E. Wetherell [Susan Warner], *Daisy* (London: Ward Lock
and Co., Limited, n.d.), pp. 304-305.

21. Norton, "Our Soldiers," *North American Review* 99 (July
1864): 172-203.

CHAPTER NINE

1. The postbellum recognition of the military careerist qua
professional (and the Prussian overtones) can be traced best in
contemporary journals, civilian as well as military. As the century
neared its close, those materials became considerably more
numerous. Articles about the military appear in *The Christian
Examiner, Lippincott's, McClure's, Century, The Magazine of American
History, The Nation*, et al., supplementing the still standard (and
still better indexed) *Harper's Monthly, Atlantic Monthly*, and *North
American Review*. After 1879, the new *United Services* magazine and

the *Journal of the Military Service Institution of the United States* illustrate the fruition of military professionalism, as well as reflecting attitudes toward it. Walter Millis, ed., *American Military Thought* (Indianapolis: Bobbs-Merrill, 1966), pp. 160-226, gives representation of government points of view; Samuel P. Huntington, *The Soldier and the State* (Cambridge, Mass.: Belknap Press, 1957), pp. 222-269, analyzes "The Creation of the American Military Profession"; and Russell F. Weigley, *History of the United States Army* (New York: The Macmillan Co., 1967), pp. 265-292, gives the essential historical background to "The Twilight of the Old Army."

2. Captain E. L. Zalinski, "The Future of Warfare," *North American Review* 61 (1890): 688-700.

3. Charles E. Munroe, "Improvements in the Science of Warfare," *The Chautauquan* 16, New Series VII (October-March 1895): 27.

4. T. Miller Maguire, "Our Art of War as 'Made in Germany,'" *Journal of the Military Service Institution of the United States* 19 (July, October 1896): 151-159, 312-321; Huntington, *Soldier and State*, pp. 30-58; Millis, *American Military Thought*, pp. 78-80.

5. Huntington, *Soldier and State*, pp. 30-58, 207-210; Weigley, *Towards an American Army* (New York: Columbia University Press, 1962), pp. 167-171; Millis, *American Military Thought*, pp. 72, 118; Alfred Vagts, *A History of Militarism: Romance and Realities of a Profession* (New York: W. W. Norton, 1937), pp. 180-228.

6. John Watts DePeyster, "Frederic the Great" in *Prussia: Its Position and Destiny*, ed. J. W. DePeyster (New York: Chasmar and Company, 1887); *The Nation* (July 28, 1870): 52, as quoted by William M. Armstrong, *E. L. Godkin and American Foreign Policy* (New York: Bookman Associates, 1957), p. 112.

7. N. H. Loring, "Prussia: Its Position and Destiny." An article first published in March 1834 and reprinted as a pamphlet in the collection by the same name; see note 6 above.

8. William Orie Long, *Literary Pioneers, Early American Explorers of European Culture* (Cambridge, Mass.: Harvard University Press, 1935), pp. 222-223; Russel B. Nye, *George Bancroft, Brahmin Rebel* (New York: Alfred A. Knopf, 1944), pp. 264-265.

9. Quoted by Richard Hofstadter, *Social Darwinism in American Thought* (Boston: Beacon Press, 1955), p. 173.

10. Richard C. Brown, "Emory Upton, the Army's Mahan," *Military Affairs* 17 (Fall 1953): 125-131; Weigley, *Towards an Ameri-*

can Army, pp. 100-126; *History of the Army*, pp. 277-281, 336-340, 396-397; Huntington, *Soldier and State*, pp. 54-55, 232.

11. Sidney Whitman, "Field Marshal Count Moltke," *The Chautauquan* 20 (January 1895): 413-417.

12. Captain T. A. Bingham, in *Journal of the Military Service Institution of the United States* 13 (1892): 666-676. General George B. McClellan, "Army Organization," *Harper's New Monthly Magazine*, 48 (April 1874): 670-680 and 49 (August 1874): 401-411.

13. "A Review of *Elements of Military Arts and History* by Edward de la Barre Duparcq and translated by G. W. Cullun," *Atlantic Monthly* 11 (April 1863): 524-525.

14. As quoted by Weigley, *Towards an American Army*, p. 171.

15. James A. Garfield, "The Army of the United States," *North American Review* 126 (1887): 454.

16. General William Carter, "The Army as a Career," *North American Review* 183 (November 1906): 870-876.

17. John W. Masland and Laurence I. Radway, *Soldiers and Scholars: Military Education and National Policy* (Princeton: Princeton University Press, 1957), pp. 76-99.

18. Zalinski, "Future of Warfare," p. 700.

CHAPTER TEN

1. The profound influences of evolutionary theories on the military image are seen in the writings of most antebellum social scientists. Especially useful here have been: John Fiske, *Outlines of Cosmic Philosophy, Based on the Doctrine of Evolution*, 2 vols. (Boston: Houghton, Mifflin and Co., 1874), II, pp. 240-254; John Fiske, *Essays Historical and Literary* (New York: The Macmillan Co., 1907), pp. 55-98; and William Graham Sumner, *What Social Classes Owe to Each Other* (Caldwell, Idaho: Caxton Printers, 1954), pp. 38-50, 63-70, 88-106; Sumner, *Andrew Jackson as a Public Man* (Boston: Houghton, Mifflin and Co., 1882), pp. 33 ff., 358 ff.; and numerous essays, especially "War" and "Discipline," available in several collections. The related business rationale and its particular picture of military men comes through in various periodical pieces, but the best illustrations of their overall slant are Andrew Carnegie, *Triumphant Democracy* (New York: C. Scribner,

1886), pp. 6-8, 25-32, 378-387; and Carnegie, *The Gospel of Wealth and Other Timely Essays*, 2 vols. (Garden City, N. Y.: Doubleday, Doran and Co., 1933). Huntington, pp. 222-230, gives an incisive explanation of the effects of "business pacifism" on civil-military relations. For the association of business and evolutionary doctrine, Richard Hofstadter, *Social Darwinism in American Thought* (Boston: Beacon Press, 1955), is basic.

2. Sumner, "War" in *Social Darwinism, Selected Essays*, ed. Stow Parsons (Englewood, N.J.: Prentice-Hall, 1963), p. 50.

3. Carnegie, *Triumphant Democracy*, p. 9.

4. Norman S. Shaler, "The Natural History of Warfare," *North American Review* 167 (1896): 328-340.

5. Sumner, "War," pp. 50-51.

6. Max Nordau, "The Philosophy and Morals of War," *North American Review* 169 (1889): 794 ff.

7. Samuel P. Huntington, *The Soldier and the State* (Cambridge, Mass.: Belknap Press, 1957), pp. 223-226; Herbert Spencer, *The Principles of Sociology*, 3 vols. (New York: D. Appleton and Co., 1883), I, pp. 473-491; Hofstadter, *Social Darwinism*, p. 184; Merle Curti, *Peace or War* (New York: Norton Co., 1936), pp. 118-120; Lewis Henry Morgan, *Ancient Society* (Cambridge, Mass.: Belknap Press, 1964), pp. 1-23.

8. Fiske, *Cosmic Philosophy*, II, p. 240 ff.; *The American Revolution*, 2 vols. (Boston: Houghton, Mifflin and Co., 1891), I, pp. 148-149, 206-243; *Essays*, pp. 55-98.

9. Fiske, *Cosmic Philosophy*, p. 252.

10. Sumner, *Social Classes*, p. 90; "War," pp. 36, 50-51 and "Discipline," pp. 24-25, in *The Conquest of the United States by Spain and Other Essays* (Chicago: Regnery, 1965).

11. Russell H. Conway and John D. Rockefeller are quoted by Ralph Gabriel, "The Gospel of Wealth of the Gilded Age," *The Course of American Democratic Thought* (New York: The Ronald Press Co., 1940), pp. 151-169. For a book length treatment of the subject, see Irvin G. Wyllie, *The Self-Made Man in America* (New Brunswick, N. J.: Rutgers University Press, 1954), especially p. 62. See also Sumner, "That it is Not Wicked to Be Rich" and "That He Who Would Be Well Taken Care of Must Take Care of Himself," in *Social Classes*, pp. 38-50, 63-70.

12. Carnegie, *Triumphant Democracy*, pp. 6-7, 27-28.

13. See, for example, James Edward Edmonds, *Fighting Fools* (New York: D. Appleton-Century Co., 1938), p. 184, and Richard

C. Brown, "Emory Upton, The Army's Mahan," *Military Affairs* 17 (Fall 1953): 125-131.

14. Huntington, *Soldier and State*, p. 226.

15. Carnegie, "Distant Possessions: The Parting of the Ways" and "Americanism Versus Imperialism" in *Gospel of Wealth*, pp. 120-165.

16. Sumner, *Andrew Jackson*, pp. 33-35, 68, 358-359.

17. Carnegie, *Triumphant Democracy*, pp. 6-7, 27-28.

18. Robin Williams, *American Society: A Sociological Interpretation* (New York: A. A. Knopf, 1963), pp. 8-12.

19. Oliver Lyman Spaulding, *The United States Army in Peace and War* (New York: G. P. Putnam's Sons, 1937), pp. 342-344.

20. Wyllie, *Self-Made Man*, pp. 34-54, 94 ff.

21. Gabriel, *American Democratic Thought*, p. 165.

22. Frederick W. Farrar as quoted by Wyllie, *Self-Made Man*, p. 9.

23. John W. Masland and Laurence I. Radway, *Soldiers and Scholars: Military Education and National Policy* (Princeton: Princeton University Press, 1957), pp. 4-5.

24. Donald W. Smythe, "The Early Years of General John J. Pershing, 1860-1917" (Ph.D. diss., Department of History, Georgetown, 1961), pp. 39-77; "Editorial Notes," *United Services* 4 (January 1881): pp. 126-127.

25. William G. H. Carter, *West Point in Literature* (Baltimore: Lord Baltimore Press, 1909), p. 870; Stephen E. Ambrose, *Duty, Honor, Country: A History of West Point* (Baltimore: Johns Hopkins Press, 1966), pp. 191-218; Huntington, *Soldier and State*, pp. 266-269.

CHAPTER ELEVEN

1. I have found no detailed first- or secondhand treatise summing up the labor-populist views of the military, but the picture can be pieced together. There are ample, though often highly charged, accounts of the emergence of big labor, the resultant wave of strikes, and the inevitable involvement of federal toops. Philip S. Foner, *History of the Labor Movement in the United States*, 2 vols. (New York: International Publishers, 1955) is a sympathetic treatment of the labor viewpoint, and Matthew Josephson in *The Politicos, 1865-1896* (New York: Harcourt, Brace and

World, 1938) gives "a procession of bullet-headed generals, cruel-lipped captains of industry, political charlatans and machine bosses who crowd the annals of our bourgeois republic." Colonel Elwell S. Otis, "The Army in Connection With the Labor Riots of 1877," *Journal of the Military Service Institution. . . ,* V (1884), pp. 292-322, and Winthrop Alexander, "Ten Years of Riot Duty," *Journal of the Military Service Institution . . .* 19 (July 1896): 1-62, are firsthand accounts from the Army and National Guard sides of the story. Robert V. Bruce, *1877: Year of Violence* (Indianapolis: Bobbs-Merrill Co., Inc., 1959) is a balanced and detailed study of the eventful opening year of military-labor confrontations.

2. Henry George, *The Menace of Privilege* (New York: Grosset and Dunlap, 1907), pp. 221-222.

3. Quoted by Foner, *History of Labor*, I, p. 471.

4. Quoted by Arthur A. Ekirch, Jr., *The Civilian and the Military* (New York: Oxford University Press, 1956), p. 117.

5. Russell F. Weigley, *History of the United States Army* (New York: The Macmillan Co., 1967), p. 281; C. Joseph Bernardo and Eugene H. Bacon, *American Military Policy: Its Development Since 1775* (Harrisburg, Pa.: Military Publishing Co., 1961), pp. 240-241; Alexander, "Ten Years of Riot Duty," p. 1 ff.; Josephson, *Politicos*, pp. 255, 563, 574-587; Frederick T. Wilson, "Federal Aid in Domestic Disturbances," Supplement to Senate Document 209, 57th Cong., 2d Sess. (Washington: Government Printing Office, 1923); Oliver Lyman Spaulding, *The United States Army in Peace and War* (New York: G. P. Putnam's Sons, 1937), pp. 369-372.

6. George, *Menace of Privilege*, pp. 203, 221 ff.; Josephson, *Politicos*, p. 255.

7. Gompers is quoted by Leonard D. White, *The Republican Era, 1869-1901* (New York: The Macmillan Co., Inc., 1958), p. 136, and Weigley, *History of the Army*, p. 282; Foner, *History of Labor*, II, p. 233.

8. "Editorial Notes," *United Service* 4 (1881): 256, 515-516; Gen. George B. McClellan, "Army Organization," *Harper's New Monthly Magazine* 49 (August 1874): 401 ff.; John M. Schofield, *An Address . . . at the U. S. Military Academy*, August 11, 1879 (West Point: U.S.M.A. Press, 1879); Capt. E. L. Zalinski, "The Future of Warfare," *North American Review* 151 (December 1890): 693.

9. Major General James B. Fry, "Origins and Progress of the Military Service Institution of the United States," *Journal of the Military Service Institution . . .* 1 (1879): 30.

10. Captain George F. Price, "The Necessity for Closer Relations. . . ," *Journal of the Military Service Institution* . . . 6 (December 1885): 329-332.

11. Foster Rhea Dulles, *Labor in America, A History* (New York: Thomas Y. Crowell Co., 1960), p. 121 ff.

12. W. R. Greg, "Popular Versus Professional Armies," *Contemporary Review* 16 (December 1870-March 1871): 351-373.

13. George, *Menace of Privilege*, p. 224.

14. Josiah Fletcher, "The Army and the People," a letter to *Journal of the Military Service Institution* . . . 7 (March 1886): 103.

15. Quoted by Ekirch, *Civilian and Military*, p. 116.

CHAPTER TWELVE

1. Postbellum political criticism was directed less at the aristocratic clique, symbolized in Jacksonian eyes by West Point, and more at the entire regular army as a useless burden than had been the case a generation earlier. *The Congressional Globe* (Washington, D.C.: Office of the Globe, 1835-1873) and *Congressional Record* (Washington, D.C.: Government Printing Office, 1873-1899) provide a running account of the debate over military expenditures and associated commentary on the army's leaders. They can be supplemented by writings of central figures. John A. Logan, *The Volunteer Soldier of America* (Chicago: R. S. Peak, 1887) is the fullest, though not fully representative, critical treatment. James A. Garfield, "The Army of the United States," *North American Review* 126 (March, June 1878) provides (in two installments) a lengthy defense of the military professionals, and in doing so also calls attention to the most persistent lines of attack. Leonard D. White, *The Republican Era, 1869-1901* (New York: The Macmillan Co., 1958), pp. 136-145 is the best summation.

2. [Godkin], "Congress on the Army," *The Nation* 26 (May 30, 1878): 352-353.

3. Honorable John A. Logan, *The Congressional Globe*, 41st Cong., 2d Sess., p. 2280. And see Samuel P. Huntington, *The Soldier and the State* (Cambridge, Mass.: Belknap Press, 1957), pp. 203-211.

4. White, *Republican Era*, p. 134.

5. *The Congressional Globe*, 40th Cong., 2d Sess., p. 1232; 40th Cong., 3d Sess., pp. 925-928; Arthur A. Ekirch, *The Civilian and*

the Military (New York: Oxford University Press, 1956), pp. 112-113; Garfield, "Army of the U. S.," p. 463; Joseph C. Bernardo and Eugene H. Bacon, *American Military Policy: Its Development Since 1775* (Harrisburg, Pa.: Military Publishing Co., 1961), pp. 236-239.

6. Oliver Lyman Spaulding, *The United States Army in Peace and War* (New York: G. P. Putnam's Sons, 1937), p. 369; Russell F. Weigley, *History of the United States Army* (New York: The Macmillan Co., 1967), pp. 270-271; William Addleman Ganoe, *The History of the United States Army* (New York: Appleton-Century Co., 1942), pp. 348-349; Bernardo and Bacon, *American Military Policy*, p. 239.

7. Thomas Nast, "Smashing and Tinkering," an illustration in *Harper's Weekly* 22 (March 16, 1878): 217; White, *Republican Era*, p. 137 ff.

8. Emory Upton, as quoted by Bernardo and Bacon, *American Military Policy*, pp. 290-291; John Gibbon, "Needed Reforms in the Army," *North American Review* 156 (February 1893): 215-217; Millis, *Arms and Men* (New York: G. P. Putnam's Sons, 1956), pp. 136-140; Weigley, *History of the Army*, pp. 285-289.

9. *The Congressional Globe*, 41st Cong., 2d Sess., Appendix, pp. 146-154, 2275-2280; Ekirch, *Civilian and Military*, pp. 113-114; Russell F. Weigley, *Towards an American Army* (New York: Columbia University Press, 1962), pp. 127-136. Logan's *The Volunteer Soldier* is a 700-page Jacksonian-come-lately attack on the regular army that praises civilian soldiers and characterizes regulars as autocratic and aristocratic. Logan typifies an element of postwar hostility that developed from unhappy Civil War experiences. In overview, it seems impressive that the regulars and civilian-soldiers worked together with as little friction as they did, yet there were a number of talented men like Logan and educator Francis Parker who, with varying degrees of justification, emerged with a deep distaste for regular officers. Logan, who had been denied a corps command by Sherman, was one.

10. Ganoe, *History of the Army*, pp. 352-354; White, *Republican Era*, pp. 135, 144; Weigley, *Towards an American Army*, pp. 137-139; Spaulding, *Army in Peace and War*, pp. 344-348 ff.; Frederick P. Powers, "West Point, the Army and the Militia," *Lippincott's Magazine* 40 (July 1887): 123 ff.

11. Bland, quoted by Ekirch, *Civilian and Military*, p. 116. The army's rebuttal was voiced by Spaulding, "The whole story is a

sad one. . . . The Army made no wars; as always someone else made the wars, and the Army, coming in when all other agencies had lost control, ended them. . . . When called into action its measures were the most moderate possible in conditions which made moderation difficult. . . ." Spaulding, *Army in Peace and War*, p. 368.

12. Weigley, *Towards an American Army*, pp. 162-190, focuses on this problem and the efforts of General Schofield and others to solve the riddle of how to achieve clear command lines and competent leadership at the top, yet subordination of the military to the civilian. See also Huntington, *Soldier and State*, p. 229 ff.; Bernardo and Bacon, *American Military Policy*, pp. 251-256.

CHAPTER THIRTEEN

1. The image of the national defender—reliable, industrious, and essential to America's welfare—was common to the supporters of the army in government, in education, in religion, and in the biographies of Civil War leaders. Walter Millis' anthology on *American Military Thought* (Indianapolis: Bobbs-Merrill, 1966) is again helpful. I have found no comprehensive studies of the religious leaders' or educators' views on war or the military profession, although Merle Curti, *Social Ideas of American Educators* (Patterson, N. J.: Pageant Books, 1959) and James Ward Smith and A. Leland Jamison, eds., *Religion in American Life*, 4 vols. (Princeton: Princeton University Press, 1961-1967) are helpful both in providing intellectual background and directing further research. It was Grant who most conspicuously personified the utilitarian's conception of the model American soldier, and it is the biographies following his death which most vividly present that picture.

2. John William DeForest, "Our Military Past and Future," *Atlantic Monthly* 44 (November 1879): 575.

3. Reverend P. W. Lyman, *The Career and Character of Ulysses S. Grant* (n.p., John L. Montague, Printer, 1885), pp. 14-15.

4. Winfield S. Hancock and James A. Garfield, from *House and Senate Joint Committee Report*, Senate Report, 555, 45th Cong., 3d Sess., II, pp. 121-125, 426-428 reprinted in Millis, ed., *American Military Thought*, pp. 163-179.

5. Francis Wayland, Jr., *Address of the President of the Board of*

Visitors to the Graduating Class of 1874, U. S. Military Academy, West Point (New York: D. van Nostrand, 1874), p. 4.

6. Lyman, *Career and Character*, pp. 8, 14-15; W. A. Clebsch, "Christian Interpretations of the Civil War," *Church History* 30 (June 1961): 221 ff.

7. Francis A. Walker, "Hancock in the War of the Rebellion," a paper read at the New York Commandery, February 4, 1891, p. 4.

8. Curti, *Educators*, pp. 41-49; William James, *Memories and Studies* (New York: Longmanns, Green, and Co., 1911).

9. Theophilus F. Rodenbough, *The National Defense: An Address at the Pennsylvania Military Academy, June 15, 1887* (New York: Public Service Publishing Co., 1887), p. 8; Russell F. Weigley, *History of the United States Army* (New York: The Macmillan Co., 1967), pp. 282-283; Curti, *Educators*, pp. 408-409; John W. Masland and Laurence I. Radway, *Soldiers and Scholars: Military Education and National Policy* (Princeton: Princeton University Press, 1957), pp. 79-80.

10. Curti, *Educators*, pp. 50-63, 194-200, 581-591; Daniel C. Gilman, *An Address Delivered to the Graduating Class of the United States Military Academy . . . June 16, 1897* (New York: D. van Nostrand, 1875), p. 19.

11. Frederick Perry Powers, "West Point, the Army and the Militia," *Lippincott's Magazine* 40 (July 1887): 111-126; *U. S. Military Academy, West Point: Boards of Visitors, Annual Reports* (Washington, D.C., Government Printing Office, 1819-to date). Compare Reports for 1884, pp. 11-17; 1885, p. 8; 1886, pp. 16-18. Paralleling the changing tone of the 1885 Board of Visitors, a growing willingness to attack military engineering is evident in the technical journals. An excellent illustration is a series of attacks and rejoinders appearing in *Engineering Magazine* in 1892, in which the Corps of Engineers is characterized as being corrupted at the source, i.e., at West Point; George Y. Wismer, "Worthless Government Engineering," *Engineering Magazine* 2 (January 1892): 427-434; with reply by Lt. Col. W. R. King, II, p. 664; and rejoinder in II, p. 743.

12. Masland and Radway, *Soldiers and Scholars*, p. 86.

13. Charles W. Eliot, *Four American Leaders* (Boston: American Unitarian Association, 1907), pp. 35-53; Eliot, "Heroes of the Civil War," *American Contributions to Civilization and Other Essays and Addresses* (New York: Century Co., 1898), p. 368; James Gordon

Steese, "Memorandum on the Criticism of West Point by Dr. Charles W. Eliot," (Washington: n.p., 1920), in the Archives of the U. S. Military Academy Library.

14. Curti, *Educators*, pp. 204, 346 ff., 369-370, 413-414. See also "Charles W. Eliot," "Francis Parker," "David Starr Jordan," in *Dictionary of American Biography*, 21 vols. (New York: Charles Scribner's Sons, 1928-1937).

15. Thomas Wentworth Higginson, "Grant," *Atlantic Monthly* 57 (March 1886): 384-388; "Grant's Memoirs, Second Volume," *Atlantic Monthly* 58 (1887): 419-424; "Some War Scenes Revisited," *Atlantic Monthly* 42 (July 1878): 1-9.

16. Hamlin Garland, "Life of Ulysses Grant," *McClure's Magazine* 8-9 (1896-1897); published later as *Ulysses S. Grant: His Life and Character* (New York: Doubleday and McClure Co., 1898), pp. vi-vii, 83, 107, 161-176.

CHAPTER FOURTEEN

1. Countless postbellum biographies of Civil War leaders were sentimental appreciations in a last great tribute to military gentlemanship, especially when they dealt with men like Generals Lee, Gordon, Thomas, Sheridan, Pickett, Jackson, Custer, and Stuart. (Representative accounts are listed in Section 1A of the Bibliography.) Some historians, too, were still picturing officers as nineteenth-century Galahads. These will be touched on briefly in the following chapter. Here I have chosen to concentrate on the image presented by the literary artists and critics, for as a group they appear to represent both the general attitudes of the postbellum period and the adjustments being made. In addition to the writings listed below, lesser known but competent works like John Esten Cooke, *Surrey of Eagle's Nest* (New York: Bunce and Huntington, 1866); Dr. S. Weir Mitchell, *In Wartime* (Boston: Houghton, Mifflin and Co., 1885); and Joseph Kirkland, *The Captain of Company K* (Chicago: Dibble Publishing Co., 1891) are equally revealing.

2. William Dean Howells, "Editor's Study," *Harper's New Monthly Magazine* 82 (January 1891): 317.

3. Honorable George W. Houk, *Report of the Annual Board of*

Visitors . . . [*1884*] (Washington, D.C.: Government Printing Office, 1884), p. 17. Also printed separately as *Address Delivered . . . at the Graduating Exercises, West Point . . . 1884* (West Point, 1884).

4. Irvin G. Wyllie, *The Self-Made Man in America* (New Brunswick, N. J.: Rutgers University Press, 1954), pp. 133-150; [Oliver Wendell Holmes], "A Review of *The Life of Major John Andre* . . . by Winthrop Sargent," *Atlantic Monthly* 28 (July 1871): 121-122; Samuel Langhorne Clemens and Charles Dudley Warner, *The Gilded Age; A Tale of Today*, 2 vols. (New York: Trident Press, 1964), II, pp. 9-10.

5. Houk, *Report*, p. 12; Garfield, "The Army of the United States," *North American Review* 126 (June 1878): 463.

6. Howells, "Editor's Study," p. 317.

7. Howells, "A Review of *The Life of Nathaniel Greene* . . . by George Washington Greene," *Atlantic Monthly* 21 (April 1868): 506-508; see also the reviews of the second and third volumes in 27 (June 1871) and 28 (October 1871), various pagination.

8. Howells, "Editor's Study," pp. 316-317; "A Review of *Memorials of the Confederate Generals* . . . by W. H. Trescott and *Oration on* . . . *General Thomas* by James A. Garfield," *Atlantic Monthly* 28 (July 1871): 124-126; "A Review of *Miss Ravenel's Conversion from Secession to Loyalty* by J. W. DeForest," *Atlantic Monthly* 20 (July 1867): 120-123.

9. Harriet Waters Preston, "Poganuc People and Other Novels," *Atlantic Monthly* 42 (October 1878): 430-437.

10. Wilfred E. Burton, "The Novels of Captain Charles King," (Ph.D. diss., Department of English, New York University, 1963); Aloysius A. Norton, "A Study of the Customs and Traditions of West Point in the American Novel" (Master of Arts thesis, English Department, Columbia University, 1950), pp. 93-95; Howells, "Editor's Study," p. 317.

11. Lucy Hazard, *The Frontier in American Literature* (New York: Frederick Ungar Publishing Co., Inc., 1961), pp. 73-78. Miss Hazard's generalization is well-founded, though it can be over-applied. Thomas Nelson Page's poignant little tale about "The Burying of the Guns" by a Confederate artillery battery following news of the surrender of Appomatox features a pseudoprofessional who is a fascinating combination of planter aristocracy and

modern soldiership, a courtly gentleman who nevertheless demands of his troops strict discipline and efficient training. Thomas Nelson Page, "The Burial of the Guns," in *Warner Library of the World's Best Literature*, ed. Charles Dudley Warner, 30 vols. (New York: Peale and Hill, 1897), 19, 10939-10960.

12. David Belasco, "The Heart of Maryland," and William Gillette, "Secret Service," in *The Best Plays of 1894-1899*, eds. John Chapman and Garrison P. Sherwood (New York: Dodd, Mead and Co., 1955); William Dunlap, *Andre: A Tragedy in Five Acts* (New York: The Dunlap Society, 1887); Richard Moody, *America Takes the Stage* (Bloomington, Ind.: Indiana University Press, 1955), pp. 150, 160-166.

13. See William I. Thrall and Addison Hibbard, "Naturalism" in *A Handbook to Literature*, rev. by C. Hugh Holman (New York: The Odyssey Press, 1960), pp. 301-304; Spiller, et al., eds., *Literary History of the United States* (New York: The Macmillan Co., 1948), pp. 1016-1038.

14. H. E. Scudder, "Recent American Fiction," *Atlantic Monthly* 55 (January 1885): 123.

15. Ambrose Bierce, *In the Midst of Life* (with an Afterword by Marcus Cunliffe) (New York: New American Library, Inc., 1961), pp. 39-80, 250-253; Bierce's "Tales of Soldiers" and "War Memoirs" are also collected in *Ambrose Bierce's Civil War*, ed. William McCann (New York: Gateway Editions, Inc., 1956); see especially pp. v-viii, 38-49, 108-117.

16. Stephen Crane, *The Red Badge of Courage* in *The Work of Stephen Crane*, ed., Wilson Follett (New York: Russell and Russell, 1963), I; Spiller, *Literary History*, pp. 1020-1022; Arthur Hobson Quinn, *American Fiction, An Historical and Critical Survey* (New York: D. Appleton-Century Co., Inc., 1936), pp. 533-535; Edward Charles Wagenknecht, *Cavalcade of the American Novel* (New York: Henry Holt and Co., 1952), pp. 214-216: Robert U. Underwood and Clarence C. Buel, eds., *Battles and Leaders of The Civil War*, 4 vols. (New York: The Century Co., 1884-1887).

17. A. C. McC., "The Red Badge of Hysteria," a letter to *Dial* 20 (April 16, 1896): 227-228.

18. Crane, "Virtue in War," in *Work*, II, pp. 177-196. Compare "The Second Generation" in *Work*, II, pp. 231-259.

19. Howells, "Editor's Study," pp. 316-317.

SECTION FIVE

1. Alfred Kazin, *On Native Grounds* (New York: Doubleday and Co., Inc., 1956), p. 37; Henry May, *The End of American Innocence* (New York: A. A. Knopf, 1959); Henry Steele Commager, *The American Mind* (New Haven: Yale University Press, 1963); Arthur Link, *The American Epoch* (New York: A. A. Knopf, 1959). See too, Harold U. Faulkner, *Politics, Reform and Expansion: 1890-1900*, (New York: Harper Co., 1959); Ray Ginger, *Altgeld's America* (New York: Funk and Wagnalls, 1958); Sidney Fine, *Laissez Faire and the General Welfare State* (Ann Arbor: University of Michigan Press, 1956); Eric Goldman, *Rendezvous with Destiny* (New York: A. A. Knopf, 1952); Ralph Gabriel, "The Religion of Humanity," *The Course of American Democratic Thought* (New York: The Roland Press Co., 1940), pp. 183-207; Richard Hofstadter, *Anti-Intellectualism in the United States* (New York: A. A. Knopf, 1963), pp. 389-407 ff.

2. James Harvey Robinson, *The New History* (New York: Macmillan Co., 1912); David L. Hoggan, *The Myth of the 'New History'* (Nutley, N. J.: The Craig Press,1965); Harry E. Barnes, *The New History and Social Studies* (New York: Century Co., 1912); Commager, *American Mind*, pp. 277-292.

CHAPTER FIFTEEN

1. The social-intellectual ferment and America's imperialistic impulses at the end of the century would have, if not immediately so, profound influences on the military image. The background material is extensive. In addition to those works cited in Note 1, Section V, Albert K. Weinberg, *Manifest Destiny: A Study of Nationalist Expansionism in American History* (Baltimore: The Johns Hopkins Press, 1938); Julius W. Pratt, *Expansionists of 1898: The Acquisition of Hawaii and the Spanish Islands* (Baltimore: The Johns Hopkins Press, 1936); and Walter Millis, *The Martial Spirit: A Study of Our War with Spain* (Boston: Houghton, Mifflin Co., 1931) are basic, though tinted by the spirit of the 1930s as well as the 1890s. Foster Rhea Dulles, *The Imperial Years* (New York: Thomas Y. Crowell Co., 1956) is more recent and balanced. In the writings of the day, impressions of the military men can be found in almost any area; but once again they must be sifted from works on tan-

gential subjects. The best summation (though often representative of rather extreme views) is in the magazines, which by this time were becoming less literary and more interested in current problems.

2. A. B. Ronne, "The Spirit of Militarism," *The Popular Science Monthly* 47 (June 1895): 234-239.

3. Twain as quoted by Louis J. Budd, *Mark Twain: Social Philosopher* (Bloomington, Inc.: Indiana University Press, 1962), p. 183.

4. Captain A. H. Russell, "What is the Use of a Regular Army in This Country?," *Journal of the Military Service Institution* . . . 24 (January 1899): 216; first printed in November 1896.

5. Robert U. Johnson and Clarence C. Buel, eds., *Battles and Leaders of the Civil War*, 4 vols. (New York: The Century Co., 1884-1888); Frank J. Cavaioli, *West Point and the Presidency* (New York: St. John's University Press, 1962), pp. 91-100; Walter Evan Davies, *Patriotism on Parade* (Cambridge, Mass.: Harvard University Press, 1955), pp. 189-214; E. L. Godkin, "The Meaning Grant's Election Would Have," *The Nation* 30 (June 3, 1880): 402-413.

6. Michael Kraus, *The Writings of American History* (Norman, Okla.: University of Oklahoma Press, 1953), p. 257 ff.; Harvey Wish, *The American Historian* (New York: Oxford University Press, 1960), pp. 265-269; Hugh Hale Bellot, *American History and American Historians* (Norman, Okla.: University of Oklahoma Press, 1952), pp. 1-36; Harry E. Barnes, *The New History and Social Studies* (New York: The Century Co., 1912); Commager, "The Transition in Historical Literature" in *The American Mind*, pp. 277-292; David L. Hoggan, *The Myth of the "New History"* (Nutley, N.J.: The Craig Press, 1965), pp. 213-225.

7. Milton Berman, *John Fiske: The Evolution of a Popularizer* (Cambridge, Mass.: Harvard University Press, 1961); and see, e.g., Fiske, *American Revolution*, 2 vols. (Boston: Houghton, Mifflin and Co., 1891), I, pp. 206-243, and *Essays, Historical and Literary* (New York: The Macmillan Co., 1907), pp. 55-98. John Esten Cooke, *Virginia, A History of the People* (New York: Houghton, Mifflin and Co., 1903), pp. 343-347.

8. James Harvey Robinson, *The New History* (New York: Macmillan Co., 1912), p. 1 ff.

9. Moses Coit Tyler, "The Party of the Loyalists in the American Revolution," *American Historical Review* 1 (October 1895): 45;

[Winthrope Sargent] "The Society of the Cincinnati," *North American Review* 77 (October 1853): 267-302.

10. John Bach McMaster, *History of the People of the United States From the Revolution to the Civil War*, 8 vols. (New York: D. Appleton and Co., 1887); Asa Bird Gardiner, "McMaster's History of the People," *Journal of the Military Service Institution. . .* , I (1887), pp. 20-23.

11. Thomas Woodrow Wilson, *Division and Reunion, 1829-1889* (New York: Longmans Green and Co., 1899), pp. 151-152, 251; Colonel Vincent J. Esposito, ed., *The West Point Atlas of American Wars*, 2 vols. (New York: Praeger, Inc., 1959), I, pp. 15-16; Robert Leckie, *The Wars of America* (New York: Harper and Row, 1968), pp. 317-377.

12. Julian Hawthorne, *History of the United States*, 3 vols. (New York: Peter Fenelon Collier, 1898), I, pp. 308-310, 314; II, pp. 843-845.

13. Admiral Stephen D. Luce, "The Benefits of War," *North American Review* 48 (April 1864): 672; J. P. Malla, "Roosevelt, Brooks Adams and Lea; The Warrior Critique of Business Civilization," *American Quarterly* 8 (Fall 1956): 216-230; Robert E. Osgood, *Ideals and Self-Interest in America's Foreign Relations* (Chicago: University of Chicago Press, 1953), pp. 58-91; C. Joseph Bernardo and Eugene H. Bacon, *American Military Policy: Its Development Since 1775* (Harrisburg, Pa.: Military Publishing Co., 1961), pp. 274-281; Weinberg, *Manifest Destiny*; Dulles, *The Imperial Years*, pp. 91-107.

14. Alfred Mahan, *Influence of Sea Power Upon History* (Boston: Little, Brown and Co., 1918); Samuel P. Huntington, *The Soldier and the State* (Cambridge, Mass.: Belknap Press, 1957), pp. 258-260, 270-272; Roosevelt is quoted by Walter Millis, *Arms and Men* (New York: G. P. Putnam's Sons, 1956), pp. 167-170; Richard Hofstadter, *American Political Tradition* (New York: A. A. Knopf, 1948), pp. 206-214; Dulles, *Imperial Years*, pp. 41-43; Lt. L. W. V. Kennan, *The Army: Its Employment During Time of Peace and the Necessity for Its Increase*, an unpublished monograph (awarded first honorable mention in an essay competition sponsored by the U. S. Infantry Society in 1896; the Board of Awards included C. F. Manderson, T. Roosevelt, and General E. A. McAlpin), p. 7.

15. Luce, "Benefits of War," pp. 675-683; Kennan, *The Army*, pp. 1-3; Richard Hofstadter, *Social Darwinism in American Thought* (Boston: Beacon Press, 1955), pp. 173-184; Roosevelt is quoted

by Dulles, *Imperial Years*, p. 118; Mahan, "The United States Looking Outward," *Atlantic Monthly* 66 (December 1890): 817-822.

16. Godkin, "Congress on the Army," *The Nation* 26 (May 30, 1878): 352-353; "The Week," *The Nation* 69 (October 12, 1899): 273-274; William Armstrong, *E. L. Godkin and American Foreign Policy* (New York: Bookman Associates, 1957), pp. 14, 185 ff., 236 ff.

17. Samuel Clemens, "The Defense of General Funston" in *The Complete Essays of Mark Twain* (New York: Doubleday, 1963); Matthew Arnold, *General Grant* (with a rejoinder by Mark Twain), ed., John Y. Simon (Carbondale, Ill.: Southern Illinois University Press, 1966); Budd, *Twain*, pp. 168-190; "Huckleberry Finn Visits West Point," *The Pointer* (December 9, 1960), pp. 13, 29.

18. Henry Cabot Lodge, *George Washington* (Boston: Houghton, Mifflin and Co., 1890), pp. 80 ff.

19. Theodore Roosevelt, "Army References," *The Outlook* 63 (December 23, 1899): 915-916; Elihu Root, "Extract from the Report of the Secretary of War for 1899" in Walter Millis, ed., *American Military Thought* (Indianapolis: Bobbs-Merrill, 1966), pp. 240-262; Russell F. Weigley, *History of the United States Army* (New York: The Macmillan Co., 1967), pp. 295-312; Bernardo and Bacon, *American Military Policy*, pp. 277-286. William Addleman Ganoe, *The History of the United States Army* (New York: Appleton-Century Co., 1942), pp. 370-385; Oliver Lyman Spaulding, *The United States Army in Peace and War* (New York: G. P. Putnam's Sons, 1937), pp. 378-380.

20. Huntington, *Soldier and State*, p. 273. Weigley, *Towards an American Army* (New York: Columbia University Press, 1962), p. 147, confirms that "the evidence of the professional journals is that the professional soldiers were by no means in the forefront of the call for an aggressive policy toward Spain."

21. Ronne, "Spirit of Militarism," p. 236.

CHAPTER SIXTEEN

1. Like chapters 2 and 8, this is an exploratory examination. Its goal is to identify—not develop fully—prominent patterns of thought about the military man in twentieth-century America. A broad sampling of sources has been considered here rather than an "in depth" search of any single vein of materials. One espe-

cially rich collection of materials, particularly for the 1950s and 1960s, is William Neale, *The U. S. Military Mind*, unpublished Master's Thesis, Georgetown University, 1958.

2. Eric Goldman, *Rendezvous with Destiny* (New York: A. A. Knopf, 1952); see, e.g., chapters II and III, pp. 10-54.

3. William Carter, "The Army as a Career," *North American Review* 183 (November 1906): 870-876.

4. Senator Carl Schurz, "Manifest Destiny," *Harper's Monthly Magazine* 137 (October 1893): 737-746.

5. Hofstadter, *Age of Reform* (New York: A. A. Knopf, 1955), p. 85 ff.

6. Bernard Mandel, *Samuel Gompers* (New York: Antioch Press, 1963), pp. 199-206; "Nelson Miles," *Dictionary of American Biography*, 21 vols. (New York: Charles Scribner's Sons, 1928-1937), p. 615; Newton F. Tolman, *The Search for General Miles* (New York: G. P. Putnam's Sons, 1968), pp. 182-185 ff.; 228-230 ff.

7. Millis, *Road to War* (Boston: Houghton, Mifflin and Co., 1935), p. 37 ff., 91-93, 209-211, 254.

8. Harry F. Ward, "Free Speech for The Army," *The New Republic* 51 (July 13, 1927): 196.

9. Stuart Chase, "The Tragedy of Waste," *The New Republic* 43 (August 12, 1925): 312-316.

10. Lewis Mumford, *Technics and Civilization* (New York: Harcourt, Brace and Co., 1934), pp. 91-95 ff.

11. C. Wright Mills, *The Power Elite* (New York: Oxford University Press, 1956). See especially chapters 8 and 9.

12. Mumford, "No: 'A Symbolic Act of War. . . ,' " *New York Times* (July 21, 1969), p. 6.

13. Merle Curti, *American Peace Crusade* (Durham, N. C.: Duke University Press, 1929); and see Edward M. Burns, *The American Idea of Mission* (New Brunswick, N.J.: Rutgers University Press, 1957).

14. T. M. Pease, "Does the Military Caste System Work in War?" *New Republic* 20 (August 6, 1919): 27-28; Mary Beard, *America Through Women's Eyes* (New York: Macmillan Co., 1933), pp. 475-476; "Revolution via Militarism," *New Republic* 42 (March 18, 1925): 86-88.

15. John Dos Passos, *Three Soldiers* (Boston: Doubleday, Doran and Co., 1921); see, e.g., pp. 109, 259, 375, 446, 466.

16. Pearl S. Buck, "The Mind of The Militarist," *Asia* 38 (January 1938): 9-10.

17. Mauritz A. Hallgren, "War," in Harold Stearns, ed., *America Now* (New York: Charles Scribner's Sons, 1938).

18. Henry Siedel Canby, "Footnotes to 1949," *Saturday Review of Literature* (August 6, 1949), p. 19 ff.; Kazin, "Mindless Young Militarists: The Hero-Victims of the American War Novel," *Commentary* 6 (December 1948): 495-501.

19. William Saroyan, *The Adventures of Wesley Jackson* (New York: Harcourt, Brace and Co., 1946), p. 123; Norman Mailer, *The Naked and The Dead* (New York: Rinehart and Co., 1948); John Hersey, *A Bell for Adano* (New York: The Modern Library, 1946). Pertinent parts of these and other "war novels" are quoted more fully by Neale, "The U.S. Military Mind."

20. George MacMillan, "A Decade of War Novels," *New York Times Book Review* (December 9, 1951), p. 6.

21. Capt. A. H. Russell, "What is the Use of a Regular Army in This Country?" *Journal of Military Service Institution* . . . 24 (January 1899): 216-231. Although published in 1899, the article was written Nov. 1896.

22. *Harper's Pictorial History of the War with Spain* (New York, n.d.).

23. Sergeant Alvin C. York, *Sergeant York: His Own Life Story* (Garden City, N. Y.: Doubleday, Doran and Co., Inc., 1928), frontispiece. Wilson is quoted by Samuel Huntington, *The Soldier and the State* (Cambridge, Mass.: Harvard University Press, 1957), p. 154. Benedict Crowell and Robert F. Wilson, *How America Went to War: The Armies of Industry* (New Haven, 1921), I, p. xxiii. For other typical postwar military and nationalistic encomia, from hundreds, see [Corporal] Slater Washburn, *One of the YD* (Boston: Houghton, Mifflin Co., 1919); [Captain] Carroll J. Swan, *My Company* (Boston: Houghton, Mifflin and Co., 1918) [dedicated to "The most loyal, the cleanest, the bravest, the best soldier in the world, the American boy in France . . ."]; Major General James G. Harbord, *Leaves From a War Diary* (New York: Dodd, Mead and Co., 1925).

24. John Bach McMaster, *The United States in The World War*, 2 vols. (New York: D. Appleton and Co., 1918), II, pp. 116-119.

25. Wilson as quoted by McMaster, I, p. 460.

26. Some representative views from national periodicals on the

interwar debates about America's soldiery and militarism are: Margery Bedinger, "The Goose Step at West Point," *New Republic* 64 (September 24, 1930): 144-146; W. E. Brougher, "Our Soldier, Friend of Peace," *National Republic* 24 (May 1936): 6-7, 18-19; H. D. Browne, "Student Soldiers in the Making," *Illustrated World* 38 (January 1923): 695-697; E. L. M. Burns, "Mind of the General," *American Mercury* 13 (February 1928): 184-189; E. Colby, "Army Officers at Civilian Colleges," *Education* 44 (June 1924): 629-635; Harvey A. DeWeerd, "Stupidities of the Military," *American Mercury* 33 (December 1934): 414-423; H. C. Engelbrecht, "Army of Men Without Hate," *World Tomorrow* 13 (April 1930): 180-181; M. H. Hedges, "On Trial: Officers Reserve Corps," *Nation* 114 (May 24, 1922): 616; H. L. M[encken], "Editorial," *The American Mercury* 18 (September 1929): 22-24; "Militarizing America's Youth," *Nation* 121 (December 16, 1925): 694; K. Moses, "Our Brutal Soldiery," *Outlook* 134 (May 23, 1923): 43-45; E. A. Ross, "Are Militarists Feeble-Minded?" *Nation* 133 (August 19, 1921): 181-183; "Techniques of Army Training," *School and Society* 15 (February 25, 1922): 228-232; E. A. Walker, "Making a Man of Him," *Educational Review* 124 (June 1927): 34-38; "Free Speech for the Army," *The New Republic* 51 (July 13, 1927): 194-196.

27. Harry Hopkins is quoted by Neale; John J. McCloy, "In Defense of the Military Mind," *Harper's Magazine* 194 (April 1947): 341-344. Henry Stimpson is quoted by McCloy, 344.

Selected Bibliography

No single work of which I am aware attempts, as we have here, to identify and trace the nation's diverse conceptions of the military careerist. There are, of course, works which contribute substantially to that end in their treatment of related subjects: American military history, military theory and policy, civil-military relations, and the like.

By far the best balanced military histories are the most recent. Earlier works contain indispensable detail but are generally defensive in outlook. Russell F. Weigley's dispassionate and scholarly *The History of the United States Army* is a major contribution, and the first in a much needed series on American military affairs under the editorship of Louis Morton. Weigley's work focuses on the polarity created by the historical arguments for a professional and for a citizen army. It is complemented by his *Towards An American Army*, a study of "the ideas on military policy expressed by professional soldiers." Walter Millis' solid and lucid *Arms and Men* relates U.S. military theory and practice to formative economic and political forces as seen in six distinguishable periods. T. Harry Williams' brief but thoughtful *Americans at War* is another that has gone beyond the narrower focus of earlier, more strictly military, histories in examining how this country has conducted its wartime affairs.

More in the area of civil and military relationships, Samuel Huntington's probing *The Soldier and the State* broke ground for the work here some years ago. His book is primarily concerned (as its sub-title says) with discovering "The Theory and Politics of Civil-Military Relations"; but in setting the historical-intellectual background, Huntington provides perceptive observations on the nation's attitudes toward its military men, especially as reflected in the political record. (Allen Guttman's chapter on "Conservatism and the Military Establishment" in *The Conservative Tradition in*

America is a recent and provocative critique of Huntington's work.) Joseph Bernardo's and Eugene Bacon's *American Military Policy* traces policy development at the governmental level from 1775, and in doing so gives favorable treatment to the Army's political problems. The sections on military affairs in Leonard B. White's studies of federal administrative history, *The Jacksonians,* . . . *1829-1861*, and *The Republican Era, 1869-1901*, provide excellent summations of governmental-military associations in the nineteenth century.

In some ways, Arthur Ekirch's *The Civilian and the Military* coincides most closely with the effort made here. It traces—with obvious sympathy—"the tradition of antimilitarism" in American thought, employing not only political records, but making full use of liberal journals and pacifist writings. (There is no counterpart to Ekirch's work. No one has fully considered, to my knowledge, the great volume of "promilitary" writings—novels, histories, periodical pieces, drama, biographies, and the like—which for over a century consistently celebrated the "virtues" of the military leader.) I have included the "antimilitary strain," here in the forms I have found it, but along with other points of view.

Soldiers and Civilians: The Martial Spirit in America, 1775-1865, by Marcus Cunliffe, was not available during the preparation of much of this study. It, too, takes a broad-based approach, though more restricted in time frame, and overlaps this work in several areas. Cunliffe's study, however, is more concerned with bringing to life selected elements of America's military attitudes in the period between the Revolution and the Civil War than in identifying the social-intellectual forces behind them. Rich with descriptive detail, its chapters, viewed in perspective, provide a mosaic rather than an analysis of the nation's martial spirit. Nor does it focus on the country's changing conception of the military leader, as we have attempted to do here.

Histories, biographies, scholarly works written in the period under consideration, and contemporary cultural studies—although they usually make little mention of the military man as a military man—were essential to this investigation, but they are far too numerous to mention. Some, typical and useful, are included in the list following. Sources found particularly helpful for each of the interior chapters are discussed in note No. 1 for Chapters 2 through 16.

Because the epilogue, Chapter 16, was added later, as an extension, the bibliography does not include works cited in that chapter, unless they were especially useful in the main text. Hundreds of valuable sources on attitudes toward the military since World War I have been consulted which will, hopefully, be employed in a planned second volume. The end-note section of Chapter 16, however, does provide a rather ample sampling of typical twentieth century materials.

I. Primary Sources

IA. Books, Nonfiction

Adams, Henry. *History of the United States of America During the Administration of Jefferson and Madison (1885-1891)*. 9 vols. New York: C. Scribner's Sons, 1889-1891.

Allen, Paul. *A History of the American Revolution.* . . . Baltimore: J. Hopkins, 1819.

American Military and Political Biography. n.p.: "Printed for subscribers," 1825.

Andrews, E. Benjamin. *A History of the United States*. New York: Charles Scribner's Sons, 1895.

Bancroft, George. *History of the United States of America.* . . . 6 vols. New York: D. Appleton, 1887.

Barnard, Henry. *Military Schools and Courses of Instruction in the Science and Art of War.* . . . New York: E. Steiger, 1872.

———. *National Education*. New York: E. Steiger, 1872.

Boynton, Capt. Edward C. *History of West Point.* . . . New York: D. Van Nostrand, 1863.

Buckingham, James Silk. *The Eastern and Western States of America*. London: Fisher, Son, and Co., 1842.

Burk, John Daly. *The History of Virginia, from Its First Settlement.* . . . 3 vols. Petersburg, Va.: Dickson and Pescud, printers, 1822.

Burr, Frank A. and Richard J. Hinton. *"Little Phil" and His Troopers. The Life of General Philip H. Sheridan.* . . . *How an Humble Lad Reached the Head of an Army*. Providence: J. A. and R. A. Reid, 1888.

Calvert, George H. *The Gentlemen*. Boston: Ticknor and Fields, 1863.

Carnegie, Andrew. *Triumphant Democracy; or, Fifty Years' March of the Republic.* New York: C. Scribner, 1886.

Clausewitz, Karl von. *On War.* Translated by O. J. Matthis Jollis. New York: Random House, 1943.

Cooke, John Esten. *Outlines from the Outpost.* Edited by Richard Harwell. Chicago: Lakeside Press, 1961.

———. *Virginia, A History of the People.* New York: Houghton, Mifflin and Co., 1903.

Cooper, James Fenimore. *The American Democrat.* . . . New York: Vintage Books, 1956.

———. *Notions of the Americans Picked Up by a Travelling Bachelor.* 2 vols. New York: Frederick Ungar Publishing Co., 1963.

DeForest, John William. *A Union Officer in the Reconstruction.* New Haven: Yale University Press, 1948.

Delafield, Major Richard. *Report on the Art of War in Europe in 1854, 1855, and 1856.* Washington: George W. Bowman, 1860.

Eliot, Charles W. *Four American Leaders.* Boston: American Unitarian Association, 1907.

Emerson, Ralph Waldo. *Representative Men.* Boston: J. R. Osgood and Co., 1876.

Fiske, John. *The American Revolution.* 2 vols. Boston and New York: Houghton, Mifflin, and Co., 1891.

———. *Outlines of Cosmic Philosophy, Based on the Doctrine of Evolution.* 2 vols. Boston: Houghton, Mifflin, and Co., 1874.

Garland, Hamlin. *Ulysses S. Grant: His Life and Character.* New York: Doubleday and McClure Co., 1898.

George, Henry. *The Menace of Privilege.* New York: Grosset and Dunlap, 1907.

———. *Social Problems.* London: Kegan, 1884.

Griswold, Rufus Wilmot (ed.). *Washington and the Generals of the American Revolution.* 2 vols. Philadelphia: Carey and Hart, 1846.

Grund, Francis. *The Americans in Their Moral, Social, and Political Relations.* 2 vols. London: Longman, *et al.,* 1837.

———. *Aristocracy in America.* 2 vols. London: R. Bentley, 1839.

Hawthorne, Julian. *History of the United States.* 3 vols. New York: Peter Fenelon Collier, 1898.

Hildreth, Richard. *The History of the United States of America.* 6 vols. New York: Harper and Brothers, 1880.

Ingersoll, L. D. *History of the War Department of the United States.* Washington: F. B. Mohun, 1879.

Irving, Washington. *The Adventures of Captain Bonneville, U.S.A.* Edited by Edgeley W. Todd. Norman, Okla.: University of Oklahoma Press, 1961.

———. *Life of George Washington.* 3 vols. New York: G. P. Putnam and Co., 1855-1859.

Latrobe, Charles J. *The Rambler in North America.* 2 vols. New York: Harper and Brothers, 1835.

Life of John C. Calhoun: Presenting a Condensed History of Political Events from 1811 to 1843. New York: Harper and Brothers, 1843.

Lodge, Henry Cabot. *George Washington.* Boston and New York: Houghton, Mifflin and Co., 1890.

Logan, Maj-Gen. John A. *The Volunteer Soldier of America.* Chicago and New York: R. S. Peale, 1887.

McClellan, George Brinton. *The Armies of Europe.* Philadelphia: Lippincott, 1861.

McMaster, John Bach. *A History of the People of the United States, from the Revolution to the Civil War.* 8 vols. New York: D. Appleton and Co., 1883-1913.

Mahan, Alfred. *The Influence of Sea Power Upon History, 1660-1783.* Boston: Little, Brown and Co., 1918.

Marshall, John. *The Life of George Washington.* 2 vols. [Philadelphia]: James Crissy and Thomas Couperthwait and Co., 1839.

Neff, Jacob K. *The Army and Navy of America.* Philadelphia: J. H. Pearsol and Co., 1845.

Parkman, Francis. *The Conspiracy of Pontiac.* Boston: Little, Brown and Co., 1913.

———. *The Oregon Trail.* Boston: Little, Brown and Co., 1873.

Robinson, James Harvey. *The New History: Essays Illustrating the Modern History Outlook.* New York: Macmillan Co., 1912.

Rodenbough, Theophilus, and William L. Haskin (eds.). *The Army of the United States.* New York: Maynard, Merrill and Co., 1896.

Rogers, Thomas J. *A New American Biographical Dictionary.* Easton, Pa.: T. J. Rogers, 1823.

Simms, William Gilmore. *The History of South Carolina.* New York: Redfield, 1860.

————. *The Life of Nathanael Greene, Major-General in the Army of the Revolution.* New York: Cooledge and Brother, [c. 1849].

Sparks, Jared (ed.). *The Library of American Biography.* 25 vols. Boston: Hilliard, Gray and Co., 1834-1848.

————. *The Life and Treason of Benedict Arnold.* New York: Harper and Brothers, 1854.

Spencer, Herbert. *The Principles of Sociology.* 3 vols. New York: D. Appleton and Co., 1880-1896.

Strong, Rev. Josiah. *Our Country: Its Possible Future and Its Present Crisis (1885).* Cambridge: Belknap Press, 1963.

Sumner, William Graham. *Andrew Jackson as a Public Man.* Boston: Houghton, Mifflin and Co., 1882.

————. *What Social Classes Owe to Each Other.* Caldwell, Ida.: Caxton Printers, 1954.

Thomas, Richard H. *Militarism, or Military Fever: Its Causes, Dangers, and Cure.* Philadelphia: no publisher listed, 1899.

Ticknor, Anna, and G. D. Hillard (eds.). *Life, Letters, and Journals of George Ticknor.* 2 vols. Boston: James R. Osgood and Co., 1876.

Tocqueville, Alexis de. *Democracy in America.* Edited by Richard D. Heffner. New York: Mentor Books, 1956.

Upton, Emory. *The Armies of Asia and Europe.* New York: D. Appleton, 1878.

————. *The Military Policy of the United States from 1775.* Washington: The U.S. Government Printing Office, 1904.

Walker, Alexander. *Jackson and New Orleans.* New York: J. C. Derby, 1856.

Weems, Mason Locke. *A History of the Life and Death, Virtues and Exploits of General George Washington.* Philadelphia: J. B. Lippincott Co., 1918.

———— and Col. Horry. *The Life of Major General Francis Marion: The Most Celebrated Partisan Officer in the Revolutionary War.* . . . New York: P. M. Davis, 1835.

Wilson, Thomas Woodrow. *Division and Reunion, 1829-1889.* New York and London: Longmans, Green and Co., 1899.

Wright, Frances. *Views of Society and Manners in America.* Edited by Paul R. Baker. Cambridge: Belknap Press, 1963.

IB. Fiction and Drama

Adams, Henry. *Democracy; An American Novel*. New York: Farrar, Straus and Young, 1952.

Amelia; or, the Faithless Briton. Boston: W. Spotswood and C. P. Wayne, 1798.

Bellamy, Edward. *The Duke of Stockbridge, a Romance of Shay's Rebellion*. Cambridge: Belknap Press, 1962.

Bierce, Ambrose. *Ambrose Bierce's Civil War*. New York: Gateway Editions, Inc., 1956.

———. *The Collected Works*. New York: Neale Publishing Co., 1909-1912.

———. *In the Midst of Life*. (With an Afterword by Marcus Cunliffe.) New York: New American Library, Inc., 1961.

Bird, Robert Montgomery. *Nick of the Woods*. New York: A. L. Burt Co., n.d.

Calvert, George H. *Arnold and Andre: An Historical Drama*. Boston: Lee and Shepard, 1876.

Caruthers, William A. *The Cavaliers of Virginia, or The Recluse of Jamestown*. . . . New York: Harper and Brothers, 1834-1835.

———. *The Knights of the Horseshoe: A Traditionary Tale of the Cocked Hat Gentry in the Old Dominion*. New York: Harper and Brothers, [1882].

Chapman, John and Garrison P. Sherwood (eds.). *The Best Plays of 1894-99*. New York: Dodd, Mead and Co., 1955.

Clemens, Samuel Langhorne and Charles Dudley Warner. *The Gilded Age; A Tale of Today*. 2 vols. New York: Trident Press, 1964.

Cooke, John Esten. *Surrey of Eagle's-Nest; or, The Memoirs of a Staff-Officer*. . . . New York: Bunce and Huntington, 1866.

———. *The Virginia Comedians; or, Old Days in the Old Dominion*. . . . New York: D. Appleton and Co., 1854.

Cooper, James Fenimore. *The Chainbearer; or, the Littlepage Manuscripts*. New York: Hurd and Houghton, 1866.

———. *The Leatherstocking Saga*. Edited by Allan Nevins. New York: Pantheon Books, 1954.

———. *The Spy; or, A Tale of the Neutral Ground*. New York: Dodd, Mead and Co., 1946.

Crane, Stephen. *The Work of Stephen Crane*. Edited by Wilson Follett. New York: Russell and Russell, 1963.

DeForest, John William. *Miss Ravenel's Conversion from Secession to Loyalty.* Edited by Gordon S. Haight. New York: Rinehart Co., 1955.

Drake, Samuel Adams. *Captain Nelson: A Romance of Colonial Days.* New York: Harper's Library of American Fiction, 1879.

Dunlap, William. *Andre: A Tragedy in Five Acts.* New York: The Dunlap Society, 1887.

Fawcett, Edgar. *A Gentleman of Leisure.* Boston: Houghton, Mifflin and Co., 1881.

Fish, Williston. *Won at West Point.* Chicago: Rand, McNally and Co., 1883.

Foster, Hannah. *The Coquette; or, The History of Eliza Wharton.* . . . Boston: Printed by Samuel Etheridge for E. Larkin, 1797.

Hale, Edward E. "The Man Without a Country," *Atlantic Monthly,* XII (December 1863), 665-679.

Hubbell, Horatio. *Arnold; or, The Treason of West Point: A Tragedy, in Five Acts.* Philadelphia: Young, printer, 1897.

Kennedy, John Pendleton. *Swallow Barn; or, A Sojourn in the Old Dominion.* New York: Hafner Publishing Co., 1962.

―――. *Horseshoe Robinson.* Edited by Ernest E. Leisy. New York: Hafner Publishing Co., 1962.

King, Capt. Charles. *Between the Lines.* New York: Harper and Co., 1888.

―――. *The Colonel's Daughter; or, Winning His Spurs.* Philadelphia: J. B. Lippincott Co., 1883.

Kirkland, Joseph. *The Captain of Company K.* Chicago: Dibble Publishing Co., 1891.

Lord, W. W. *Andre; A Tragedy in Five Acts.* New York: Charles Scribner, 1856.

Mitchell, S. Weir. *In Wartime.* Boston: Houghton, Mifflin and Co., 1885.

Moody, Richard (ed.). *Dramas from the American Theater, 1762-1909.* New York: World Publishing Co., 1966.

Noah, M. M. *Marion; or, the Hero of Lake George: A Drama in Three Acts.* . . . New York: E. Murden, 1822.

―――. "She Would Be a Soldier" in *Dramas from the American Theater, 1762-1909.* New York: World Publishing Co., 1966.

Page, Thomas Nelson. "The Burial of the Guns: in *Warner Library of the World's Best Literature.* Vol. 19. New York: Peal and Hill, 10937-10960.

Paulding, James Kirke. *The Old Continental; or, The Price of Liberty.* New York: Paine and Burgess, 1846.

Quinn, Arthur Hobson (ed.). *Representative American Plays, From 1767 to the Present Day.* New York: Appleton-Century-Crofts, Inc., 1953.

Rowson, Susanna. *Charlotte Temple. A Tale of Truth.* New York: Optimus Printing Co., n.d.

Simms, William Gilmore. *Katherine Walton; or, The Rebel of Dorchester.* New York: J. W. Lovell Co., n.d.

————. *The Partisan: A Romance of the Revolution.* New York: Harper and Brothers, 1835.

————. *The Yemassee.* Boston: Houghton, Mifflin and Co., 1961.

Thompson, Daniel Pierce. *The Green Mountain Boys: A Historical Tale.* . . . Boston: Bazin and Ellsworth, n.d.

[Warner, Susan], Elizabeth Wetherell. *Daisy.* London: Ward Lock and Co., Limited, n.d.

IC. Articles and Periodicals

Alexander, Winthrop. "Ten Years of Riot Duty," *Journal of the Military Service Institution of the United States*, XIX (July 1896), 1-62.

[Austin, I. J.] "The Military Academy," *North American Review*, LVII (October 1843), 269-292.

Austin, J. B. "Manifest Destiny," *Lippincott's Magazine*, IV (August 1869), 183-186.

Berwich, Edward. "American Militarism," *Century*, XLVII (December 1893), 316-317.

Bingham, Capt. T. A. "The Prussian Great General Staff and What It Contains That Is Practical from an American Standpoint," *Journal of the Military Service Institution of the United States*, XIII (July 1892), 666-676.

Boynton, Capt. Edward Carlisle. "History of West Point," *North American Review*, XCVIII (April 1864), 530-550.

Bronson, T. B. "The Value of Military Training and Discipline in Schools," *School Review*, II (May 1894), 281-285.

Carter, Brig-Gen. William. "The Army as a Career," *North American Review*, CLXXXIII (November 1906), 870-876.

[Clark, J. F.] "Military Drill in Schools," *Christian Examiner*, LXXVI (March 1864), 232-240.

[Cooke, John Esten.] "Memoirs of Generals Lee, Gates, Stephen, and Darke," *Harper's New Monthly Magazine*, XVII (1858), 500-511.

Cooke, Philip St. George. "One Day's Work of a Captain of Dragoons, and Some of Its Consequences," *Magazine of American History*, XCIII (July 1887), 35-44.

Dana, Charles A. "Reminiscences of Men and Events of the Civil War," *McClure's Magazine*, X-XI (November 1897-October 1898), various pagination. (A series appearing in nine installments.)

Dapray, Capt. John A. "Are We a Military People?" *Journal of the Military Service Institution of the United States*, XXIII (November 1898), 371-391.

DeForest, John William. "Caesar's Art of War and of Writing," *Atlantic Monthly*, XLIV (September 1879), 273-288.

———. "Our Military Past and Future," *Atlantic Monthly*, XLIV (November 1879), 561-575.

DePeyster, John Watts. "Anthony Wayne," *The Magazine of American History*, XV (February 1886), 127-143.

"Editorial Notes," *United Services*, IV (January 1881), 126-127.

Emerson, Ralph W. "American Civilization," *Atlantic Monthly*, IX (April 1862), 502-511.

Finley, Lt. John P. "Washington as a Soldier," *The United Service*, XVII (April 1897), 235-246.

Fiske, John. "Manifest Destiny," *Harper's Monthly*, LXX (March 1885), 578-590.

———. "Sociology and Hero-Worship," *Atlantic Monthly*, XLVII (January 1881), 75-84.

Fletcher, Josiah. "The Army and the People," *Journal of the Military Service Institution of the United States*, VII (March 1886), 103.

Flower, B. O. "Plutocracy's Bastiles: Or Why the Republic Is Becoming an Armed Camp," *Arena*, X (October 1894), 601-621.

"Fort Benton," *Montana—The New Northwest*, XXII (1879), 1-2. (A magazine published by Thomas Dowse of St. Paul, Minnesota.)

Franklin, W. B. "National Defense," *North American Review*, CXXXVII (May 1883), 594-604.

Fry, Maj-Gen. James B. "Origin and Progress of the Military Service Institution of the United States," *Journal of the Military Service Institution of the United States*, I (1879), 20-32.

Gardiner, Asa Bird. "McMaster's History of the People," *Journal of the Military Service Institution of the United States*, VIII (December 1887), 435-446.

Garfield, James A. "The Army of the United States," *North American Review*, CXXVI (March, June 1878), 197-216, 442-465.

Garland, Hamlin. "Life of Ulysses Grant," *McClure's Magazine*, VIII-IX (December 1896-October 1897), various pagination. (A series later published in book form; see Section IA.)

Garrison, W. P. "Effects of Soldiering on Character and Physique," *The Nation*, VII (September 10, 1868), 214-215.

Gibbon, John. "Needed Reforms in the Army," *North American Review*, CLVI (February 1893), 212-218.

Godkin, E. L. "The Absurdity of War," *Century*, LII (January 1897), 486-490.

[Godkin, E. L.] "The Church in the War," *The Nation*, LXVI (May 19, 1898), 377-378.

[———.] "Congress On the Army," *The Nation*, XXVI (May 30, 1878), 352-353.

[———.] "The Meaning Grant's Election Would Have," *The Nation*, XXX (June 3, 1880), 412-413.

[———.] "Military Morality," *The Nation*, LXIX (October 12, 1899), 273-274.

[———.] "The Week," *The Nation*, LXII (January 1896), 1.

Greg, W. R. "Popular Versus Professional Armies," *Contemporary Review*, XCI (December 1870-March 1871), 351-373.

Griffin, Eugene. "Our Sea-Coast Defenses," *North American Review*, CXLVIII (January 1888), 64-73.

Harbord, Lt. J. G. "The Necessity of a Well Organized and Trained Infantry at the Outbreak of War, and the Best Means to be Adopted by the United States for Obtaining Such a Force," *Journal of the Military Service Institution of the United States*, XXI (July 1897), 1-27.

Hawthorne, Nathaniel. "Chiefly About War Matters. By a Peaceable Man," *Atlantic Monthly*, X (July 1862), 43-61.

Hazewell, C. C. "Fighting Facts for Fogies," *Atlantic Monthly*, XIII (April 1864), 393-412.

Higginson, Thomas Wentworth. "Grant," *Atlantic Monthly*, LVII (March 1886), 384-388. (A review of the first volume of Grant's Memoirs.)

———. "Grant's Memoirs, Second Volume," *Atlantic Monthly*, LVIII (October 1886), 419-424.

———. "Some War Scenes Revisited," *Atlantic Monthly*, XLII (July 1878), 1-9.

[Holmes, Oliver Wendell.] "A Review of *The Life of Major John Andre, Adjutant-General of the British Army of America* by Winthrop Sargent," *Atlantic Monthly*, XXVIII (July 1871), 121-122.

———. "My Hunt after 'The Captain,' " *Atlantic Monthly*, X (December 1862), 738-764.

Howard, Lt. Guy. "The Standing Army of the United States," *The Chautauquan*, XVII: new series VIII (April-September 1893), 156-161.

Howard, Maj-Gen. O. O. "The Example of Washington: An Address Delivered Before the Cadets of the Military Academy at West Point," *United Service*, IV (1881), 505-614.

Howells, William Dean. "Editor's Study," *Harper's New Monthly Magazine*, LXXXII (January 1891), 317.

———. "A Review of *The Life of Nathanael Greene, Major-General in the Army of the ·Revolution* by George Washington Greene," *Atlantic Monthly*, XXI, XXVII, XXVIII (April 1868; June 1871; October 1871), various pagination. (The basic work was published in three volumes and each was reviewed separately as indicated.)

———. "A Review of *Memorials of the Confederate Generals Pettigrew and Elliott* by W. H. Trescott and *Oration on . . . General Thomas* by General James A. Garfield," *Atlantic Monthly*, XXVIII (July 1871), 124-126.

———. "A Review of *Miss Ravenel's Conversion from Secession to Loyalty* by J. W. DeForest," *Atlantic Monthly*, XX (July 1867), 120-123.

———. "A Review of *Ohio in the War* by Whitelaw Reid," *Atlantic Monthly*, XXI (February 1868), 252-254.

Hurd, John Codman. "A Review of *History of West Point* by Captain Edward C. Boynton," *Atlantic Monthly*, XIII (February 1864), 258-261.

King, Lt. Col. W. R. "Government Engineering Defended," *Engineering Magazine*, II (February 1892), 664-674.

Leslie, Miss. "Recollections of West Point," *Graham's Magazine* (April 1842), pp. 207-209, 290-295.

Lowell, James Russell. "General McClellan's Report," *North American Review*, XLVIII (April 1864), 550-566.

Luce, Rear-Adm. Stephen D. "The Benefits of War," *North American Review*, CLIII (1891), 672-683.

McC., A. C. "The Red Badge of Hysteria," *Dial*, XX (April 16, 1896), 227-228. (A letter to the editor, signed as shown.)

McClellan, Gen. George B. "Army Organization," *Harper's New Monthly Magazine*, XLVIII (April 1874), 670-680; XLIX (August 1874), 401-411.

McMaster, John Bach. "The North in the War," *The Chatauquan*, XV: new series VI (April-September 1892), 152-157.

Mahan, Alfred T., "The United States Looking Outward," *Atlantic Monthly*, LXVI (December 1890), 817-822.

Maguire, T. Miller. "Our Art of War as 'Made in Germany,'" *Journal of the Military Service Institution of the United States*, XIX (July, October 1896), 151-159, 312-321.

Michie, Peter Smith. "Caste at West Point," *North American Review*, CXXX (June 1880), 604-611.

Miles, Gen. Nathan A. "Military Europe," *McClure's Magazine*, XI (May-October 1898), 129-142, 253-269, 353-364.

"Military Academy at West Point," *American Quarterly Review*, XXII (September and December 1837), 71-131.

"Military Idea of Manliness," *Independent*, LIII (April 18, 1901), 874-875.

"Military Presidents," *The United States Magazine and Democratic Review*, XXVI (June 1850), 481-498.

Mitchel, F. A. "How to Make West Point More Useful," *North American Review*, CLIX (July 1894), 61-66.

Molineaux, Gen. E. L. "Riots in Cities and Their Suppression," *Journal of the Military Service Institution of the United States*, IV (October 1883), 335-370.

Munroe, Charles E. "Improvements in the Science of Warfare," *The Chautauquan*, XVI: new series VII (October 1892-March 1893).

"New Applications of Science to War," *Nature*, XVII (1877), 361.

Nordau, Max. "The Philosophy and Morals of War," *North American Review*, CLXIX (December 1899), 787-797.

Norton, Charles Eliot. "A Review of *Twelve Years of a Soldier's Life in India*, letters of Major W. S. R. Hodson," *Atlantic Monthly*, V (January 1860), 124-215.

———. "Our Soldiers," *North American Review*, XCIX (July 1864), 172-203.

Otis, Elwell S. "The Army in Connection With the Labor Riots of 1877," *Journal of the Military Service Institution of the United States*, V (1884), 292-323.

Parker, Capt. James. "The Military Academy as an Element in the System of National Defense," *Harper's New Monthly Magazine*, XCV (July 1897), 295-304.

[Peabody, A. P.] "War Indefensible on Christian Principles," *Christian Examiner*, XVIII (July 1835), 368-389.

Powers, Frederick Perry. "West Point, the Army and the Militia," *Lippincott's Magazine*, XL (July 1887), 111-126.

Preston, Harriet Waters. "Poganuc People, and Other Novels," *Atlantic Monthly*, XLII (October 1878), 430-437.

Price, Capt. George F. "The Necessity for Closer Relations Between the Army and the People, and the Best Method to Accomplish the Result," *Journal of the Military Service Institution of the United States*, VI (December 1885), 303-332.

"A Review of *Elements of Military Arts and History* by Edward de la Barre Duparcq and translated by G. W. Cullum," *Atlantic Monthly*, XI (April 1863), 524-525.

"A Review of *Lectures and Annual Reports on Education* by Horace Mann," *Atlantic Monthly*, XIX (April 1867), 512.

Ronne, A. B. "The Spirit of Militarism," *The Popular Science Monthly*, XLVII (June 1895), 234-239.

Roosevelt, Theodore. "Army Reforms," *The Outlook*, LXIII (December 23, 1899), 915-916.

Ropes, J. C. "General McClellan," *Atlantic Monthly*, LIX (April 1887), 546-559. (A review of *McClellan's Own Story*.)

Russell, Capt. A. H. "What is the Use of a Regular Army in This Country?," *Journal of the Military Service Institution of the United States*, XXIV (January 1899), 216-231. (Written in November 1896.)

[Sargent, Winthrope.] "The Society of the Cincinnati," *North American Review*, LXXVII (October 1853), 267-302.

Schurz, Carl. "Manifest Destiny," *Harper's Monthly Magazine*, LXXXVII (October 1893), 745.

[Scott, A. L.] "National Defence," *Putnam Monthly Magazine*, V (February 1855), 122-128.

Scudder, H. E. "Recent American Fiction," *Atlantic Monthly*, LV (January 1885), 121-132.

Shaler, N. S. "The Last Gift of the Century," *North American Review*, CLXI (December 1895), 674-684.

——. "The Natural History of Warfare," *North American Review*, CLXII (March 1896), 328-340.

Temple, Lieutenant. "The Military Academy," *North American Review*, XXXIV (January 1832), 246-261.

[Tuckerman, H. T.] "A Review of *The Gentleman* by George H. Calvert," *Atlantic Monthly*, XI (June 1863), 787-788.

Tyler, Moses Coit. "The Loyalists in the American Revolution," *American Historical Review*, I (October 1895), 24-45.

Wagner, Lt. Arthur L. "The Military Necessities of the United States and the Best Provisions for Meeting Them," *Journal of the Military Service Institution of the United States*, V (September 1884), 237-271.

"West Point Military Academy," *North American Review*, LII (January 1841), 22-30.

[Whiting, Henry.] "Army of the United States," *North American Review*, XXIII (October 1826), 245-274.

Whitman, Sidney. "Field Marshal Count Moltke," *The Chautauquan*, XX (January 1895), 413-417.

Wismer, George Y. "Worthless Government Engineering," *Engineering Magazine*, II (January 1892), 427-434. (With reply by Lt. Col. W. R. King in II, 664 and rejoinder in II, 743.)

Young, Lt. R. W. (LLB). "Legal and Tactical Considerations Affecting the Employment of the Military in the Suppression of Mobs. . . ," *Journal of the Military Service Institution of the United States*, IX (March, June 1888), 67-80; 249-286.

Zalinski, Capt. E. L. "The Future of Warfare," *North American Review*, CLI (December 1890), 688-700.

ID. Other Primary Sources, Collected and Separate

American State Papers, Class V, Military Affairs. 7 vols. Washington: Gales and Seaton, 1832-1861.

Annals of the Congress of the United States . . . March 3, 1789-May 27, 1824. Washington : Gales and Seaton, 1834-1856.

Austin, Iver James. *An Address Delivered Before the Corps of Cadets at the United States Military Academy [June 17, 1842].* New York: Wiley and Putnam, 1842.

Bancroft, George. *Literary and Historical Miscellanies.* New York: Harper and Brothers, 1855.

Banning, Hon. H. B. "The Object of Our Army," an appendix to *The Use of the Army in Aid of the Civil Power* by G. N. Leiber. Washington: U.S. Government Printing Office, 1898.

Barnard, Henry. *Henry Barnard on Education.* Edited by John S. Brubacker. New York: Russell and Russell, 1965.

Bayard, Samuel J. *Address Delivered Before the Graduating Class of Cadets, June 16, 1854.* Camden: Office of the Camden Democrat, 1854.

Benton, Thomas Hart. *Abridgement of the Debates of Congress, from 1789 to 1865.* 16 vols. New York: D. Appleton and Co., 1857-1861.

Blau, Joseph Leon (ed.). *Social Theories of Jacksonian Democracy.* New York: Liberal Arts Press, 1954.

The Book of Peace: A Collection of Essays. Boston: George C. Beckwith, 1845.

Bryant, William Cullen. A letter to Hon. Lewis Cass, Secretary of War, dated March 19, 1834; in Clements Library, Ann Arbor, Michigan.

Carnegie, Andrew. *The Gospel of Wealth and Other Essays.* 2 vols. Garden City, N.Y.: Doubleday, Doran and Co., Inc., 1933.

Carnegie, Andrew. *Miscellaneous Writings.* 2 vols. Edited by Burton J. Hendrick. Garden City, N.Y.: Doubleday, Doran and Co., Inc., 1933.

Channing, William Ellery. *Discourses on War.* Boston: Ginn and Co., 1903.

————. "The Passion for Power," in the *Warner Library of the World's Best Literature.* Vol. 6, 3513-3522.

Clemens, Samuel Langhorne. *The Complete Essays of Mark Twain.* New York: Doubleday, 1963.

The Congressional Globe. Debates and Proceedings of Congress, 23d Con-

gress, 1st Session to 42d Congress, 1833-1873. Washington, D.C.: Office of the Globe, 1835-1873.

Congressional Record, Containing the Proceedings and Debates of . . . Congress [1873-1899]. Vols. I-XXXII. Washington, D.C.: Government Printing Office, 1873-1899.

Crane, Stephen. *The War Dispatches of Stephen Crane.* Edited by P. W. Stallman and E. R. Hagerman. New York: New York University Press, 1964.

DePeyster, John Watts. "Frederic the Great" in *Prussia: Its Position and Destiny.* (A series of pamphlets.) New York: Chasmar and Company, 1887.

Eliot, Charles W. *American Contributions to Civilization and Other Essays and Addresses.* New York: Century Co., 1898.

Everett, William. *Oration in Honor of Colonel William Prescott.* Boston: University Press, 1896. (Delivered in Boston, October 14, 1895.)

Fiske, John. *Essays, Historical and Literary.* New York: The Macmillan Co., 1907.

Gilman, Daniel C. *Address Delivered to the Graduating Class of the United States Military Academy, . . . June 16, 1897.* New York: D. van Nostrand, 1875.

Greeley, Horace. *An Overland Journey.* New York: Alfred A. Knopf, 1964.

Hawthorne, Nathaniel. *Tales, Sketches and Other Papers.* Vol. XII of *The Complete Writings of Nathaniel Hawthorne.* Boston: Houghton, Mifflin and Co., 1893.

Houk, Hon. George W. *Address Delivered . . . at the Graduating Exercises, West Point . . . 1884.* West Point: U.S.M.A. Press, 1884.

Ingersoll, Robert. *Complete Lectures of Colonel R. G. Ingersoll.* Chicago: J. Regan and Co., n.d.

Johnson, Robert Underwood, and Clarence Clough Buel (eds.). *Battles and Leaders of the Civil War.* 4 vols. New York: The Century Co., 1884-88.

Kennon, Lt. L. W. V. *The Army: Its Employment During Time of Peace and the Necessity for Its Increase.* An unpublished monograph printed for the U.S. Infantry Society in 1896.

Lieber, G. Norman. *The Use of the Army in the Aid of the Civil Power.* Washington: U.S. Government Printing Office, 1898. (War Department Document No. 64, Office of the Judge-Advocate General.)

Loring, N. H. *Prussia: Its Position and Destiny.* New York: Chasmar and Co., 1887. (An article first published on March 1, 1834, and reprinted as a pamphlet in a series by the same name.)

Lyman, Reverend P. W. *The Career and Character of Ulysses S. Grant.* John L. Montague, Printer, 1885. (An address delivered in the Congressional Church, Belchertown, Mass.)

Millis, Walter (ed.). *American Military Thought.* Indianapolis: Bobbs-Merrill, 1966.

Page, Thomas Nelson. *The Old South: Essays Social and Political.* New York: C. Scribner's Sons, 1905.

Parkman, Francis. *Letters of Francis Parkman.* 2 vols. Edited by William R. Jacobs. Norman, Olka.: University of Oklahoma Press, 1960.

[Partridge, Captain Allen.] *The Military Academy at West Point, Unmasked: or, Corruption and Military Despotism Exposed, by Americanus.* Washington: no publisher given, 1830.

Rayner, Hon. Kenneth. *An Address Delivered Before the Graduating Class of the United States Military Academy . . . 1853.* New York: John F. Trow, 1853.

Reed, Hon. Thomas Buck. *An Address to the Cadets at West Point . . . Delivered at the Request of The Board of Visitors. . . .* New York: J. Seymour, 1827.

Rodenbough, Theo. F. *The National Defense: An Address at the Pennsylvania Military Academy, June 15, 1887.* New York: Public Service Publishing Co., 1887.

Schofield, Maj-Gen. John M. *An Address . . . to the Corps of Cadets, U.S.M.A., Monday, August 11th, 1879.* West Point, U.S.M.A. Press, 1879.

———. *Remarks . . . Upon the Reorganization of the Army.* Washington: U.S. Government Printing Office, 1876.

Seymour, General Truman. "Military Education, A Vindication of West Point." Williamstown, Mass., 1864. (Reprinting of a letter appearing in *The Army and Navy Journal* of September 24, 1864.)

Smith, Hon. Ashbel. *Address Delivered . . . Before the Officers and Cadets at the United States Military Academy . . . June 16, 1848.* New York: W. R. Burroughs, 1848.

Staunton, Major to Lt. Colonel Sylvannus Thayer. A letter dated 26 January 1822. Manuscript held by United States Military Academy Library, West Point, New York.

Sumner, William Graham. *The Conquest of the United States by Spain and Other Essays.* Chicago: Regnery, 1965.

————. *Social Darwinism, Selected Essays.* Edited by Stow Parsons. Englewood, N.J.: Prentice-Hall, 1963.

Ticknor, George. *West Point in 1826.* An unpublished and undated extract of a letter to his wife written while serving as a member of the annual Board of Visitors; given to the United States Military Academy by his daughter and held in the Academy Library Archives.

Turner, Gordon B. (ed.). *A History of Military Affairs in Western Society Since the Eighteenth Century.* New York: Harcourt, Brace and Co., 1953.

U.S. Military Academy, West Point. Board of Visitors, Annual Reports. West Point: U.S.M.A. Press, and Washington: Government Printing Office, 1819- . (A collection of separate reports; bound under single cover in the U.S.M.A. Library.)

Walker, Gen. Francis A. *Hancock in the War of the Rebellion.* A paper read by General Walker at a meeting of the New York Commandery, February 4, 1891.

Wayland, Francis, Jr. *Address of President of the Board of Visitors to the Graduating Class of 1874, U.S. Military Academy, West Point.* New York: D. van Nostrand, 1874.

II. Secondary Sources

IIA. Books, Nonfiction

Allen, H. C. and C. P. Hill (eds.). *British Essays in American History.* New York: St. Martin's Press, 1951.

Ambrose, Stephen E. *Duty, Honor, Country: A History of West Point.* Baltimore: Johns Hopkins Press, 1966.

Beers, Henry P. *The Western Military Frontier.* Philadelphia: The University of Pennsylvania, 1935.

Bentley, Eric. *A Century of Hero-Worship.* Philadelphia and New York: J. B. Lippincott Co., 1944.

Bernardo, C. Joseph and Eugene H. Bacon. *American Military Policy: Its Development Since 1775.* Harrisburg, Pa.: Military Publishing Co., 1961.

Boorstin, Daniel J. *The Americans.* 2 vols. New York: Random House, 1958.

Bruce, Robert V. *1877: Year of Violence.* Indianapolis: Bobbs-Merrill Co., Inc., 1959.

Bryan, William Alfred. *George Washington in American Literature, 1775-1865*. New York: Columbia University Press, 1952.

Burns, Edward M. *The American Idea of Mission*. New Brunswick, N.J.: Rutgers University Press, 1957.

Cady, Edwin Harrison. *The Gentleman in America*. Syracuse, N.Y.: Syracuse University Press, 1949.

Calhoun, Daniel Hovey. *The American Civil Engineer: Origins and Conflict*. Cambridge: Harvard University Press, 1960.

Carter, William G. H. *West Point in Literature*. Baltimore: Lord Baltimore Press, 1909.

Cavaioli, Frank J. *West Point and the Presidency: The Voters Attitude Toward the Military Elite*. New York: St. John's University Press, 1962.

Centennial of the United States Military Academy at West Point, New York: 1802-1902. 2 vols. Washington: Government Printing Office, 1904.

Cowie, Alexander. *The Rise of the American Novel*. New York: American Book Co., 1951.

Cramer, Clarence H. *Royal Bob: The Life of Robert G. Ingersoll*. New York: Bobbs-Merrill Co., Inc., 1952.

Curti, Merle. *American Peace Crusade*. Durham, N.C.: Duke University Press, 1929.

———. *The Growth of American Thought*. New York: Harper and Brothers, 1951.

———. *Peace or War: The American Struggle, 1636-1936*. New York: Norton Co., 1936.

———. *Social Ideas of American Educators*. Patterson, N.J.: Pageant Books, 1959.

Davies, Wallace Evan. *Patriotism on Parade: The Story of the Veterans' and Hereditary Organizations in America, 1783-1900*. Cambridge, Mass.: Harvard University Press, 1955.

Dictionary of American Biography. 21 vols. New York: Charles Scribner's Sons, 1928-1937.

Downey, Fairfax. *Indian-Fighting Army*. New York: Scribner's Sons, 1941.

———. *Indian Wars of the U.S. Army, 1776-1885*. Garden City, N.Y.: Doubleday and Co., Inc., 1963.

Dulles, Foster Rhea. *The Imperial Years*. New York: Thomas Y. Crowell Co., 1956.

———. *Labor in America*. New York: Thomas Y. Crowell Co., 1960.

Dupuy, R. Ernest. *The Compact History of the United States Army.* New York: Hawthorn Books, Inc., 1956.

——— and Trevor N. Dupuy. *Military Heritage of America.* New York: McGraw-Hill Book Co., 1956.

Edmonds, James Edward. *Fighting Fools.* New York: D. Appleton-Century Co., 1938.

Ekirch, Arthur A., Jr. *The Civilian and the Military: A History of the American Anti-Militarist Tradition.* New York: Oxford University Press, 1956.

Fishwick, Marshall Wm. *American Heroes, Myth and Reality.* Washington, D.C.: Public Affairs Press, 1954.

Floan, Howard Russell. *The South in Northern Eyes, 1831-1861.* Austin: University of Texas Press, 1958.

Foner, Philip S. *History of the Labor Movement in the United States.* 2 vols. New York: International Publishers, 1955.

Forman, Sidney. *West Point, A History of the United States Military Academy.* New York: Columbia University Press, 1950.

Franklin, John Hope. *The Militant South.* Cambridge: Harvard University Press, 1956.

Gabriel, Ralph. *The Course of American Democratic Thought.* New York: The Ronald Press Co., 1940.

Ganoe, William Addleman. *The History of the United States Army.* New York: Appleton-Century Co., 1942.

Goebel, Dorothy B. and Julius Goebel. *Generals in the White House.* Garden City, N.Y.: Doubleday, Doran Co., Inc., 1945.

Guttman, Allen. *The Conservative Tradition in America.* New York: Oxford University Press, 1967.

Hamilton, Holman. *Zachary Taylor.* 2 vols. Indianapolis: Bobbs-Merrill Co., 1941-1951.

Hart, James D. *The Popular Book: A History of America's Literary Taste.* Berkeley: University of California Press, 1961.

Hazard, Lucy. *The Frontier in American Literature.* New York: Frederick Ungar Publishing Co., Inc., 1961.

Hicks, John D. *The Populist Revolt.* Minneapolis: University of Minnesota, 1931.

Hofstadter, Richard. *The American Political Tradition.* New York: A. A. Knopf, 1948.

———. *Anti-Intellectualism in the United States.* New York: A. A. Knopf, 1963.

———. *The Development and Scope of Higher Education in the United States.* New York: Columbia University Press, 1952.

────. *Social Darwinism in American Thought*. Boston: Beacon Press, 1955.

Hoggan, David L. *The Myth of the "New History."* Nutley, N.J.: The Craig Press, 1965.

Hugins, Walter. *Jacksonian Democracy and the Working Class: A Study of the New York Workingman's Movement, 1829-1837*. Stanford: Stanford University Press, 1960.

Huntington, Samuel P. *The Soldier and the State*. Cambridge, Mass.: Belknap Press of Harvard University Press, 1957.

Jacobs, James Ripley. *The Beginning of the U.S. Army, 1783-1812*. Princeton: Princeton University Press, 1947.

Janowitz, Morris. *Sociology and the Military Establishment*. New York: Russell Sage Foundation, 1959.

Josephson, Matthew. *The Politicos, 1865-1896*. New York: Harcourt, Brace and World, 1938.

Kluckhohn, Clyde. "American Culture and Military Life," an appendix to *Report of U.S. Working Group on Human Behavior under Conditions of Military Service*. Washington: Department of Defense Research and Development Board, 1951.

Liddell Hart, Basil Henry. *Sherman: Soldier, Realist, American*. New York: Praeger, 1958.

Long, Orie William. *Literary Pioneers, Early American Explorers of European Culture*. Cambridge, Mass.: Harvard University Press, 1935.

Masland, John W. and Laurence I. Radway. *Soldiers and Scholars: Military Education and National Policy*. Princeton: Princeton University Press, 1957.

Meyers, Marvin. *The Jacksonian Persuasion: Politics and Belief*. Stanford: Stanford University Press, 1957.

Miller, John C. *The Federalist Era, 1789-1801*. New York: Harper and Brothers, 1960.

Millis, Walter. *Arms and Men: A Study in American Military History*. New York: G. P. Putnam's Sons, 1956.

────. *The Martial Spirit, A Study of Our War With Spain*. Boston: Houghton, Mifflin and Co., 1931.

Mott, Frank Luther. *A History of American Magazines, 1741-1905*. 4 vols. Cambridge, Mass.: Harvard University Press, 1938.

Nevins, Allan. *America Through British Eyes*. New York: Oxford University Press, 1948.

Nye, Russel B. *George Bancroft, Brahmin Rebel*. New York: Alfred A. Knopf, 1944.

Osgood, Robert E. *Ideals and Self-Interest in America's Foreign Relations.* Chicago: University of Chicago Press, 1953.

Pratt, Julius W. *Expansionists of 1890: The Acquisition of Hawaii and the Spanish Islands.* Baltimore: Johns Hopkins Press, 1936.

Prucha, F. P. *Broad Ax and Bayonet.* Madison, Wis.: State Historical Society of Wisconsin, 1953.

————. *A History of the American Drama.* . . . 2 vols. New York: Appleton-Century-Crofts, Inc., 1943.

Reed, Perley Isaac. *American Characters in Native American Plays Prior to 1870.* Columbus: Ohio State University Bulletin, Vol. XXII, 1918.

Riker, William H. *Soldiers of the States: The Role of the National Guard in American Democracy.* Washington: Public Affairs Press, 1957.

Schlesinger, Arthur M., Jr. *The Age of Jackson.* Boston: Little, Brown and Co., 1950.

Smith, Henry Nash. *Virgin Land; The American West as Symbol and Myth.* Cambridge: Harvard University Press, 1950.

Spaulding, Oliver Lyman. *The United States Army in Peace and War.* New York: G. P. Putnam's Sons, 1937.

Spiller, Robt. E. *et al.* (eds.). *Literary History of the United States.* 2 vols. New York: The Macmillan Co., 1948.

Sprout, Harold and Margaret. *The Rise of American Naval Power.* Princeton: Princeton University Press, 1939.

Taylor, Wm. R. *Cavalier and Yankee: The Old South and American National Character.* New York: George Braziller, 1961.

Turner, Gordon B. (ed.). *A History of Military Affairs in Western Society Since the Eighteenth Century.* New York: Harcourt, Brace, 1953.

Utley, Robert. *Frontiersmen in Blue, 1845-1865.* New York: Macmillan Co., 1967.

Vagts, Alfred. *A History of Militarism: Romance and Realities of a Profession.* New York: W. W. Norton, 1937.

Wagenknecht, Edward Charles. *Cavalcade of the American Novel.* New York: Henry Holt and Co., 1952.

Ward, John William. *Andrew Jackson, Symbol for an Age.* New York: Oxford University Press, 1955.

Wecter, Dixon. *The Hero in America, A Chronicle of Hero-Worship.* New York: C. Scribner's Sons, 1941.

Weigley, Russell Frank. *Towards An American Army.* New York: Columbia University Press, 1962.

———. *History of the United States Army*. New York: The Macmillan Co., 1967.

Weinberg, Albert K. *Manifest Destiny; a Study of Nationalist Expansionism in American History*. Baltimore: The Johns Hopkins Press, 1938.

Wesley, Edgar B. *Guarding the Frontier: A Study of Frontier Defense from 1815 to 1825*. Minneapolis: University of Minnesota Press, 1935.

White, Leonard D. *The Jacksonians, A Study in Administrative History, 1829-1861*. New York: The Macmillan Co., 1954.

White, Leonard D. *The Republican Era: 1869-1901*. New York: The Macmillan Co., 1958.

Williams, T. Harry. *Americans at War*. New York: Collier Books, 1962.

Wish, Harvey. *The American Historian*. New York: Oxford University Press, 1960.

Wyllie, Irvin G. *The Self-Made Man in America*. New Brunswick, N.J.: Rutgers University Press, 1954.

Young, Otis E. *The West of Philip St. George Cooke, 1809-1895*. Glendale, Calif.: A. H. Clark Co., 1955.

IIB. Articles and Periodicals

Bell, Daniel. "Power Elite—Reconsidered," *American Journal of Sociology*, LXIV (November 1958), 238-250.

Bone, Robert A. "Irving's Headless Hessian: Prosperity and the Inner Life," *American Quarterly*, XV (Summer 1963), 167.

Boorstin, Daniel J. "America and the Image of Europe," *Perspective, U.S.A.*, XIV (1956), 5-19.

Brown, Richard C. "Emory Upton, The Army's Mahan," *Military Affairs*, XVII (Fall 1953), 125-131.

Carpenter, Hazen C. "Emerson at West Point," *The Pointer*, XXVII (June 12, 1951), 5, 27.

Clebsch, W. A. "Christian Interpretations of the Civil War," *Church History*, XXX (June 1961), 212-230.

Davis, David Brion. "Some Ideological Functions of Prejudice in Ante-Bellum America," *American Quarterly*, XV (Summer 1963), 115-125.

Eisinger, C. E. "American War Novel," *Pacific Spectator*, IX (Summer 1955), 272-287.

England, J. Merton. "The Democratic Faith in American Schoolbooks, 1783-1860," *American Quarterly*, XV (Summer 1963), 191-199.

French, David P. "James Fenimore Cooper and Fort William Henry," *American Literature*, XXXII (March 1960), 28-38.

"Huckleberry Finn Visits West Point," *The Pointer* (December 9, 1960), 13, 29.

Ives, C. B. "Billy Budd and the Articles of War," *American Literature*, XXXIV (March 1962), 31-39.

Lasswell, Harold D. "The Garrison State," *American Journal of Sociology*, XLVI (January 1951), 455-468.

Lipset, Seymour M. "Value Patterns of Democracy," *American Sociological Review*, XXVIII (August 1963), 515-531.

"The Macs and the Ikes: America's Two Military Traditions," *American Mercury*, LXXXV (October 1952), 32-39.

Malla, John P. "Roosevelt, Brooks Adams and Lea; The Warrior Critique of Business Civilization," *American Quarterly*, VIII (Fall 1956), 216-230.

Martin, Terrence. "Social Institutions in the Early American Novel," *American Quarterly*, IX (Spring 1957), 72-84.

Prucha, Francis P. "The United States Army as Viewed by British Travellers, 1825-60," *Military Affairs*, XVII (Fall 1953), 113-124.

Sackett, J. J. "Captain Charles King, U.S.A.," *Midwest Quarterly*, III (October 1961), 69-80.

Smylie, J. E. "Protestant Clergymen and American Destiny, Prelude to Imperialism, 1865-1900," *Harvard Theological Review*, LVI (October 1963), 297-311.

Somit, Albert. "The Military Hero as Presidential Candidate," *Public Opinion Quarterly*, XII (Summer 1948), 192-200.

Sprout, Harold. "Trends in the Traditional Relations between Military and Civilian," *American Philosophical Society, Proceedings*, XIIC (1948), 264 ff.

Williams, T. Harry. "The Attack on West Point During the Civil War," *Mississippi Valley Historical Review*, XXV (March 1939), 491-504.

IIC. Other Secondary Sources, Miscellaneous and Unpublished

Brown, Richard C. "Social Attitudes of American Generals, 1898-1940." An unpublished Ph.D. thesis, University of Wisconsin, 1951.

Burton, Wilford C. "The Novels of Charles King—1844-1933." An unpublished Ph.D. dissertation, Dept. of English, New York University, 1963.

Denton, Edgar. "The Formative Years of the Military Academy." An unpublished Ph.D. dissertation, Dept. of History, Syracuse University, 1964.

Langley, Harold D. "The Humanitarians and the United States Navy, 1798-1862." An unpublished Ph.D. dissertation, University of Pennsylvania, 1961.

Norton, Alloysius A. "A Study of the Customs and Traditions of West Point in the American Novel." An unpublished Master of Arts thesis, Dept. of English, Columbia University, 1950.

Skelton, William B. "The American Army Officer Class, 1820-1860: A Social Intellectual Study." An unpublished Ph.D. dissertation, Northwestern University, 1964.

Smythe, Donald W. "The Early Years of General John J. Pershing: 1860-1917." An unpublished Ph.D. dissertation, Georgetown University, 1961.

Steese, James Gordon. "Memorandum on the Criticism of West Point by Dr. Charles W. Eliot." Washington: no publisher listed, 1920. In the Archives of the U.S. Military Academy Library.

Wilson, Frederick T. *Federal Aid in Domestic Disturbances*. A Supplement to Senate Document 209, 57th Cong., 2d Sess. Washington: Government Printing Office, 1923.

Index